The Arts in Higher Education

Series Editor
Nancy Kindelan
Department of Theatre
Northeastern University
Boston, MA, USA

The role the arts play in higher education continues to be a complex and highly debated topic, especially in the changing climate of North American education. Showcasing cutting-edge research, this series illuminates and examines how engagement in the arts helps students meet the challenges and opportunities of a twenty-first century life and workplace by encompassing a wide range of issues from both scholars and practitioners in the arts. Key topics the series will cover include: evolving interdisciplinary degrees that include the arts; creating innovative experiential/pedagogical practices in the arts; discovering new methods of teaching and learning that involve the arts and technology; developing inventive narrative forms that explore social issues through play making; exploring non-traditional sites for creative art making; demystifying the process of creative thinking (especially as creativity relates to business practices, scientific thought, inter-active media, and entrepreneurial activities); engaging the arts in understanding global perspectives; and illustrating how the arts create life-long skills that help students manage a challenging job market. While the scope of the series is focused on the arts in higher education in North America, the series may also include scholarship that considers the total educational spectrum from K through 16, since there is now interest in creating a seamless educational progression from kindergarten through the baccalaureate degree.

More information about this series at
http://www.palgrave.com/gp/series/14452

Michelle Hayford • Susan Kattwinkel
Editors

Performing Arts as High-Impact Practice

palgrave
macmillan

Editors
Michelle Hayford
Theatre, Dance, & Performance Technology
University of Dayton
Dayton, OH, USA

Susan Kattwinkel
Theatre and Dance
College of Charleston
Charleston, SC, USA

The Arts in Higher Education
ISBN 978-3-030-10290-6   ISBN 978-3-319-72944-2   (eBook)
https://doi.org/10.1007/978-3-319-72944-2

© The Editor(s) (if applicable) and The Author(s) 2018
Softcover re-print of the Hardcover 1st edition 2018
This work is subject to copyright. All rights are solely and exclusively licensed by the Publisher, whether the whole or part of the material is concerned, specifically the rights of translation, reprinting, reuse of illustrations, recitation, broadcasting, reproduction on microfilms or in any other physical way, and transmission or information storage and retrieval, electronic adaptation, computer software, or by similar or dissimilar methodology now known or hereafter developed.
The use of general descriptive names, registered names, trademarks, service marks, etc. in this publication does not imply, even in the absence of a specific statement, that such names are exempt from the relevant protective laws and regulations and therefore free for general use.
The publisher, the authors, and the editors are safe to assume that the advice and information in this book are believed to be true and accurate at the date of publication. Neither the publisher nor the authors or the editors give a warranty, express or implied, with respect to the material contained herein or for any errors or omissions that may have been made. The publisher remains neutral with regard to jurisdictional claims in published maps and institutional affiliations.

Cover illustration: © Roman Rvachov / Alamy Stock Photo

Printed on acid-free paper

This Palgrave Macmillan imprint is published by the registered company Springer International Publishing AG part of Springer Nature.
The registered company address is: Gewerbestrasse 11, 6330 Cham, Switzerland

Acknowledgments

We would like to thank Nancy Kindelan for bringing us together; the Leadership Institute of the Association for Theatre in Higher Education for community and inspiration; our friends and families for support, love, and patience; and our colleagues and students for sustaining our passion for higher education.

Contents

1 **Introduction: Why Frame the Performing Arts as High-Impact Practice?**   1
   Calls for Creativity   6
   From Plato to LEAP: How the Arts Are Still Being Left Out of the Conversation   8
   A Call to Action   13
   Bibliography   18

2 **First-Year Seminars and Experiences**   21
   Devising Pedagogies for First-Year Theatre and Performance Studies Students — James Davis   25
   A Performance Project to Accomplish FYE Learning Outcomes for Non-Performing Arts Students — Susan Kattwinkel   33
   Bibliography   42

3 **Common Intellectual Experiences**   45
   Rites/Rights/Writes and the University Experience — Richard K. Chenoweth   50
   Bibliography   60

4	**Learning Communities**	63
	Connecting Music and Computer Science: An Interdisciplinary Learning Community for First-Year University Students — Bill Manaris and Blake Stevens	68
	Social Innovation Through Purpose, Performance, and Story — Brian LaDuca	82
	Bibliography	96
5	**Writing-Intensive Courses**	101
	Program Notes in the Classroom — K. Dawn Grapes	105
	Performing the Australian Crawl — James Brock	111
	Bibliography	119
6	**Collaborative Assignments and Projects**	121
	The Ampersand Festival: A Case Study in Theatre as High-Impact Educational Practice — Claire M. McDonald	125
	An Ethical Balancing Act: Student Labor and Project-Based Learning — Angela Sweigart-Gallagher and Kristin Hunt	136
	Bibliography	145
7	**Undergraduate Research**	147
	Research: Digesting Creative Food — Kathy L. Privatt	156
	Questioning Through Doing: Shaping Praxis Through the Individual Dance Project — Malaika Sarco-Thomas	163
	Bibliography	178
8	**Diversity and Global Learning**	181
	The "Real" Versus the "Represented" Self: First-Year Students Seek Identity Through Kanye West — Julius D. Bailey	190
	Making Brighter Connections — Michelle Hayford and Katie O'Leary	198
	Bibliography	213
9	**Service Learning and Community-Based Learning**	217
	Performative Organizing: "Spark-ing" Civic Leadership and Inclusive Modes of Public Narrative — Michelle Hayford and Brandon W. Kliewer	225

Preparing to Engage the Community with Public Speaking Performance Classes — Trudi Wright 234
Bibliography 247

10 **Internships** 251
Experiential Learning in Dance Education: Collaborative Teaching to Develop Professional Practice — Marissa Beth Nesbit 255
Beyond the Proscenium: Internships at Washington College — Michele Volansky 263
Bibliography 271

11 **Capstone Courses and Projects** 273
Cultivating a Successful Dance Capstone Course — Gretchen S. McLaine 279
(Never) Mind the Gap: Preparing Professional Musicians at the Royal Academy of Music, London — Marc Ernesti 289
Bibliography 299

Index 303

List of Figures and Tables

Fig. 1.1	Chart of HIP characteristics in the performing arts	5
Fig. 4.1	A sample of a JythonMusic program transcribing J.S. Bach's Canon No. 1 of the Fourteen Canons on the Goldberg Ground (see http://bit.ly/bachCanon1)	72
Fig. 4.2	A Laptop Orchestra Performance of Terry Riley's "In C" (see video—http://bit.ly/charlestonLaptopOrchestra)	73
Fig. 4.3	"Daintree Drones" by Kenneth Hanson—sonification of digital image by computer programming (see https://vimeo.com/64110119)	77
Fig. 4.4	"Lugna" by John Thevos and Katherine May—sonification of digital image by computer programming (see https://vimeo.com/64109534)	78
Fig. 4.5	"Manhattan Solstice" by Caroline Freeman (née Bowman)—sonification of digital image by computer programming (see https://vimeo.com/64101616). Photo courtesy of Robinson McClellan, Rutgers University	78
Fig. 4.6	Mask-making at the Institute of Applied Creativity for Transformation	91
Fig. 4.7	Mask-making at the Institute of Applied Creativity for Transformation	92
Fig. 7.1	Cycle of action research. Image: Valencia College	167
Fig. 7.2	Selected IDP topics, University of Malta, 2015–2017	169
Fig. 7.3	"Contact improvisation skills for bellydance" IDP workshop. Photo by Yasmin Falzon	170
Fig. 7.4	"Embodied drawing" IDP workshop. Photo by Eszter Joo	171
Fig. 7.5	Robin Nelson's PaR modes of knowing	174
Fig. 9.1	Persuasive presentation peer evaluation form	238
Fig. 9.2	Persuasive presentation peer evaluation form	239

Table 4.1	Fall 2016 ACT I schedule providing scaffolding and top-level definitions of the three-part themes that supported the overarching outcomes of the semester	88
Table 11.1	DANC 441 Capstone Project Rubric (sample) for *Motion Capture for Labanotation*	285
Table 11.2	Required elements of e-portfolio for DANC 441	288

CHAPTER 1

Introduction: Why Frame the Performing Arts as High-Impact Practice?

This book investigates how the performing arts in higher education nationally contribute to the "high-impact practices," as identified by the Association of American Colleges and Universities (AAC&U). These ten practices have been promoted since 2008 as best practices to deliver quality educational experiences for undergraduates. These HIPs, as they are known, have been implemented at institutions of all types across the country (and internationally) and are consistently assessed and analyzed. Both studies of individual HIPs and those of the implementation of HIPs as a whole have concluded, as Kilgo, Sheets, and Pascarella did in their longitudinal study of HIP implementation, that

> This finding—that high-impact practices have an overall positive effect on student learning and development—has significant practical implications for institutions of higher education. Institutions should strive to provide students with opportunities to engage in high-impact practices, particularly practices such as undergraduate research and active and collaborative learning, which are shown to have vast positive impact for student learning and development.[1]

Using the well-known map of the HIPs for illustrating the centrality of performing arts practices in higher education, we call for increased participation by performing arts programs in general education and campus initiatives, with specific case studies as a guide. This book both illustrates why

© The Author(s) 2018
M. Hayford, S. Kattwinkel (eds.), *Performing Arts as High-Impact Practice*, The Arts in Higher Education,
https://doi.org/10.1007/978-3-319-72944-2_1

performing arts programs should be finding ways to attract non-majors to their courses (and institutions should be encouraging/requiring students to take performing arts courses) and how performing arts programs can take their pedagogies to the larger campus community, outside the arts curriculum.

This book is beneficial as academia is looking to expand the emphasis on STEM education to *STEAM* (science, technology, engineering, ARTS, mathematics) education and the role of creativity for all majors as a means to deliver important educational outcomes and promote undergraduate scholarship and research. When disciplines can effectively make the case for how they capture the high-impact educational practices identified by AAC&U, they can contribute to the efforts of their institution in delivering a strong liberal arts education that best serves students to meet the careers of the future.

Unfortunately, the performing arts disciplines have been slow to make this argument for themselves, and there is a pressing need to assert the value and role of the performing arts in contributing to the high-impact educational practices that upper administrators have committed to deliver to students. What is at stake is nothing less than the viability of performing arts programs to continue to serve students in their pursuit of a liberal arts education, the articulation of the necessity of adding the "A" of Arts to STEM in the move toward STEAM, and the exploration of creativity as the nexus of innovation in academia as an emerging best practice.

Our hope is that this book, the first to explicitly link the performing arts to the HIPs, will result in the implementation of best practices in the contributions of the performing arts in liberal education, and advocacy for greater inclusion of the performing arts in general education and campus initiatives to better meet the educational needs of students. The case studies provide models for leveraging the performing arts as HIPs in higher education classrooms and studios. We hope to spur future research into the efficacy and assessment of the performing arts as HIPs, and provide educators tools to consider the viability and relevance of their programs and course work to their students' educational goals and the mission of liberal arts education.

Higher education has come under scrutiny during times of economic recession and uncertainty in recent years, as lawmakers consider the value of a college education to deliver high-paying jobs to graduates and contribute to the health and wealth of the economy. We have seen an unprecedented devaluing of liberal arts education, as political pundits have privileged vocational or trade schools as better paths to careers that would contribute to the economy. Rick Scott, governor of Florida, for example, has suggested that anthropology programs be cut in favor of shifting funding to STEM disciplines. In 2011, Governor Scott asked, "Is it a vital interest of the state to have more anthropologists? I don't think so."[2] Similarly, in 2015, Republican presidential candidate Marco Rubio revealed his contempt for liberal arts education when he stated, "I don't know why we have stigmatized vocational education. Welders make more money than philosophers. We need more welders and less [sic] philosophers."[3]

In this devaluing of liberal arts education, all humanities, social sciences, and the arts have come under fire and have been forced to make the case for how their non-STEM discipline prepares students for viable careers. As a result, non-STEM disciplines have turned to explaining and demonstrating the value of a liberal arts education, trumpeting the success of their graduates in pursuing a variety of career paths.[4] The case for the arts in all levels of education has been made multiple times and should not need further defense. Vast amounts of research shows that arts education, in all its varieties, benefits all demographics of K–12 students by aiding in their development of higher-order thinking skills and habits, as well as in personal characteristics such as motivation, engagement, and self-awareness.[5] Recently, the recognition of these benefits has extended beyond traditional arts exposure and participation to include arts integration across the curriculum. Arguing for arts integration rather than simply arts education, Gene Diaz and Martha Barry McKenna, in their book *Preparing Educators for Arts Integration: Placing Creativity at the Center of Learning*, note that "when the use of what are sometimes known as 'studio habits' or 'creative processes' become integral to teaching, possibilities open up, and students' imaginations can lead to new and alternative ways of knowing and being."[6]

In institutions of higher education, however, where arts departments were not commonly seen until the twentieth century, the arts are often still viewed as discrete disciplines with little connection to the rest of the university. Although photos of artists at work and in performance grace the pages of public relations publications, and potential donors and visiting VIPs are taken to art openings and performances in order to show off the university's "culture," the arts are rarely seen as an essential element of the "well-rounded education" most institutions aim to provide. But the AAC&U, a powerful consortium for upper administrators nationally to gather and share best practices, conduct research, and provide white papers advising best practices in academia, has provided the performing arts with a powerful argument for relevancy in their research on HIPs. The identification of the ten HIPs is the result of the AAC&U's research into which well-documented and thoroughly researched educational practices increase student retention rates and student engagement. Their publication, "High-Impact Educational Practices: What They Are, Who Has Access to Them, and Why They Matter" has been extremely influential in shaping the current landscape of general education and the approach to liberal arts education throughout academia.[7] The National Survey of Student Engagement (NSSE) has added Study Abroad and Research with Faculty as two additional HIPs. An 11th HIP has recently been identified—e-portfolios.[8] We made the decision to stick with the ten HIPs discussed in the 2008 AAC&U document because the additional three can be at least partially implied in the original ten, and reference to all are included in the following chapters. But a word should be said about "Research with Faculty" as a HIP excelled at by the performing arts. In all the disciplines currently taught in institutions of higher education, only the sciences come close to achieving the variety and ubiquity of research pursued jointly by students and faculty in the performing arts. Although all disciplines have opportunities for faculty and students to research together—archeological digs, lab experiments, and so on, research in most disciplines rarely demands the extended time together that research in the performing arts does. And the results of that research rarely take the form of public dissemination that showcases the work of multiple students and faculty, as is common in theatre, dance, and music. Every one of the HIPs discussed in this book demands a high level of student–faculty interaction when they are practiced in the performing arts. Whether students are majors in the discipline or just taking one course in performance practice, close interaction with faculty is essential to course assignments. In the performing arts, students rarely complete an assignment alone and then turn it in for faculty assessment; they collaborate with the faculty member throughout the process. Again, many disciplines incorporate these practices as crucial elements of their pedagogy, but only in the performing arts is "Research with Faculty" absolutely fundamental to the learning process.

It should also be noted that courses in the performing arts are frequent users of what are known as "good practices"—pedagogical techniques and habits that facilitate undergraduate learning and retention. First identified by Chickering and Gamson in 1987[9] and affirmed, adjusted, and assessed consistently since then, these practices, articulated by Kuh and O'Donnell as characteristics of HIPs that work, include "interactions with faculty and peers about substantive matters," "periodic, structured opportunities to reflect and integrate learning," "opportunities to discover relevance of learning through real-world applications," "frequent, timely, and constructive feedback," "significant investment of time and effort by students over an extended period of time," "performance expectations set at appropriately high levels," "experiences with diversity," and "public demonstration of competence."[10] Each of these practices lies at the heart of undergraduate performing arts study (see Fig. 1.1).

Characteristic of High-Impact Practices	Appearance in the Performing Arts
interactions with faculty and peers about substantive matters	In classrooms, studios, rehearsal and performance spaces, interaction with faculty and peers is continuous, with contact hours in the performing arts exceeding all other disciplines
periodic, structured opportunities to reflect and integrate learning	Preparing for frequent live performances provides regular, structured opportunities to put theory into practice, reflect on and integrate learning from the classroom/studio to the stage
opportunities to discover relevance of learning through real-world applications	Performance as public dissemination of creative scholarship is a real world application
frequent, timely, and constructive feedback	Happens in classrooms/studios, during rehearsals for performance, during performance from audience, and post-performance from faculty
significant investment of time and effort by students over an extended period of time	Every performance is the result of significant investment of time and effort over an extended period of time
performance expectations set at appropriately high levels	Excellence in creative scholarship is always sought
experiences with diversity	The performing arts excel in exposing students to issues in diversity, and grappling with diversity issues raised by performance
public demonstration of competence	Live public performance is dissemination of creative scholarship

Fig. 1.1 Chart of HIP characteristics in the performing arts

Performances at the course and college performance level (outside student clubs) cannot happen without frequent and sustained contact between students and faculty, conducted at a professional level. All performing arts, even solo performances, demand collaboration and mutually beneficial work between students and significant investments of time. Even the most critically based performance programs (those focused on the critique and theorizing of performance forms) generally encourage students to acquire significant experience working on realized performances (active learning) that result in public performance.

CALLS FOR CREATIVITY

In survey after survey, business leaders consistently name job skills in which the performing arts excel as their top priorities. According to the 2016 PayScale Workforce Skills Preparedness Report, 36% of business managers feel that recent college graduates are lacking in the soft skill of "interpersonal skills/teamwork."[11] The AAC&U's own 2013 study of employers showed that 71% of employers thought that colleges could do a better job teaching "the ability to innovate and be creative" and 67% thought that colleges could do a better job teaching "teamwork skills and the ability to collaborate with others in diverse group settings." Furthermore, 74% of respondents said that developing "the skills to conduct research collaboratively" would help students succeed.[12] And yet, when constructing their survey of chief academic officers (CAOs) two years later (in collaboration with the same research organization), they chose not to ask about these skills that are taught more intentionally in the performing arts than anywhere else on campus.[13] Although other disciplines certainly are capable of teaching "the ability to work well in teams" and "the ability to be creative and innovative in solving problems,"[14] the performing arts accomplish these priorities as a matter of course.

In 2013 Dan Berrett outlined efforts at a growing number of colleges and universities to include creativity among student learning outcomes in order to better prepare students for this demand from business leaders. In some cases creativity is infused across the curriculum and faculty of all disciplines are trained in its pedagogy, and in other cases specific courses are developed. In fact, according to Berrett, "Practically focused programs in business have been among the first to embrace creativity and design thinking in their curricula."¹⁵ Significantly, most of these creativity requirements do not explicitly connect creativity to the arts, and do not even look to the arts for guidance in how to teach creativity. How are the arts to remain relevant in higher education when they are not recognized for their greatest strengths?

That question will become more urgent as the creativity agenda accelerates. In 2014, Steven J. Tepper published a think piece in the *Chronicle of Higher Education* citing a rise in self-focused creativity on the part of college students and calling on colleges to immerse their students in "Bigger Than Me" creative experiences. Citing surveys indicating a sharp rise in self-centeredness and a corresponding decrease in empathy over the last several decades, the latter perhaps connected to media overload and new creative formats that focus on the self via social media, Tepper advocated for experiences that contribute to "feeling a sense of purpose," "helping solve a collective problem," "putting ourselves in another's shoes," and "adopting a different perspective." After relating a number of course assignment examples, Tepper points out that the arts are a natural home for such experiences. "In spite of the perception that the arts primarily promote individual expression and voice," he says,

> many of the core competencies developed through arts training create opportunities for "bigger than me" experiences. In arts classes, students hone their empathic imagination, routinely shift contexts, ask "what if" questions, try out multiple perspectives, and, in the words of [Liz] Lerman, experience the "free fall" of recognizing that reality is up for grabs and their assumptions about the world might not be shared.¹⁶

The number one recommendation for undergraduate education by the 2008 Harvard Task Force on the Arts was to "[i]ntroduce arts-practice into the General Education curriculum of the College and more broadly into the undergraduate curriculum as a whole."¹⁷ Their explanation includes the statement that "[a]ctivities such as quantitative reasoning, historical analysis, social analysis, expository writing, and laboratory experiment and observation are today self-evidently part of the general curriculum for undergraduates, so too, the activities of arts-practice, such as filmmaking, creative writing, and dramatic performance should be an accepted, pedagogically well-supported component of the curriculum."¹⁸

From Plato to LEAP: How the Arts Are Still Being Left Out of the Conversation

Ever since Plato denied art's ability to convey truth,[19] and Immanuel Kant decided that anything aesthetic cannot be considered rationally, the arts have suffered from a crisis of legitimacy in higher education.[20] Rehabilitating the role of the arts in liberal education has been an ongoing project, and one that is presently urgent. Kevin Moll questions how selected art forms could ever have been removed from the "Great Books" movement in Prolegomena to Any Future Great Books of Music: Reconsidering Liberal-Arts Paradigms in a Postmodern Age:

> [I]f we are prepared to concede (as many educators evidently are unwilling to do) that some sort of liberal-arts paradigm might be worth perpetuating within our secondary and tertiary curricula, then the content of that program must be broadened to include the study of substantial contributions to the visual and sounding arts, as well as theatre, dance, and cinema. The essential point here is that a grounding in the fine arts must constitute an integral part of any curricular program that calls itself "liberal." Indeed, those disciplines should never have been allowed to become marginalized through the presumptive view expressed by a single body of educationalists, namely, that such fields of endeavor do not participate sufficiently in its Platonic constellation of "great ideas"—notwithstanding the specious aura of objectivity by which that claim was derived.[21]

The editors of the Great Books collections, which were first published in 1952 and are touted as the foundation of a liberal education, are indicted here for promoting their narrow view of "great ideas" that made the cut in the "Great Books" series.[22] That the performing arts can be so sweepingly discredited is not new, but the scorn the liberal arts are facing today holds the academy responsible in new ways that are affecting operating budgets, program cuts, elimination of majors, and threats to all disciplines considered impractical in times of economic hardship. The wars over what constitutes a liberal arts education are not over, as Moll conveys:

> At this time, it is inconceivable that any single paradigm of liberal studies could be proposed that would be acceptable universally. We may even be reaching the end of the era in which it is acceptable *at all*. If the liberal arts are to survive in our postmodern–globalist–relativist intellectual milieu, and in the face of the utilitarian preoccupation with preprofessional majors that

now prevails, it must be the task of faculty at each individual institution to develop a vision of what such an education is to be. And that is the way it seems to be working out at the college level, with a wide range of schemes being implemented. In any case, I believe it is a categorical imperative that the option of pursuing a broad-based agenda of study centered on the humanities be retained in our curricula of higher education, and that the fine arts should comprise an integral component of any such program.[23]

It is precisely Moll's observation of the various visions of liberal arts being played out at each institution that compels us to publish this book. Each of us at our own institution will play a vital role in determining how the performing arts are, or are not, included in the vision of the liberal arts. We would like to take for granted that our colleagues in all disciplines have come around to understand what Bennett Reimer calls "the special cognitive status of the arts and the authentic, essential ways they involve people in intelligent, reasoned, mindful experiences that yield a powerful form of knowledge of their outer and inner worlds."[24] But economic crises have taken their toll, legislatures have utilized their power to dictate scarcity, and threatened colleagues can take on a less enlightened view when faced with cuts to their own programs and agendas. We cannot put our guard down, and need to remind administrators at every turn why the performing arts are foundational to a liberal arts education.

The arts in general, and the performing arts in particular, are rarely included in discussions of efficacious pedagogies or skills necessary for a well-rounded education. This despite the wide-spread calls from business leaders for higher education graduates with skills that would be considered more central to the arts than any other discipline. In 2012, David Oxtoby published the article "The Place of the Arts in a Liberal Education" about the AAC&U's Liberal Education and America's Promise (LEAP) initiative in *Liberal Education*. He noted that "'Study' of the arts is mentioned in LEAP rubrics, but not creation or performance; 'teamwork' is another LEAP outcome, but it appears as a generic goal that one could apply not only to a group of students performing a play or ensemble music, but also to everything from group classroom presentations to laboratory work. The rest of the LEAP initiative barely connects to the arts."[25] The LEAP initiative has not addressed this lacuna in the intervening years. Although one of the LEAP Essential Learning Outcomes is Critical and Creative Thinking, the VALUE rubric on Creative Thinking doesn't emphasize *doing* art. The introduction notes that "[c]reative thinking in higher education can only be expressed productively within a particular domain. The student must have a strong foundation in the strategies and skills of the domain in order to make connections and synthesize."[26] This statement implies that creativity must be disciplinary and not attempted until a student has acquired an intellectual understanding of creation within the discipline. That goes against prevailing views of creativity that insist creativity in the arts can be introduced without a foundation, unlike in the sciences.[27] It also seems to suggest that creative thinking cannot arise out of interdisciplinary work, and must be a destination rather than an investigative process.

The AAC&U's most recent strategic plan states: "Science and the other STEM fields are important to Americans' global future. But rich learning about history, diverse cultures, languages and literatures, the creative and performing arts, philosophical traditions, religions, and political systems is equally fundamental to Americans' global future and success."[28] Once again, this includes the arts as a subject of study, not as a practice. Similarly, the 2015 AAC&U survey of CAOs on trends in general education lists learning outcomes that address skills and knowledge, none of which include creativity skills. The list of skills they asked about includes public speaking, but no other skill explicitly involving creating thinking.[29] When so many institutions are paying attention to calls from American businesses for graduates with creative and innovation skills, why were those learning outcomes not included in the survey of CAOs? One explanation may be that the AAC&U, like many institutions of higher education and individual academics, still conceive of the arts as a subset of the humanities, with the same practices and occasional innovative forms of scholarship. In a letter to the authors, responding to questions about the place of the arts in AAC&U studies and projects, President Lynn Pasquerella wrote, "I am convinced that the future of the humanities, including the arts, lies in the cultivation of humanities practice, both in traditional and innovative ways." She lauded artists who engage humanistic questions and others "whose work makes a connection between humanities questions and endeavors and the products of cultural expression." Referring to the age-old criticism of the humanities as a pursuit for the elite, Pasquerella warned that public institutions of higher education—the schools that serve the broadest range of the population—will have to increase their public practice and "be a visible force in the lives of the broadest possible segments of society."[30] President Pasquerella's references to "practice" are welcome, because it is through practice—both pedagogical and public—that the performing arts have the most to offer the academy.

In terms of pedagogical and research practice, the performing arts have about as much in common with the humanities as the sciences do. The arts in general, and the performing arts in particular, approach research and pedagogy in fundamentally different ways from the traditional humanities. Certainly there is humanities-style pedagogy and research in the performing arts, where we investigate human endeavors and artifacts in traditional formats and publish our research for narrow audiences of fellow scholars. But in our classrooms it is far more common to see embodied pedagogy that incorporates subjective response, and the publication of our research most often takes the form of public performance in front of live audiences made up of non-expert fellow citizens. Because the very basis of our work is the interaction of human bodies and ideas, our teaching and research is, and has always been, public practice.

The public nature of our teaching and research is not only about format, but also intention. Although arts practice may be seen inside higher education as a merely aesthetic examination of humanistic questions, the arts, and performing arts in particular, have always had direct interaction with and impact on, the wider society. Even at its most conservative and traditional, performing arts research has always been presented to the public with the purpose of changing society for the better. This goal has become even more focused in the last half century with the rise of the arts as civic practice, in which artists take their skills into the community in order to facilitate the civic-minded work of public partners. The work of artists, often trained and working in institutions of higher education, having a direct impact on civic life, can be found in the writing and practice of Augusto Boal (theatre), Liz Lerman (dance), and Brynjulf Stige (music), to name only a few examples.[31] Current activity of artists in public practice can be found by looking at the web pages of professional organizations such as The Center for Performance and Civic Practice, as well as in the wide range of literature on arts therapies. However, institutions of higher education have been slower to catch on to this shift to more direct civic engagement in the arts. But the number of degree programs that focus on art in public practice is growing every year, and relevant courses are appearing in traditional studio-oriented programs at an even higher rate. We are ahead of the curve in being "a visible force in the lives of the broadest possible segments of society." But it is incumbent upon performing arts departments to cultivate such work by acquiring the professional development to teach and model ethical creative collaborations in communities, and to share our methodologies and long history of public service with our institutions.[32]

Fortunately, there has been some progress in the recognition of the arts as both important subject matter and relevant practice. In 2015, the AAC&U added "knowledge of the arts" to the list of "knowledge areas" addressed by learning outcomes in a survey of higher education administrators. In the previous survey, conducted in 2008, institutions were not asked about the arts. Clearly the addition was needed, because in the 2015 survey, 85% of institutions reporting a common set of learning outcomes for all students claimed to have learning outcomes addressing "knowledge of the arts," placing the arts in the middle of all subject areas listed.[33] Also, the new approach to general education being championed by AAC&U includes experiential education that is "[r]equired, sustained, assessed," and calls for expanding HIPs so that they are "required, sustained, included in all general education pathways,"[34] directions that provide an open door for the performing arts to take a central role in general education.

These signs of progress, set against the continued bias against the arts and the lack of knowledge about the real-world applications of our work, are just some of the reasons why departments of performing arts must assert ourselves in HIPs. The conflation of the arts with the humanities will be dangerous for the arts as attacks on the humanities increase and as each discipline must justify its continued existence in the university setting. The performing arts are not simply humanities disciplines with fun forms of scholarship and unique ways of considering human activity. The performing arts have long-established relationships with the community outside the university, and time-tested pedagogies that are uniquely suited for training students for the growing creative economy. We must learn to articulate our research goals, showcase our successes in impacting society, and demonstrate the power of our pedagogies. We must show institutions and organizations of higher education that we have unique skills and structures that are vital to the future of higher education.

The arts in general exist in a perilous place within higher education. While some administrators and faculty may see them as traditional liberal arts and sciences educational disciplines, others see them as living outside that tradition. While that outsider status may work well for disciplines such as business, education, architecture, or engineering, all of which often occupy central locations in undergraduate institutions, the performing arts do not share those disciplines' enjoyment of acceptance and value by society at large. Schools of the above-mentioned disciplines may continue to co-exist happily in institutions with new general education programs, benefitting from the well-rounded educations their majors are achieving and justifying their continued existence through public support, but performing arts disciplines (despite the evidence that our graduates succeed, thrive, and are content post-graduation)[35] may find themselves having an even more difficult time justifying faculty lines and attracting students if we do not find our way into skills-based general education programs and HIPs.

It is incumbent on performing arts departments to take action by involving themselves directly in general education initiatives and by putting forward their pedagogies and programs as models of HIP best practices. We need to assert the relevance of the performing arts to the AAC&U HIPs, widely recognized as the gold standard for college campuses nationwide for the following urgent reasons: (1) to advocate for the performing arts as a thriving contributor to the goals of liberal arts education; (2) to encourage performing arts departments to participate as fully as possible within the realm of general education and to provide models to help them increase that participation; and (3) to ensure the attendant creative capacity and cultural literacy attained by students via their explorations in the performing arts, regardless of major.

A Call to Action

This book is a call to action. There is a call to action in each chapter regarding implementing the respective HIPs at your institution. The call to action is for higher education administrators and organizations to include the performing arts in their considerations of the HIPs in general education and learning outcomes. It is a call to performing arts departments, programs, and faculty to advocate for themselves as valuable contributors to HIPs, general education, and the learning outcomes desired for all college students. And it is a call to performing arts faculty to use the HIPs with their own majors in intentional ways, to better prepare them for life after college. All of these groups can benefit from the vast amount of literature that exists on HIPs, and from the ongoing theorization and research being done by the AAC&U and other organizations working to improve higher education. One specific tool that may be helpful is the AAC&U "High-Impact Practices for Administrators Tool."[36] Administrators and performing arts faculty need to make sure that the performing arts are included in all areas possible, and reach out to inquire into how they can contribute both to the HIPs as they are practiced on our campuses and to general education reforms as they are instituted.

This call to action comes at a precarious time for the liberal arts, but it could be a particularly fortuitous time for the performing arts. In times of crises, there is an opportunity to better position ourselves in the shakeup. Many colleges and universities are taking inventory, and determining that radical change needs to occur within general education, student learning outcomes, and assessment. The performing arts can put our best foot forward into the fray and make the case for the centrality of our disciplines in delivering the most prized educational practices. In his provocatively titled article Strategy for American Humanities: Blow Them Up and Start Again, Toby Miller argues for all the disciplines in the humanities to integrate vocational training into curriculum.[37] The performing arts are ahead of this message: we already integrate professional practice into our disciplines, and we only need to be more intentional about the delivery and messaging of this merge.[38] We also need to be explicit about how the performing arts align with institutional mission. The revision of general education is a prime time to make this alignment clear, and to seize the resultant broader student exposure and engagement.[39]

Too often, performing arts departments leave ourselves out of the conversation. The arts have historically been discounted as frivolous so their skills have been ignored, and some arts faculty prefer to be left alone, accustomed to, and finding comfort in, the isolation. Furthermore, during times of prosperity some arts educators have prioritized educating professional artists, and there is the impression that using our skills in the business world or in communities for civic practice is demeaning the art. Sometimes arts programs are resistant to participating in general education and want only to be training future artists. When asked to perform at VIP university events, yet wounded in territorial curriculum wars, arts faculty are understandably wary of being perceived as service-only departments without intrinsic disciplinary merit. But we cannot retreat our way out of this predicament. We must be our own champions until conceptions of the liberal arts promote the performing arts as self-evident to a comprehensive education.

What follows are ten chapters, one for each HIP, that contain an introductory review of the literature and research and case studies demonstrating the ways in which the performing arts contribute to the particular HIP in question throughout colleges and universities nationally, and internationally (in a couple of cases). Chapter 2 looks at *First-Year Seminars and Experiences*, and common First-Year Experience learning outcomes and how they line up with common performing arts learning outcomes, necessitating greater participation by performing arts faculty. Chapter 3 is about *Common Intellectual Experiences*, and discusses how the performing arts are finding their way into general education curricula and experiences. Chapter 4 is on *Learning Communities*, and examines how performing arts pedagogies enrich those of other disciplines. The performing arts can add embodiment and practice to any discipline, and the combination is beneficial in a transdisciplinary integration. *Writing Intensive Courses* are the subject of Chapter 5, which explores how we teach creativity. Why are students of all majors not encouraged to take courses that teach writing in artistic forms in (partial) fulfillment of their writing-intensive course requirements?

Chapter 6 is about *Collaborative Assignments and Projects* and describes how these projects are at the heart of what the performing arts do all the time—and promote the same skills being pushed so much in contemporary higher education. Although the humanities feel excluded by the new emphasis on skills, performing arts programs should not. We already teach team building and communication skills. *Undergraduate Research* is the subject of Chapter 7, which advocates that our students involved in creative scholarship need to be acknowledged for their contributions to the institution's research profile. This is important for equity reasons, as the perception of what "counts" as undergraduate research relates to the distribution of grant funds, visibility, and overall support on campuses. The HIP of *Diversity/Global Learning* is discussed in Chapter 8, which details how performing artists wrestle with issues of diversity and global learning constantly, from the historical context of creative works, to casting, to presentation, and beyond. How are the performing arts poised to engage students in self-reflexivity and increase their cultural competence? Chapter 9 covers *Service Learning and Community-Based Learning* in the performing arts and details how students engage with communities in numerous ways during their undergraduate years. With the rise of applied performing arts companies and the increasing visibility of applied performing arts practices, academic performing arts programs are beginning to embrace service and community-based learning with community and non-profit partners in the social service sector. Chapter 10 is about *Internships* in the performing arts as practical and experiential learning that leads to viable career paths. Finally, Chapter 11 looks at *Capstone Courses and Projects* and considers how we are preparing our performing arts majors as they near graduation. How do we build capstone outcomes into courses throughout a student's matriculation, so that they can demonstrate longitudinal progress in their learning? Taken together, the case studies presented in each chapter point the way toward a full integration of the performing arts in our students' liberal education, and answer our urgent call with innovations that articulate the performing arts as high-impact educational practices.

Notes

1. Cindy A. Kilgo, Jessica K. Ezell Sheets, and Ernest T. Pascarella, "The Link between High-Impact Practices and Student Learning: Some Longitudinal Evidence," 523.
2. Zac Anderson, "Rick Scott Wants to Shift University Funding Away from Some Degrees."
3. Glenn Whitehouse, "Learning the Truth About Rubio's Welder vs Philosopher Remark."
4. See AAC&U's initiative "Liberal Education and America's Promise" [LEAP] or the Strategic National Arts Alumni Project [SNAAP].
5. The ArtsEdSearch website contains links to over 200 studies examining a wide range of arts practices and their positive impacts on everything from critical thinking skills to high school dropout rates.
6. Gene Diaz, Martha Barry McKenna, eds. *Preparing Educators for Arts Integration: Placing Creativity at the Center of Learning*, 4–5.
7. George D. Kuh and Carol Geary Schneider, *High-Impact Educational Practices: What They Are, Who Has Access to Them, and Why They Matter*.
8. C. Edward Watson, George D. Kuh, Terrel Rhodes, Tracy Penny Light, and Helen L. Chen. *ePortfolios—The Eleventh High Impact Practice*.
9. Arthur W. Chickering and Zelda F. Gamson. *Seven Principles for Good Practice in Undergraduate Education*. Originally published in the AAHE Bulletin, 3–7.
10. George D. Kuh, Ken O'Donnell, and Sally Reed, *Ensuring Quality and Taking High-Impact Practices to Scale*.
11. Payscale.com.
12. Hart Research Associates, "It Takes More Than a Major: Employer Priorities for College Learning and Student Success," survey conducted by Hart Research Associates and AAC&U.
13. The 2015 survey did ask about "Research skills and projects," but not about collaborative research or any form of teamwork skills.

14. See AAC&U, *How Should Colleges Prepare Students to Succeed in Today's Global Economy?* (Results of a national poll by Peter D. Hart Research Associates, 2007) quoted in "Top Ten Things Employers Look for in New College Graduates."
15. Dan Berrett, "The Creativity Cure," *The Chronicle of Higher Education.*
16. Steven J. Tepper, "Thinking 'Bigger Than Me' in the Liberal Arts."
17. See Harvard's "Report of the Task Force on the Arts."
18. Harvard, 21.
19. See Tom Rockmore, *Kant on Art and Truth after Plato.*
20. See Immanuel Kant, *Critique of Judgement.*
21. Kevin N. Moll, "Prolegomena to Any Future 'Great Books of Music': Reconsidering Liberal-Arts Paradigms in a Postmodern Age," 70–71.
22. Robert Maynard Hutchins and Mortimer Jerome Adler, "The Great Ideas Today."
23. Moll, "Prolegomena to Any Future 'Great Books of Music,'" 78.
24. Bennett Reimer, "The Nonconceptual Nature of Aesthetic Cognition," 112.
25. David Oxtoby, "The Place of the Arts in a Liberal Education."
26. See AAC&U, VALUE Creative Thinking rubric.
27. For a good summary of the research on how creativity works, see R. Keith Sawyer, *Explaining Creativity: The Science of Human Innovation.*
28. See the AAC&U's most recent Strategic Plan.
29. See the AAC&U's *Recent Trends in General Education Design, Learning Outcomes, and Teaching Approaches.*
30. All quotes from president Pasquerella from a personal email to the authors, May 23, 2017.
31. The editors would like to thank Susan Gardstrom for introducing us to the work of Brynjulf Stige.
32. See Chapter 9 for more information and case studies about how the performing arts contribute to service learning and community-based learning. Professional development for faculty can be found through various organizations within the performing arts disciplines. One particularly rich community of performing arts leaders convenes each summer at the Association for Theatre in Higher Education's Leadership Institute (often comprising dance scholars as well).
33. See AAC&U and Hart Research Associates, *Trends in Learning Outcomes Assessment.* The percentage was 72% among all institutions (including those that do not have common sets of learning outcomes for all students), also right in the middle of the set of subject areas.
34. Paul L. Gaston, *General Education Transformed.*
35. See survey data collected by Strategic National Arts Alumni Project [SNAAP].

36. The tool can be downloaded at https://pullias.usc.edu/wp-content/uploads/2016/06/HIPs-for-Admins-Tool-Formatted.pdf and its explanation can be found at: Adrianna Kezar, and Elizabeth Holcombe, "Support for High-Impact Practices: A New Tool for Administrators."
37. Toby Miller, "Strategy for American Humanities: Blow Them Up and Start Again."
38. See Chapter 11 about capstone projects and experiences for more information on how the performing arts should deliver intentional vocational training that includes and goes beyond performance training, to produce a more agile and entrepreneurial graduate.
39. See Scott M. Fuess and Nancy D. Mitchell, "General Education Reform: Opportunities for Institutional Alignment."

Bibliography

Anderson, Zac. 2011. Rick Scott Wants to Shift University Funding Away from Some Degrees. *Herald Tribune*, October 10.
Association of American Colleges & Universities (AAC&U). aacu.org. "How Should Colleges Prepare Students to Succeed in Today's Global Economy?" quoted in "Top Ten Things Employers Look for in New College Graduates." http://www.aacu.org/leap/students/employers-top-ten. Accessed June 2017.
———. aacu.org. Recent Trends in General Education Design, Learning Outcomes, and Teaching Approaches. https://www.aacu.org/sites/default/files/files/LEAP/2015_Survey_Report2_GEtrends.pdf. Accessed Mar 2017.
———. aacu.org and Hart Research Associates. Trends in Learning Outcomes Assessment. https://www.aacu.org/sites/default/files/files/LEAP/2015_Survey_Report3.pdf. Accessed 11 Aug 2017.
———. aacu.org. About LEAP. https://www.aacu.org/leap. Accessed 23 Aug 2017.
———. aacu.org. VALUE Creative Thinking Rubric. https://www.aacu.org/value/rubrics. Accessed 23 Aug 2017.
———. aacu.org. Strategic Plan 2013–2017: Big Questions, Urgent Challenges: Liberal Education and American's Global Future. https://www.aacu.org/about/strategicplan. Accessed 23 Aug 2017.
Berrett, Dan. 2013. The Creativity Cure. *The Chronicle of Higher Education*, April 1.
Chickering, Arthur W., and Zelda F. Gamson. 1987. Seven Principles for Good Practice in Undergraduate Education. *AAHE Bulletin* 3: 7.
Clayton, Michelle, Mark Franko, Nadine George-Graves, André Lepecki, Susan Manning, Janice Ross, and Rebecca Schneider. 2013. Inside/Beside Dance Studies: A Conversation: Mellon Dance Studies in/and the Humanities. *Dance Research Journal* 45 (3): 5–28.

Diaz, Gene, and Martha Barry McKenna, eds. 2017. *Preparing Educators for Arts Integration: Placing Creativity at the Center of Learning*, 4–5. New York: Teachers College Press.

Fuess, Scott M., Jr., and Nancy D. Mitchell. 2011. General Education Reform: Opportunities for Institutional Alignment. *The Journal of General Education* 60 (1): 1–15.

Gaston, Paul L. 2015. *General Education Transformed: How We Can, Why We Must*. Washington, DC: Association of American Colleges and Universities.

Hart Research Associates. 2013. It Takes More Than a Major: Employer Priorities for College Learning and Student Success. *Liberal Education* 99. https://www.aacu.org/sites/default/files/files/LEAP/2013_EmployerSurvey.pdf. Accessed June 2017.

Harvard University. 2008. Harvard.edu. Report of the Task Force on the Arts, December. http://www.harvard.edu/sites/default/files/content/arts_report.pdf.

Hutchins, Robert Maynard, and Mortimer Jerome Adler. 1981. The Great Ideas Today. *Encyclopædia Britannica*.

Kant, Immanuel, and Sir James Creed Meredith. 1952. *The Critique of Judgement. Translated with Analytical Indexes by James Creed Meredith*. Oxford: Oxford University Press.

Kezar, Adrianna, and Elizabeth Holcombe. 2017. Support for High-Impact Practices: A New Tool for Administrators. *Liberal Education* 103 (1): n1.

Kilgo Cindy, A., Jessica K. Ezell Sheets, and Ernest T. Pascarella. 2015. The Link Between High-Impact Practices and Student Learning: Some Longitudinal Evidence. *Higher Education* 69 (4): 523.

Kuh, George D. 2008. *High-Impact Educational Practices: What They Are, Who Has Access to Them, and Why They Matter*. Washington, DC: Association of American Colleges and Universities.

Kuh, George D., Ken O'Donnell, and Sally Reed. 2013. *Ensuring Quality and Taking High-Impact Practices to Scale*. Washington, DC: Association of American Colleges and Universities.

Miller, Toby. 2012. Strategy for American Humanities: Blow Them Up and Start Again. *Times Higher Education*, 8.

Moll, Kevin N. 2016. Prolegomena to Any Future "Great Books of Music": Reconsidering Liberal-Arts Paradigms in a Postmodern Age. *The Journal of Aesthetic Education* 50 (4): 45–85.

Oxtoby, David W. 2012. The Place of the Arts in a Liberal Education. *Liberal Education* 98 (2): 36–41.

PayScale Human Capital. Payscale.com. 2016 Workforce-Skills Preparedness Report. http://www.payscale.com/data-packages/job-skills. Accessed 23 Aug 2017.

Reimer, Bennett. 1986. The Nonconceptual Nature of Aesthetic Cognition. *Journal of Aesthetic Education* 20 (4): 111–117.

Rockmore, Tom. 2013. Kant on Art and Truth After Plato. *Washington University Jurisprudence Review* 6: 45.

Sawyer, R. Keith. 2011. *Explaining Creativity: The Science of Human Innovation.* Oxford: Oxford University Press.

Strategic National Arts Alumni Project (SNAAP). http://snaap.indiana.edu/. Accessed 23 Aug 2017.

Tepper, Steven J. 2014. Thinking 'Bigger Than Me' in the Liberal Arts. *The Chronicle of Higher Education*, September 19.

Watson, C. Edward, George D. Kuh, Terrel Rhodes, Tracy Penny Light, and Helen L. Chen. 2016. ePortfolios–The Eleventh High Impact Practice. *International Journal* 6 (2): 65–69.

Whitehouse, Glenn. 2015. Learning the Truth About Rubio's Welder vs Philosopher Remark. *Naples Daily News*, December 4.

CHAPTER 2

First-Year Seminars and Experiences

First-Year Seminars and Experiences are the most widespread and researched curricular innovation in higher education of the past 30 years. Although they differ greatly from one institution to the other, First-Year Experiences (FYEs) and seminars are regularly tasked with a host of learning outcomes that range from intellectual and personal development to need for cognition. This is an ambitious set of learning and development outcomes for one course to tackle, but research shows that ambitious and successful FYE programs have a significant impact on student retention and academic and personal success throughout their college careers.[1]

There is no definitive list of FYE learning outcomes, but there are a set of outcomes that are shared by large percentages of programs and which are regularly assessed. In the original High-Impact Educational Practices document, Kuh lists "critical inquiry, frequent writing, information literacy, collaborative learning, and other skills that develop students' intellectual and practical competencies"[2] as the qualities of effective FYEs. He also notes that they offer opportunities for students to connect with faculty research. The First-Year Seminar student learning goals at most institutions reflect these, and can be divided into three major categories: (1) intellectual skills such as active reading, critical thinking, intensive writing in different formats and disciplines, and similar college-wide goals introduced in the FYE; (2) academic skills and habits like knowledge of the academic resources on campus, test-taking and note-taking, and appreciation of the traditions and strengths of their own institution and a development of intellectual curiosity; and (3) personal development skills like the ability to collaborate with and understand the contributions of others, the pursuit of and development of a personal code of ethics, leadership abilities, self-reflection, and so on. The intellectual and institutional goals of the First-Year Seminar are regularly met in performing arts First-Year Seminars, and it can be argued that the performing arts are especially effective at some of these goals—active reading and critical thinking particularly—because of the "outside the box" thinking demanded in creative endeavors. The personal development goals, where students learn to consider their own subjectivity both as unique individuals and as part of a larger social structure, are perhaps where the performing arts are uniquely suited, no matter what type of FYE they serve.

Structurally, FYEs are also probably the most amorphous of the high-impact practices (HIPs) and have the potential to impact the greatest number of the essential learning outcomes of a liberal education. The five main types of First-Year Seminar range from extended orientation seminars to in-depth academic seminars[3] and are sometimes seen as "catch-alls" for every academic and life skill that faculty, administrators, and board members would like college students to acquire. At many institutions, other HIPs are bundled into FYEs, both for the sake of financial and other practical exigencies, and because educators understandably want students to begin integrating their curricular and co-curricular experiences and applying their education to real-world situations early in their college careers. All of the other HIPs except for undergraduate research, internships, and capstone courses can be easily bundled into an FYE either as a pedagogy or as a dimension of content. And since FYEs are so widely studied and assessed, research showing the efficacy of incorporating other HIPs into FYEs can lead administrators to believe that it can all be done at once.[4] Unfortunately, no one class (or even set of first-year classes, as some schools structure their FYEs) can incorporate every other HIP or instill every good habit that students will need to succeed in college and in life. When institutions attempt to make everything happen in the first year, they risk overwhelming students and diluting the potential that FYEs have to get students off on the right foot in their educational journey. This wide variation in both structure and purpose of FYEs only helps to emphasize that when it comes to first-year students, *what* is taught is not nearly as important as *how* it is taught. Efficacious pedagogies for first-year students are how the courses achieve their learning outcomes and are where the performing arts can make their greatest contribution.

Because of the wide range of course types and goals across institutions, it can be difficult to measure what pedagogies "work" in FYEs. But regardless of the course style or goals, pedagogies that draw on the performing arts are particularly useful and efficacious for first-year students. Arts-informed pedagogies have been gaining traction in K–12 education for years, and students come to college with both experience with arts pedagogies and the expectations that they will spend time being asked to think creatively and work collaboratively. Whereas the No Child Left Behind Act's narrowed focus on testing in reading and math had significant negative impacts on arts instruction,[5] the Every Student Succeeds Act of 2015 (if it is allowed to continue) opens K–12 education's focus from "Core Academic Subjects" to a "well-rounded" education, providing greater space for interdisciplinarity, and offers funding for integrating the arts into STEM (science, technology, engineering, mathematics). When paired with the fact that nearly half of new college students report that in high school they were involved at least "some" with performing or visual arts programs, it becomes clear that first-year college students are likely to be open to performance pedagogies that promote interdisciplinary thinking and real-world connections.[6]

First-Year Seminars and Experiences that involve practical, creative work in the performing arts expose students to important personal development habits early in their college careers. They provide opportunities for close, non-lecture-oriented contact with faculty and expose students to older peers who are already successful in the academic environment. Practical skills and habits are taught, not solely through lectures or small class projects, but via performance projects in which skill acquisition is necessary in order to complete a successful, often public, presentation. Time management and personal responsibility are consistently emphasized in light of other academic responsibilities so that habits learned in the performance classroom will translate into other courses. The performing arts most commonly involve participation in someone else's creation, and in order to participate effectively, the student must consider the needs and desires of others, often others from very different backgrounds from their own. They must compromise in service of the greater project, and learn how to argue for their own ideas. Regular collaboration gives rise to leadership skills. Because creation involves self-reflection, students begin to develop self-actualization and ethical processes.

The case studies in this chapter examine the use of performative pedagogies in courses that, although they focus on content related to the performing arts, might easily be taught with traditional lecture-style techniques. Susan Kattwinkel writes about her use of performance creation to embody ethical debate in a course on theatre and ethical choice. Embodied pedagogy offers a deeply personal, empathic entrance into the difficult social concepts that first-year college students are often encountering for the first time. Jim Davis outlines a devised theatre project that responds to a survey of political opinions among fellow students in the university. His use of established theatre practice and coaching techniques in an assignment designed to help students productively engage with difficult real-world conversations is an excellent example of how first-year students can be brought into the world of intellectual debate. In both cases students learn to integrate personal experience and opinion with those of others to create complex and reasoned responses to difficult and important social issues.

Call to action:

- Administrators of FYE programs should recruit performing arts faculty to teach in the program. Performing arts FYE courses can offer both rigorous coursework and active, interesting pedagogies that contrast with the large survey courses that first-year students are likely to have as the majority of their schedule. The ease of incorporating interdisciplinary work into performing arts courses also helps prevent first-year students from "pigeonholing" their courses into disciplines and failing to see the connections across the curriculum. The close connections with faculty and other students that are formed by performing arts pedagogies also help bond students to the institution, raising retention rates and strengthening institutional loyalty.
- Performing arts departments must take a more active role in their school's FYE programs. FYE courses are an excellent opportunity to recruit new students to performing arts programs. Students who have no plans to be arts majors, or whose parents disapprove of that choice, are often drawn to the one first-year course that isn't a large lecture class. If the course is academically rigorous enough, they may reconceive of the performing arts as a legitimate major and convince their parents of the same. At the very least, students who enjoy their FYE class are likely to take more courses in that discipline during

their college career. In institutions where departments must play the "numbers game" of justifying their majors by teaching as many non-majors as possible, FYE courses are terrific places to show off faculty and pedagogies that students will want to experience again.
- Performing arts departments should make sure that their own majors are incorporating skills learned in their First-Year Seminars into their major studies. Arts students often have the benefit of close-knit student communities within their majors, but they often segregate themselves within those communities, and this can isolate them from other students and decrease their interactions with students with experiences and beliefs different from their own. Especially for students hoping to make a living in the arts, it is crucial that they maintain relationships with students who will be their future audiences, in the interests of understanding the desires and needs of the wider population. Aside from other general education courses that can, unfortunately, take the form of large impersonal lectures inspiring little contact among students in the class, FYE courses can be the first and last place performing arts students interact regularly and personally with students outside the arts.

Devising Pedagogies for First-Year Theatre and Performance Studies Students

James Davis
Kennesaw State University
Kennesaw, GA, USA

> I don't think I will ever experience an election that will be as polarizing and terrifying as this one.[7]

It will probably come as no surprise that this student was writing about the 2016 presidential election.

It will also come as no surprise that the 2016 presidential election presented unique challenges to those of us who work with first-year students. While the action and rhetoric of the 2016 presidential election was stressful to nearly everyone, they were particularly problematic for students who were facing the challenges of college for the first time.

I teach at Kennesaw State University (KSU), long regarded for its ground-breaking programs for first-year students, and hold a joint appointment in the Department of First-Year Studies (the academic home of our learning communities, LCs) and the Department of Theatre & Performance Studies (TPS). While my primary department home is First-Year and Transition Studies, my academic training is in theatre, and I teach upper-division courses and serve as a director and dramaturg in the TPS production season. This joint appointment, while it may result in more department meetings, allows me to frequently demonstrate the value of theatre pedagogies for first-year students.

At KSU all first-year full-time students with fewer than 15 semester hours are required to complete a First-Year Seminar or enroll in an LC.[8] We have numerous seminars and LCs focused on specific disciplines and areas of interest, all of which address four specific learning outcomes: life skills, strategies for academic success, campus and community connections, and foundations for global learning.[9]

A central focus of my teaching and service is our LC for first-year TPS majors, called "The World of the Scholar Artist." This LC has been in existence since 2007 and links Introduction to Theatre Studies and the university's First-Year Seminar. I teach the First-Year Seminar, which addresses "life skills, strategies for academic success [...] and foundations for global learning," as well as departmental and discipline-specific material to help our new majors navigate the complexities of KSU's theatre program.[10] In fall of 2016, we had two sections of our LC. I taught both sections of our First-Year Seminar and two other faculty members taught individual sections of Introduction to Theatre Studies.

Departmental research[11] has indicated that students enrolled in LCs at Kennesaw State have higher grade point averages (GPAs), develop a greater holistic understanding of material covered in their courses, and are more deeply embedded in campus culture than those students who are not. Anecdotally, this level of achievement is also reflected in the Department of Theatre & Performance Studies, with increased participation of students who enrolled in LCs in their first year in our mainstage production season as actors, designers, stage-managers, dramaturgs, and other production positions.

A central mission of the Department of Theatre & Performance Studies is to combine academic and creative work to create original, socially relevant theatre—often using devised original performances as a way to develop and present research. In the past, the TPS First-Year LC has met this challenge and created projects as diverse as working with Augusto Boal's Theatre of the Oppressed, original performances based on the Turkish *Karagöz* shadow puppet theatre tradition and one-minute plays about de-extinction developed in collaboration with an upper-level biology course. However, as 2016 brought an extremely contentious presidential election which raised myriad political, cultural, and economic issues (as well as highlighting their numerous intersections), it provided a unique opportunity to put our department's central mission into practice.

Similar goals are present in the First-Year Seminar I taught as part of the LC. The course, called "Be The Change," uses concepts from community engagement, specifically research- and skills-based community-based learning projects, to introduce larger issues relevant to first-year students. While there is course content focusing on traditional first-year curriculum (time management, study skills, etc.), much of our seminar meets these specific learning outcomes through dramaturgical research, ensemble work, and rehearsal and revision, which ultimately came together in the creation of an original performance. Working in collaboration with my colleagues who taught the other courses in the LC, I decided that we would collect information based on the political and cultural attitudes of other students enrolled in First-Year Seminars and use this data to create original, short, collaborative, ensemble driven, devised performances.

Generally speaking, devised performance is "an alternative to the dominant literary theatre tradition" and can "start from an infinite number of possibilities, such as an idea, image, concept, object, poem, piece of music, or painting, and the precise nature of the end product is unknown."[12] This openness was particularly useful for this project in that it created an opportunity for the LC students to engage with diverse ideas and opinions, empowered them to make important creative decisions, and positioned the rehearsal and research process on an equal footing with the performance.

While I wanted the students to have the freedom to explore the topics creatively, I did impose three non-negotiable rules. The first was "yes and"—a rule from improvisational theatre where one actor makes a statement and the second accepts it and adds onto it. "Yes and" required students to listen to a variety of ideas about the projects and think about how they could accept and expand on them rather than discounting them immediately and going with their initial, and at times, underdeveloped, instincts and choices. Or, as Tina Fey explains in her book *Bossypants*, "If I start a scene with 'I can't believe it's so hot in here,' and you just say, 'Yeah…' we're kind of at a standstill. But if I say, 'I can't believe it's so hot in here,' and you say, 'What did you expect? We're in hell' [...] now we're getting somewhere."[13] This was particularly useful in the early stages of the devising process when students were brainstorming and attempting to engage material.

The second rule was "therefore/but"—a story structure strategy practice by Trey Parker and Matt Stone, the creators of *South Park*. According to Parker, when *South Park* writers create an episode, each scene in a script should be followed by "either the word 'therefore,' or 'but,'" to create an organic flow into the next scene, as well as creating an action that motivates the script's next action.[14] By considering this, and being aware of how one action impacts another, it helped students to create work that followed a linear and logical structure.

The third, and possibly the most difficult rule for the students, was "no cynicism." The intent of this rule was to address the prevailing attitude in circulation during fall 2016 that both the presidential candidates were generally dishonest, motivated solely by self-interest, and equally unqualified for the job. As cynicism is utterly antithetical to both significant civil discourse and creativity, I assigned a step in the project that would allow the students to step outside of their narrow perceptions of the candidates and, hopefully, challenge some of their preconceived beliefs. In this phase, each student was assigned to identify five ideas, policies or professional qualifications that they viewed as a positive for both Mr. Trump and Secretary Clinton. This step in the project encouraged the students to view both candidates more objectively, and as one reflected, "engage with those positives and negatives (and) learn more about our political system than I ever thought imaginable." "This," according to a different student, "forced us to look across political party lines and at least attempt to understand the other side's point of view." While this may not have eliminated cynicism entirely, it was a "first step in coming together with people who have different views."

This was the most difficult rule to enforce throughout the process as many of the students automatically defaulted to cynicism when they were generating material that was critical of the candidates. One student reflected that "It was really hard for us to talk about the candidates in a non-cynical way," but engaging with the material in a way that challenged them to be creative "made talking about politics easier for me."

The first step in the devising process was to determine what political and cultural issues the LC students themselves were concerned with. To do that, students filled out an anonymous survey that allowed them to reflect on and communicate their political context and beliefs. The survey asked them to, using a 1–10 scale where 1 was "Very Liberal" and 10 was "Very Conservative," rank their personal political beliefs as well as those of their families and hometown/community. They were also asked to identify five political/cultural issues that concerned them the most, who or what has generally had the most influence on the development of their political/cultural beliefs, and whether or not they had ever changed their minds about a deeply held political/cultural belief.[15]

Once the surveys were returned, we discussed the findings—specifically the definitions and misperceptions of "Liberal" and "Conservative"—and identified the six issues that the LC students thought were the most relevant to their lives: immigration reform, climate change, police brutality, increasing the minimum wage, gun control and the rising cost of college. Once these issues were identified, the students and I developed a more focused questionnaire that was distributed to 12 sections of the First-Year Seminar—some of which were part of other LCs—as well as a number of standalone sections. Our target audience of respondents was fairly diverse, and, as nearly all of our first-year students enroll in LCs during their first semester, representative of students from a number of majors and areas of interest.

The new questionnaire asked the other students enrolled in First-Year Seminars to identify one of the six issues, and then asked a series of questions about that issue, as well as others that would provide additional context and understanding. The first section focused on the issue selected by the respondent:

- What is your opinion on the issue you selected?
- How specifically does this issue affect all of us?
- Who/What has most influenced your beliefs on this topic?
- What does your family believe about this issue? Do they agree with you?

They were also asked:

- If you currently support one of the candidates, please list four specific policies/beliefs of theirs that appeal to you.
- How have you handled situations where you or others have encountered prejudiced actions or attitudes?
- What other thoughts/opinions/ideas do you have about important issues or our current political climate?

While the majority of responses were detailed and thoughtful, one of the most compelling bits of data was the reply to the question about whether or not the student supported one of the presidential candidates. A large number of respondents left the response blank—indicating either that they couldn't identify four of a candidate's policies/beliefs that they found appealing, or, possibly, that they didn't support a specific candidate. Of those that did answer, support was roughly equally divided among Donald Trump, Secretary Clinton, and Senator Bernie Sanders, who had lost the Democratic nomination and been out of the race for over a month when the questionnaire was circulated.

From "I do not support one of the candidates," and "I don't like any of them… Obama was better," through "n/a," "I hate them all," and "lol, this election sucks," responses indicated equal parts apathy and antipathy toward the major presidential candidates. While this was interesting and illustrative of how our cadre of first-year students regarded the election, it also forced us to see how cynicism had infused the political and cultural discourse.

Once the questionnaires were returned, students were grouped according to their interest and encouraged to react reflexively to the material. This was challenging, as most of the students had come from traditional, playwright/director-centric theatre training. But I tried to instill a sense of exploration and play by using theatre games and reminding them that the entire experience was an experiment. Throughout this process, I attempted to create an egalitarian environment, inspired by Konstantin Stanislavsky's concept of ensemble which placed "artistic aims above individual vanity."[16] Stanislavsky believed that in order for a performance to be successful, each member of an ensemble had to contribute equally. This was particularly applicable to this project as the entirety of it was based on the TPS majors' responses to the student questionnaire and it was imperative that they all contribute. Luckily, as the rehearsal and devising process started approximately two months into the semester, the students had already bonded and were willing collaborators. Because of this, one student wrote, "we were able to openly discuss how [these issues affect] the world and the people around us […] because we were able to discuss this there weren't really any topics off the table."

As this project existed well beyond the traditional classroom structure, I also had to step out of my standard "professor mode" and move into a place where I could simultaneously contribute as a member of the creative ensemble, as well as offer guidance, critique and instruction. For this, I used the idea of the sidecoach as developed and defined by Viola Spolin.

Spolin was a Chicago teacher and theatre artist whose work in the 1950s and 60s was central to the development of the style of improvisational theatre that would eventually become The Second City, one of the most influential theatre companies of the late twentieth century. (Incidentally, Spolin was also a pioneer in Creative Drama, a rehearsal technique and performance genre that uses games to develop spontaneous, interactive performances—many of which have been reinterpreted into the ice breakers and warmups used in academic and corporate settings.) According to Spolin, a sidecoach is simultaneously a member of the ensemble, as well as a leader who offers support, encouragement and guarantees the artist "time and space for movement, interaction and transformation."[17]

While the original intent of the project was to reflect the political and cultural attitudes of our fall 2016 first-year students, there were times when external forces compelled us to recalibrate. For example, approximately halfway through the devising process, the infamous *Access Hollywood* video of Donald Trump bragging that he could "grab (women) by the pussy" emerged. A number of students reacted immediately and discussed creating work in response to it. While sexual assault and rape culture were not included in the topics initially identified by the students, both had emerged as major issues in the campaign. As one student wrote, "our next possible president said he could sexually assault women and get away with it [...] he says it is because he is a celebrity, yet so many men get away with assaulting women on a day to day basis. That is why this needed to be introduced because it is a prevalent issue in our society." I was initially hesitant; however, I also wanted the project to be driven by the students' interests, so I agreed, and the issue was integrated into the whole.

Alison Oddey writes, "the very nature and eclecticism of the devising experience [...] makes it impossible to articulate a single theory of how theatre is devised, when every professional company or group works in a unique way with different intentions, interests, and concerns."[18] This was very much the case in our experience. After assigning groups and helping them clarify their topics, I attempted to let the students discover and create their individual pieces with only minimal sidecoaching. If I did anything right in this project, I was always being completely honest with the students about having no preconceptions about what they would create. While many of them felt confused and frustrated by this, it also provided an opportunity for them to explore their material in ways that I would have never come up with. One student wrote that this approach created a "safe space for creating the devised piece. I was able to be in a collaborative environment with people who wanted to create and inform. I was able to share my beliefs in a community of people that I trust."

Another benefit of this hands-off/sidecoaching approach was that groups could engage material using their own specific skill sets. For example, one group who was dealing with issues surrounding gun control found that they all had dance training as well as some experience with American sign language, which they incorporated into their final product. Obviously, there was no way of knowing this beforehand, and it created a compelling piece, but it had other unintended benefits as well—"Pulling my love of dance and sign language together to create this performance really empowered me in a way I could not have ordinarily conceived." While this was a fortuitous happenstance, it would not have happened in a more formalized, structured environment.

Ultimately, the nearly 50 students in the two sections of our First-Year Seminar created 12 original pieces inspired by our questionnaire. There were three Saturday Night Live-style sketches, five spoken word pieces, three dance/movement pieces and one hip-hop performance. Each group performed in our black box theatre for an audience of other first-year students, many of whom had responded to our survey on their political and cultural beliefs. Based on post-show talkbacks and in-class written reflections, both audiences and performers found that reframing the raw information we had in a creative context made it more accessible. One audience member commented that having ideas presented in a metaphorical way—specifically in a piece about police brutality—helped her develop greater empathy toward victims of violence.

One of the challenges of teaching this course is trying to meet the prescribed learning outcomes while simultaneously preparing the students for our TPS program's academic and creative rigor. After a decade of teaching the course, I've found that the best way to do that is through a long-term, in-depth, student-driven creative project that integrates them in a holistic way rather than dealing with each outcome separately. While this does make assessment difficult, it allows students to work in an environment that encourages collaboration and creativity—the elemental building blocks of theatre—while being introduced to research practices, academic discipline, and new, diverse ways of thinking about their own cultural context. One student reflected "I learned how a group can thrive if they work creatively and collaboratively because everybody wanted to make this piece great and everybody had ideas. And even though not all of our ideas were perfect for the piece, we worked really well together (because of our shared commitment to the project)."

A Performance Project to Accomplish FYE Learning Outcomes for Non-Performing Arts Students

Susan Kattwinkel
College of Charleston
Charleston, SC, USA

I have taught in the College of Charleston's FYE almost every year since I became the program's founding director in 2007, including in the years since 2012 when a new faculty member entered the rotating position. I have taught both Introduction to Theatre as part of an LC, and standalone First-Year Seminar (FYSM) courses with varying topics. Out of an average class size of 18, I have never had more than about a quarter of the students who plan to be arts majors. Students come from across the college curriculum, including science majors, social science and humanities majors, and a significant number of business majors. Over that decade and with this wide variety of students, I have slowly developed a series of assignments that I can use whatever the course topic that both meets the goals of the school's FYE and introduces them to performance pedagogies that provide a deeper immersion into the ideas of the course than many traditional teaching methods. My use of embodied pedagogies stems from my belief that the performance of ideas offers an exploration of those ideas that demands a greater immersion in them than are necessary for a traditional research paper. The projects also force students to collaborate on their knowledge and process information empathically, both of which are learning skills that FYE programs generally hope to instill.

The College of Charleston FYE program has three main goals—Knowledge of Campus Services, Information Literacy, and Integrative Learning. By the completion of the course, students are expected to be able to:

- Identify and use the appropriate academic resources and student support services at the College of Charleston
- Use appropriate tools and search strategies for identifying particular types of information specific to the discipline
- Evaluate the relevance, quality, and appropriateness of different sources of information
- Recognize and classify the information contained within a bibliographic citation

- Access and use information ethically and legally
- Use appropriate critical thinking skills and problem-solving techniques in appropriate disciplinary contexts
- Make connections across disciplines and/or relevant experiences[19]

The three main goals are listed on all FYE course syllabi, along with references to class assignments that will address each outcome. The first goal (addressed in the first bulleted learning outcome) is covered in peer-led synthesis seminars that are attached to every FYE course. The second and third goals (outcomes 2–7) are the responsibility of the faculty teaching the course. Assignments connected to the information literacy outcomes (outcomes 2–5) are often addressed in library assignments that connect students to an embedded librarian who may provide library orientation, quizzes, or projects, and is available to students throughout the semester for research consultation. The final two outcomes, under the Integrative Learning goal, encourage faculty to both incorporate disciplinary pedagogies and connect course material and pedagogies either to specific other courses (especially in the case of LCs) or to other learning experiences.

The mix of majors (and undecided students) that I find in my FYE courses means walking a line between the traditional pedagogical practices that most new college students expect and introducing them to the artistic practices of theatre. Within the Department of Theatre and Dance our Introduction to Theatre courses are expected to have a certain amount of theatre practice in them, and class sizes are kept relatively small so that group projects can allow students to experience the writing, design, and performance processes alongside their exposure to basic theatrical history and literature. When taught as part of an LC with courses from other departments, the Introduction to Theatre classes retain the praxis element, often studying and creating theatre that connects thematically with the other class in the LC. The First-Year Seminars taught by theatre and dance faculty are not required to include praxis elements, but often do, and I've made it a point to include as much active learning and theatrical practice as possible without making students worry that they will be judged based on aesthetic criteria.

New college students expect the learning process to be an additive one, where they accumulate knowledge parsed out by faculty and textbooks, and hope they can remember as much as possible for tests and put it in their own words for papers. This authority dependence makes it difficult for students to acquire higher-order learning skills like critical and adaptive thinking and the developmental capacities necessary for personal maturation. As Magolda et al. summarize it, "Thinking critically and learning from mistakes requires more complex ways of making meaning of knowledge and acknowledging one's role in constructing it."[20]

Over the last couple of decades, education researchers have come to a conclusion that performance scholars have always known—knowledge resides in the whole body, not just in the brain, and embodied learning can add not only a depth of understanding, but whole aspects of knowledge not accessible through traditional Eurocentric mind-centered pedagogical practices. Class discussion about ethical ideas can easily reproduce common social hierarchies, despite the best efforts of faculty to introduce parity of opportunity and judgment. They often mirror everyday life, in which those students with privilege are more comfortable and experienced expressing their opinions, and in which the opinions of the less privileged are often ignored even when they are expressed. But when all students are embodying a fictional character who shares (or doesn't share) their own subjectivity, normally silent students will often speak up to defend their character, because the fictional situation offers an opportunity for justice that they don't often perceive in the real world. Tammy J. Freiler has outlined the different theoretical approaches to embodied learning, and summarizes embodiment as "a way to construct knowledge through direct engagement in bodily experiences and inhabiting one's body through a felt sense of being-in-the-world."[21]

As Wagner and Shahjahan have noted, embodied pedagogies can make students uncomfortable and puzzle faculty accustomed to mind-centered acquisition of knowledge, and can therefore be dangerous practices for untenured or contingent faculty to use.[22] However, even students from other disciplines expect a certain amount of unconventional practice from performing arts classes, where embodiment is regularly considered a part of knowledge acquisition and demonstration. Therefore, courses in the performing arts are given a certain amount of leeway by reluctant students, which may then transfer to courses they take later in other disciplines. In many areas of the country, students may already be accustomed to arts pedagogies, including embodiment, from their k-12 education. The Every Student Succeeds Act of 2015 encourages the use of arts pedagogies across the curriculum, and some states have been working to bring arts education in various forms to all k-12 students for decades, like the

Arts in Basic Curriculum Project in South Carolina, which was formed in 1987 to "achieve quality, comprehensive arts education ... for all students in South Carolina."[23]

I have created a series of assignments that culminate in a final performance project designed to address the Integrative Learning goal of our FYE program. Initially the goals of the assignment were to have students work collaboratively, get them to respond to difficult course readings in a creative, personal format, and to help them make connections across their courses and outside activities. Over the many times I have used this assignment I have added elements to the project in order to connect it more clearly to early assignments in the semester, to focus on the College Reads common reading book, and to incorporate the Information Literacy goal of the FYE program. The version of the project that I'll discuss here will be the most recent version that most fully incorporates the learning outcomes of College of Charleston FYE program. The last two times I used it were in a First-Year Seminar titled "Theatre and Ethical Choice," in which we read basic philosophical readings on ethics and a selection of plays that deal with ethical choices, and discuss theatre's approach to ethical quandaries.

Assignment 1: Ethics and the College Reads Book

Like many common read programs, the College of Charleston's College Reads program involves a book that is provided to all incoming freshmen (but also read in many upper-division courses), a visit from the book's author that includes a large public address as well as smaller group meetings, and multiple relevant activities throughout the school year. For their Synthesis Seminar (a weekly class focusing on study and life skills, taught by an upper-class peer facilitator), all students in FYE courses write a personal response to a prompt about the College Reads book. This is not a graded assignment in the Synthesis Seminar, but rather a prompt for self-reflection and a method for kick-starting class conversation.

As the first step in this project, I continued that conversation in the FYSM, and shared a list of ethically focused themes that I had pulled from their response papers. I then placed the students in pairs that corresponded to the themes of the book that they had most connected with. In those pairs, the students discussed what scenes or elements of the book had led them to choose the particular ethical issue that they had.

They then imagined a situation in college life that involves the same ethical quandary. They defined characters, described the scene in one sentence, and then began writing dialogue. Once they had established the ethical issue in their scene, I made them pass the scene along to a different pair of writers. Those writers read the scene to that point and then continued writing more dialogue, advancing the story. A third pair of writers completed the scene, finding a way to resolve the ethical situation in the scene.

The scenes were then read out loud. The students were amused at how their scenes changed under the guidance of other writers, and it prompted a conversation about how different people respond to the same ethical dilemma. Not all the scenes ended up with the ethical decision that the first writers had planned. We were also able to discuss how dramatizing an ethical dilemma made it more recognizable, but also how it placed restrictions on the amount of detail that could be related. Because we were focusing on the ethical issues rather than on the theatre, students who had never written in a dramatic form before were not intimidated. The assignment was a good warm-up for the final project and illustrated the benefits of problem-solving in a theatrical format.

Assignment 2: Ethics and Bibliography

Throughout the semester the class read and discussed a number of plays that dramatize ethical dilemmas. Plays like *Antigone, Hamlet, An Enemy of the People*, and Jennifer Haley's *The Nether* illustrate the cognitive processes that people go through when faced with an ethical dilemma in real life. One of the goals of the class is for students to recognize that different people approach ethical dilemmas in different ways, and that personal experience and cultural backgrounds may lead people to different decisions. Class discussion about the issues of the plays illustrated that they did not always agree with their peers, but I wanted to show that such variation in interpretation extends to more mature and experienced writers as well.

The students were put in groups, one group for each of the plays we read in class, and given a library assignment—find two reviews of productions of the play and two scholarly articles about the play and annotate the bibliographic entry in terms of the ethical themes of the play. The librarian for the class showed them resources for finding both types of sources and provided directions for correct citation.

Assignment 3: Final Project

In preparation for the final project we made a list of the major ethical themes in each of the plays we had read and connected them to the ethical issues in the College Reads book. Students then wrote a paragraph naming which of the themes they connected with most and why. I used those paragraphs to create the final groups. The final project was to write and perform a short play (5–7 minutes) inspired by an episode in the College Reads book. Several class periods were devoted to the project, and students met outside of class to write and rehearse. The plays were presented during the final exam period. The following directions were used the year that the school's College Reads book was Anand Giridharadas' *The True American* and reflect some general theatrical concepts we had discussed throughout the semester in the context of the plays we read.

Rules for your play:

- Everyone in the group must be in the play.
- Your play must connect to *The True American* (see justification) in some way, even if it's just as an inspiration.
- In your play, at least one character must be put in a situation where they must make an ethical choice or compromise. Remember, ethics involve other people, so just making a personal sacrifice isn't enough.
- Your play must take place in one scene—no time jumps or cuts. The time of the play is the time of the presentation.
- Your play must be realistically presentable. So no trucks or explosions on stage, unless you're doing a highly stylized play and want to do symbolic explosions. (But then the whole play must be in that style.) If you need something to happen that would be realistic on a stage but which you can't do in our classroom (e.g., the lights go out or there's a sound effect), you can have someone who is not in the play read stage directions during the performance.
- You should bring props and costumes that you need. They can be representative. (E.g., if you have a police officer in your play, it is sufficient to make a badge to indicate who they are. You don't need a full costume.)
- It should be memorized. Know your lines!

For the final project, all you'll be turning in is your script and a brief justification.

Your justification should include:

- the ideas/incidents/page numbers (if relevant) from *The True American* that inspired your play
- a brief description of why you picked that aspect of the book to dramatize and how you think it connects to ethical considerations in life
- a brief explanation of how you thought your selection should be dramatized and why—for example, it should be realistic, like a dream play, full of symbolic imagery, like a docudrama, and so on
- your script, in script format (use one of the ones we read as a model), with all stage directions, list of characters, and so on
- Don't forget to title your play!

In every iteration of this project I have emphasized the rehearsal element. Although the course does not teach acting skills and most of the students have little to no acting experience, it is important that they perform the ethical dilemma as well as write it.

In the process of rehearsal, students discover that the *way* that something is said may have as much impact as *what* is said. Because students automatically gravitate toward excessive drama and humor in their scenes if they are having fun with the assignment, they then must face the difficulty of making their ethical argument in an atmosphere not conducive to measured ethical decisions. The first assignment of the project, in which students wrote scenes and then read them out loud, introduced this problem as the serious dialogue they had written became humorous when read out loud. The presence of physical bodies acting out written lines also forces students to confront the identity politics of everyone in their group, as students negotiate how ideas are relayed differently depending on the performer's subjectivity.

Groups that incorporate unusual physical activity into their scene are also confronted with the inequities and assumptions that physical bodies present. Students must consider the cultural construction of bodies when they physicalize ideas, whereas simple writing or reading can allow them—especially white students—to "universalize" their characters, ignoring the implications of race and class. For example, one group wrote a scene in which one student convinces another to steal a wallet, the instigator wanting money for socializing and the eventual thief needing money for basic necessities. Once the group started to cast and rehearse their play, the racial diversity of the students in the group inspired lengthy conversations about how the ethical dilemma might read to an audience depending on which actor they cast in which role.

Being asked, often for the first time, to come to their own conclusions (based on ethical sources and personal experience) about difficult social debates, rather than simply accepting the voice of authority, first-year students in traditional lecture classes can easily bypass this new responsibility. Faced with philosophical readings and a professor's lecture, they may choose the voice of authority with which they are most comfortable and present that opinion as their own. But when they must write an ethical decision to be voiced by a character, and then embody that decision, it becomes a personal issue—one which they need to fully understand in order to physicalize.

Although the final project does not have the same rule about connecting their play to college life that the first assignment does, most groups end up writing plays that could happen to them or other college students. Faculty often complain about being expected to tie all course material to the lives of students in order to make it "relatable," and suggest that millennials expect the world to relate to them rather than making the effort to relate to the outside world. In this project, students make that leap on their own, relating realistic (if fictional) events about college students to ethical debates presented in books about cultures vastly different from their own. In 2015 the College Reads book was *The Good Soldiers* by David Finkel, who was embedded with the US military during the 2007 troop surge in Iraq. 2015 was not only a year when American wars abroad were very much in the news, but the two months before first-year students arrived on campus saw the murders of nine churchgoers at the Emanuel AME Church just a block from the College of Charleston campus and the removal of the confederate battle flag from the statehouse in Columbia, SC. Debates about protests, war, and violence permeated the campus. One of the groups in my class that year presented a particularly poignant play about how a group of college friends reacts when one of them decides to enlist and another is against the war. The following year—the year the students read *The True American*, which is about the immigrant Raisuddin Bhuiyan who forgave the white supremacist who shot him in the wake of 9/11—a group created a play about campus protests and what are ethical responses to differing ideas about free speech.

Of course, not all the final projects have contained the depth of synthesis and empathy as the projects described here. But having to present their research publicly (to an audience of their classmates) ensures a certain amount of reflection, intention, and seriousness on the part of students. Students often reference the final project on their course evaluations as both the most difficult and most enjoyable part of the course. Embodied pedagogy encourages investment of time and energy from students, allows students to "make it about them" simply through physical mobilization, and assists students in using both the logical and empathic parts of their brain to form responses to course content.

NOTES

1. Ryan D. Padgett, Jennifer R. Keup, and Ernest T. Pascarella, "The Impact of First-Year Seminars on College Students' Life-Long Learning Orientations"; Robert Dean Reason, Patrick T. Terenzini, and Robert J. Domingo, "Developing Social and Personal Competence in the First Year of College"; Tracy L. Skipper, *What Makes the First-Year Seminar High Impact? An Exploration of Effective Educational Practices.*
2. George D. Kuh, *High-Impact Educational Practices: What They Are, Who Has Access to Them, and Why They Matter,* 9.
3. As identified in Jayne Elise Brownell and Lynn Ellen Swaner. *Five High-Impact Practices: Research on Learning Outcomes, Completion and Quality,* 5–6.
4. For examples of FYEs in combination with other HIPs, see Martha J. LaBare, ed., "First-Year Civic Engagement: Solid Foundations for College, Citizenship, and Democracy"; Jean-Philippe Faletta, Jo A. Meier, and J. Ulyses Balderas, "High-Impact Practices: Integrating the First-Year Experience"; Adrienne Redding, Jeanne Lahaie, and Jonathon Bush, "One-on-One 'Intensive' Instruction: Faculty and Students Partnering for Success in First-Year Writing."
5. F. Robert Sabol, "Summary of Findings from NCLB: A Study of its Impact on Art Education Programs," and Ron Whitehorne, "NCLB: Taking a Toll on Arts and Music Education."
6. The most recent (2016) BCSSE survey revealed that 46% of new college students reported that in high school they were involved at least "some" with performing or visual arts programs. See "BCSSE Summary Report 2016."
7. All of the quotes from students in this article are taken from student reflections written both immediately after the performances and as part of the final exam one month later. In some instances they have been edited for clarity and concision.

8. "First-Year Requirement," *First-Year Requirement,* Kennesaw State University.
9. "Learning Outcomes," *First-Year Requirement,* Kennesaw State University.
10. "KSU 1101: First-Year Seminar," *2016–17 Undergraduate Catalog,* Kennesaw State University.
11. "Learning Communities," *Department of First-Year and Transition Studies,* Kennesaw State University.
12. Alison Oddey, *Devising Theatre: A Practical and Theoretical Handbook,* 4, 7.
13. Tina Fey, *Bossypants,* 84.
14. Dave Itzkioff, "Hello! Matt Stone and Trey Parker Crash a Class at N.Y.U."
15. While I obviously encouraged the students to be as honest and forthright as possible in their answers, I did ask them not to select abortion as one of the issues that concerned them. As a citizen, I'm acutely aware of the importance of issues of choice and women's health; however, as an educator I've seen it create deep rifts within academic and creative communities. While this was an arbitrary limitation on my part, the students managed to identify a multitude of other more accessible issues.
16. Jean Benedetti, *Stanislavski: His Life and Art—a Biography,* 61.
17. Viola Spolin, *Theatre Games for Rehearsal: A Director's Handbook,* 10.
18. Oddey, *Devising Theatre,* 2–3.
19. "Program Outcomes," *First-Year Experience.*
20. Marcia B. Baxter Magolda, Patricia M. King, Kari B. Taylor, and Kerri M. Wakefield, "Decreasing Authority Dependence During the First Year of College," 419.
21. Tammy J. Freiler, "Learning Through the Body," 41.
22. Anne E. Wagner and Riyad A. Shahjahan, "Centering Embodied Learning in Anti-Oppressive Pedagogy," 251.
23. "Mission & History," *Arts in Basic Curriculum.*

Bibliography

BCSSE Summary Report 2016. http://bcsse.indiana.edu/pdf/2016/BCSSE16% 20Institutional%20Report%20(Grand).pdf. Accessed 14 July 2017.

Benedetti, Jean. 1990. *Stanislavski: His Life and Art—A Biography.* London: Methuen Drama.

Brownell, Jayne Elise, and Lynn Ellen Swaner. 2010. *Five High-Impact Practices: Research on Learning Outcomes, Completion and Quality.* Washington, DC: Association of American Colleges and Universities.

Faletta, Jean-Philippe, Jo A. Meier, and J. Ulyses Balderas. 2016. High-Impact Practices: Integrating the First-Year Experience with Service Learning and Study Abroad. In *Handbook of Research on Effective Communication in Culturally Diverse Classrooms,* ed. Katia Gonzalez and Rhoda Frumkin, 337–355. Hershey, PA: Information Science Reference.

Fey, Tina. 2011. *Bossypants*. New York: Little, Brown.
First-Year Requirement. *First-Year Requirement*. http://uc.kennesaw.edu/fyts/prospective/requirement.php. Accessed 24 July 2017.
Freiler, Tammy J. 2008. Learning Through the Body. *New Directions for Adult and Continuing Education*: 37–47. https://doi.org/10.1002/ace.304. Accessed 6 July 2017.
Itzkioff, Dave. 2011. Hello! Matt Stone and Trey Parker Crash a Class at N.Y.U. *The New York Times*, September 8.
KSU 1101: First-Year Seminar. *2016–17 Undergraduate Catalog*. http://catalog.kennesaw.edu/index.php?catoid=29. Accessed 30 June 2017.
Kuh, George D. 2008. *High-Impact Educational Practices: What They Are, Who Has Access to Them, and Why They Matter*. Washington, DC: Association of American Colleges and Universities.
LaBare, Martha J., ed. 2008. First-Year Civic Engagement: Solid Foundations for College, Citizenship, and Democracy. http://citeseerx.ist.psu.edu/viewdoc/download?doi=10.1.1.474.7700&rep=rep1&type=pdf. Accessed 13 Aug 2017.
Learning Communities. *Kennesaw State University Department of First-Year and Transition Studies*. http://uc.kennesaw.edu/fyts/programs/learningcommunities/index.php. Accessed 30 June 2017.
Learning Outcomes. *First-Year Requirement*. http://uc.kennesaw.edu/fyts/programs/fys/learning_outcomes.php. Accessed 24 July 2017.
Magolda, Marcia B. Baxter, Patricia M. King, Kari B. Taylor, and Kerri M. Wakefield. 2012. Decreasing Authority Dependence During the First Year of College. *Journal of College Student Development* 53 (3): 418–435.
Mission & History. *Arts in Basic Curriculum*. http://www.abcprojectsc.com/about/mission-history/. Accessed July 2017.
Oddey, Alison. 1996. *Devising Theatre: A Practical and Theoretical Handbook*. Abingdon: Routledge.
Padgett, Ryan D., Jennifer R. Keup, and Ernest T. Pascarella. 2013. The Impact of First-Year Seminars on College Students' Life-Long Learning Orientations. *Journal of Student Affairs Research and Practice* 50 (2): 133–151.
Reason, Robert Dean, Patrick T. Terenzini, and Robert J. Domingo. 2007. Developing Social and Personal Competence in the First Year of College. *The Review of Higher Education* 30 (3): 271–299.
Redding, Adrienne, Jeanne Lahaie, and Jonathon Bush. 2016. One-on-One 'Intensive' Instruction: Faculty and Students Partnering for Success in First-Year Writing. *Language Arts Journal of Michigan* 32 (1): 17–24.
Sabol, F. Robert. Summary of Findings from NCLB: A Study of Its Impact on Art Education Programs. *National Art Education Association*. https://arteducators-prod.s3.amazonaws.com/documents/455/b496a8f0-4a04-4d79-ba10-058240e7191b.pdf?1452930373. Accessed 14 July 2017.

Skipper, Tracy L. 2017. *What Makes the First-Year Seminar High Impact? An Exploration of Effective Educational Practices*. Research Reports on College Transitions No. 7. Columbia: National Resource Center for The First-Year Experience and Students in Transition.

Spolin, Viola. 1985. *Theatre Games for Rehearsal: A Director's Handbook*. Evanston, IL: Northwestern UP.

Wagner, Anne E., and Riyad A. Shahjahan. 2015. Centering Embodied Learning in Anti-Oppressive Pedagogy. *Teaching in Higher Education* 20: 244–254. https://doi.org/10.1080/13562517.2014.993963.

Whitehorne, Ron. 2006. NCLB: Taking a Toll on Arts and Music Education. *Philadelphia Public School Notebook*, May 24. http://thenotebook.org/articles/2006/05/24/nclb-taking-a-toll-on-arts-and-music-education. Accessed 14 July 2017.

CHAPTER 3

Common Intellectual Experiences

In a 2015 Association of American Colleges and Universities (AAC&U) survey of chief academic officers, two in five (41%) reported that they incorporate or offer a common intellectual experience as part of the undergraduate curriculum.[1] Nowhere, however, does the report define what is meant by "common intellectual experience" in the survey or how administrators completing the survey might have interpreted the phrase. It is likely that even those familiar with the language of the high-impact practices (HIPs) interpret the concept in many different ways. Kuh's language in the original HIP document refers to "a set of required common courses or a vertically organized general education program that includes advanced integrative studies and/or required participation in a learning community."[2] Most commonly, when "common intellectual practices" are defined outside of Kuh's language, authors refer to curricular structures, usually involving general education. For example, Deryl K. Hatch et al. define them as "Shared curricular and cocurricular options for students that include participation in a set of required common courses or organized general education program. May center on broad themes, such as technology."[3] One curricular manifestation is the Integrated Experience, a course designed to help students directly apply the skills and knowledge gained from their general education courses to their disciplinary major.[4] Often, First-Year Experience courses, instituted with a common theme, double as common intellectual experiences.

© The Author(s) 2018
M. Hayford, S. Kattwinkel (eds.), *Performing Arts as High-Impact Practice*, The Arts in Higher Education,
https://doi.org/10.1007/978-3-319-72944-2_3

The awareness of HIPs has coincided with a change in the way many institutions conceive of and structure their general education programs, leading to their incorporation of common courses or thematically integrated classes shared by large numbers of students. In his article "Disrupting Ourselves: The Problem of Learning in Higher Education," Randy Bass outlines higher education's long-term movement from core curricula that force students to internalize large amounts of content before practicing application to inquiry-based learning and integrative studies that ask students to acquire the content they need as they attempt to solve problems. As Bass puts it, "the optimal way to learn is reciprocally or spirally between practice and content."[5] This change in approach has coalesced in recent years with the growing attention to skills-based learning that directs students to practice critical thinking, thick reading, and group work as well as writing and other communication skills during the process of knowledge acquisition and application. Through common courses or themed curricula in which they approach "big questions" from varying disciplinary viewpoints, students learn to see their education as a way of looking at and processing problems rather than as a set of knowledge that differs by major.

In 2013, the AAC&U began a sweeping project on general education designed to help institutions of higher education rethink how they achieve student learning outcomes in general education programs. As described on their web page:

> AAC&U's General Education Maps and Markers (GEMs) initiative is designed to develop principles through which institutions of higher education can create general education curricula that focus on core proficiencies, intentional educational pathways within and across institutions, and students' engagement in work that allows assessment of their demonstrated accomplishments in inquiry- and problem-based learning. ... This new approach to general education is a dramatic departure from current practice, with implications both for institutional programs and practices and for higher education as a whole.[6]

One of the publications associated with this effort is Paul L. Gaston's *General Education Transformed: How We Can, Why We Must*. In the foreword to the report, former AAC&U president Carol Geary Schneider writes, "When general education is organized mainly as an á la carte menu of disconnected survey courses, and when it is taught in huge lectures that emphasize content delivery over critical inquiry while neglecting students' own active participation in their learning, it falls far short of its intended horizon-expanding purposes."[7] She echoes Gaston's call to "colleges and universities to organize general education as a catalyst for integrative and applied learning."[8] General education programs that emphasize "integrative and applied learning" will be very hospitable to performing arts programs if we lobby successfully for our place there.

Although more and more institutions are embracing general education programs that emphasize applied learning,[9] few of them consider the performing arts—where applied learning is a staple of our pedagogy—appropriate for common intellectual experiences. Currently, a very small minority of colleges and universities has an arts requirement as part of their general education program, and, anecdotally, fewer than half accept arts practice courses (as opposed to humanities-style, "study of" courses) for any general education requirement. There has been no national study on the inclusion of the arts in general education programs, but recent examinations of school requirements show a small but growing number of institutions recognizing the importance of arts pedagogy to a well-rounded liberal education. The Council of Public Liberal Arts Colleges (COPLAC) is a group of 30 schools "dedicated to the advancement of high-quality, public liberal arts education in a student-centered, residential environment."[10] Of those 30 schools, 6 require an arts practice course as part of their general education requirements. Another 13 allow arts practice courses to count for their humanities or other general education requirement.[11]

The inclusion of the arts as part of general education is far lower among larger public universities. On the 2017 *U.S. News and World Report* list of top 25 public universities, only 1 shows a general education requirement that can only be met by arts practice courses. But 17 accept some practice courses in fulfillment of an Arts and Humanities-type requirement. Interestingly, quite a few of the schools on that list have a general education requirement titled "Visual and Performing Arts" or "Creative Expression," and often define that requirement in their catalog as fulfilling a need for students to experience the creative process. However, the lists of courses that can be taken to fulfill that requirement are most often dominated by traditional humanities-style arts courses, with course descriptions that emphasize the history, theory, and literature of an art form rather than exposing students to the practice of it. Whether that is the result of academic turf wars between arts and humanities departments or a sign that arts pedagogies are being employed across the curriculum in ways not apparent from course descriptions will have to be determined by more thorough studies. Certainly our hopes are that the AAC&U and other higher education organizations will undertake such studies in the coming years.

Outside the structure of general education programs, other forms of common intellectual experiences exist as co-curricular experiences designed to help students synthesize their course work with broad societal questions. E-portfolios are sometimes seen as common intellectual experiences because they provide all students with a common method for processing their curricular and extra-curricular experiences.[12] Other individual experiences viewed for their power to help students synthesize learning include field experiences like mission trips, Alternative Spring Break, and so on.[13] These "one-offs" are about introducing students to a community of scholars where everyone is talking about one topic from the point of view of different disciplines. Very often these experiences are created for first-year students. It is common practice today for colleges to create experiences to introduce new students as quickly as possible to an ethos of learning that they hope will pervade their college careers. The idea that there is a shared membership of lifelong learners to which new students are being inducted drives extra-curricular efforts such as convocation, common read programs, college-wide explorations of socially relevant "themes," and expanded orientations. The hope is that students and faculty will filter the content of their courses through these common conversations in order to participate in the investigation of important social issues through multiple disciplinary lenses.

Common reads, usually aimed at first-year students but occasionally campus-wide efforts, are one of the most conventional forms of co-curricular common intellectual experiences. Nadelson and Nadelson, following on earlier research, note that the purposes of such programs are usually "used to foster students' exploration of values and ethics, increase awareness of cultural diversity, deepen feelings of being part of a community, and integrate social and academic campus experiences."[14] Especially when they are aimed at first-year students, most programs share the goals of that at Nipissing University in Canada, which aims "to foster a sense of community and belonging through a common academic experience, and to introduce new students to the level of critical thinking, literacy and analysis necessary in a university environment."[15] Generally, common reads are chosen by a committee of faculty, staff, and students from across the university, offering plenty of opportunity for performing arts faculty to encourage common intellectual experiences that position the arts as a vital element of a well-rounded education.

The case study in this chapter exists across the several types of common intellectual experiences discussed in this introduction. The Rites/Rights/Writes (RRW) experience at the University of Dayton (UD) was designed as an Arts Immersion Experience for first-year students, attended after a full school year of thematically connected events offered by faculty and campus groups from disciplines across the university. The event was a sort of first-year capstone experience, a performative integration of concepts discussed in multiple courses in the Common Academic Program (CAP). Richard K. Chenoweth discusses the many elements of this program that both introduced first-year students to their university education through interdisciplinary scholarship and capped off their first year with a common intellectual experience that examined the common theme through the perspective of the arts.

Call to action:

- As more institutions move away from the old content-based core curriculum toward an experiential, problem-based, thematic general education program, performing arts programs must insist on being part of the conversation or risk being left behind.
- Performing arts faculty should join committees on general education reform, common reads, and so on as often as possible. Faculty in other disciplines often need explanations of how the performing arts are relevant in cross-disciplinary educational initiatives.
- Administrators of arts schools and programs should consider their performances as potential common intellectual experiences for students from all disciplines. Reach out to other departments to find ways for them to incorporate performances into their courses.
- Universities frequently implement "theme days" or college-wide themed initiatives as part of accreditation or grant projects. Performing arts departments can connect with these programs via their performance programs. When choosing a season of concerts or plays, consider works that speak to those themes and market those performances accordingly.

Rites/Rights/Writes and the University Experience

Richard K. Chenoweth
University of Dayton
Dayton, OH, USA

> American concert life, generally, is securely divorced from American intellectual life. ... Classical music occupies a more isolated niche in the world of contemporary culture than do film, dance, or theatre. (Joseph Horowitz, *Moral Fire: Musical Portraits from America's Fin de Siècle*, University of California Press, 2012)

Origins

Throughout my almost 50-year career as a professional performing musician, I remained curious about the listener-and-observer participants' reactions to the arts and if they experienced lasting and distinctive intellectual growth as a result of their artistic encounters. Based on my experiences, while there was no doubt that music and other art forms created emotional and sometimes immediate responses, I wondered about those impressions—the life-changing moments, the context of the music, and the aural and visual sensations that could create opportunities for intellectual curiosity and understanding that went beyond momentary and superficial reactions.

It occurred to me that the artist-to-audience experience could be enriched if there were an attempt not only to explain the historical context (usually found in program notes or brief comments from the stage or gallery that included vignettes and personal information about the artists/creators) but to organize efforts to establish connections on a deeper level. Suppose there were a program that asked questions about the arts where the answers informed the participants about a particular work in a more profound way? What were the cultural environments and influences on an artistic creator? What social issues were prevalent and topical when specific works were conceived? What were the connections to other fine arts, music, theatre, and dance, as well as their interrelatedness to the humanities and sciences? Would it be possible to gain deeper insight into the creative process and the thoughts of the artistic creator? Would an understanding of the creative process open new pathways to inspire innovation and perception in other areas of study? Finally, as a member of an academic community that observed college students' dwindling interest and engagement in the performing fine arts (compared with those genres that reflected current popular trends), was there a way to remove the impression of concert music—symphonic music, opera, and ballet—as existing only for elite consumption and entertainment? Could a process be formulated that examined and revealed the arts with a clear demonstration of their creativity, value, profundity, humanity, and *necessity*?

My research into existing resources found that while there are numerous arts organizations currently supporting initiatives in higher education, many of them serve as advocacy groups for continued or increased arts funding, as umbrella organizations that collect curricular models and rationales for arts courses, and those that encourage and display faculty research. It seemed that there was, in fact, an opportunity to creatively combine the outreach and audience development initiatives of professional performing arts organizations with the needs and intellectual imperatives of the academic community.

During the final four years (2012–2016) of my academic career at UD, I was appointed to the Graul Chair in Arts and Languages, an endowed chair with broad latitude in its stated research agenda and campus activities. Since one of the primary missions of that position was to communicate the importance of the arts and languages to both the campus and the local community, there was an opportunity to establish a program exploring these questions in a detailed manner and to apply my interest in developing a unique and more comprehensive model for understanding and appreciating the arts. Fortunately, the university was completing a broad curriculum revision that emphasized, among other criteria, common intellectual experiences and experiential learning. One intent of the RRW project was to serve as an umbrella opportunity for the entire CAP process. To complement the new curricular plan, my programmatic concept included the creation of broad themes and academic topics that embraced many subjects, allowing latitude for interpretation, connection, intersections of perspectives, and diversity, while at the same time culminating in attendance at a targeted capstone performance by either the Dayton Philharmonic Orchestra (DPO), the Dayton Opera, or the Dayton Ballet, on a rotating yearly basis. (These three groups had recently combined their fund-raising, marketing, and administrative offices, resulting in the creation of a unique collaborative arts organization called the Dayton Performing Arts Alliance, or DPAA.) The students would experience a performance by award-winning professional ensembles as part of this program, attending the concerts off-campus in a superior world-class theatre, the Benjamin and Marion Shuster Performing Arts Center, located in the center of downtown Dayton.

As the concept for this program evolved, I wanted to avoid offering a college-level "young person's concert": my hope was that by the time students attended the performance, they would have received multiple perspectives on the specific work and related topics from their professors in the arts, humanities, and sciences, and through class discussion, symposia, panels, films, complementary and thematically related on-campus performances, student-initiated activities, and guest lectures.

I worked closely with community professional ensembles: the music director of the DPO, Neal Gittleman, was instrumental in buying into the concept. The DPO had already established a concert series, *Classical Connections*, in which a piece was explained during the first half of the concert with examples and then performed in its entirety in the second half. As we discussed the concept, we felt that it would be very effective if we could examine Stravinsky's music for the ballet, *Rite of Spring*, a revolutionary work and agent for change in contemporary music. Since the following year was the one-hundredth anniversary of that work, the DPO was planning to program it on a *Classical Connections* concert, so we agreed that this would be an excellent opportunity to initiate this program and engage the students and faculty in wide-ranging discussions about revolution and change. Its controversial premiere—one that challenged the contemporary concepts of music and dance—as well as the turbulent time in which it was written (1913) meant that there were numerous possibilities for discussions about music, dance, theatre, historical context, the effects of change, and the impact of this work on contemporary thought and culture. At the same time, the chair of the UD Political Science Department suggested that we collaborate on co-sponsoring events that emphasized human rights, since that department was planning to host an international symposium on trends in human rights advocacy, in conjunction with the establishment of a Center for Human Rights.

With full and enthusiastic support of the university administration, the DPAA, and other local arts groups, we developed the concept and philosophy of RRW. Simply stated: humans create habits (*rites*), which become societal expectations (*rights*), which are then expressed through the written word (*writes*), including poetry, fine arts, literature, music, film, dance, and other means of creative expression. This initiative would subsequently evolve into a multi-year extended cross-curricular program that would consider the question, "What does it mean to be human?" while focusing on the impact and role of the arts and how creativity in the arts intersects with other academic subjects in the humanities and sciences.

Implementation

Once the foundation for the concept and focus of RRW was established, informational meetings were held over the course of the academic year with faculty, administrators, student groups, standing and *ad hoc* university committees, and local community groups about this new program. A key factor in gaining traction and enthusiasm for RRW was the adoption by the College of Arts and Sciences Humanities faculty of a First-Year Arts Immersion experience as an alternative to a "first-year read." The idea of combining this experience with a common curricular focus was very appealing to faculty who saw this as an opportunity to illuminate their own research through the perspective of the arts, while relating it to their specific fields of study and discovering intersections with other academic areas. I also spoke with College of Arts and Sciences department chairs and program directors, at faculty meetings, and with individual faculty while seeking support from the directors of the various university arts departments and programs.

Communication and Marketing

Another important component contributing to the success of this initiative was communicating the themes, topics, events, and other actions associated with RRW and linking them to ongoing or newly created campus and community activities.

Initially, we developed a website as a central information source. The website quickly became an important part of the initiative, because it listed schedules, participants, detail pages for each event, and links to other related university departments and units, as well as links to local arts organizations, videos, articles, and other resource materials. It was updated on a daily basis and included model in-class syllabi. We were able to create an arts nexus that encouraged a broad overview of the arts activities on campus, and the community and their relationship to special events, classes, and activities specifically designed to support RRW.

By the time we launched RRW, we had assembled a small but highly effective creative team that assisted with other marketing aspects: personnel from the university marketing department, advancement, and other units collaborated on the design of a distinctive brand. A logo and banners utilizing this unique graphic element were displayed throughout the campus to advertise major RRW events. We also sent a monthly e-blast called

"This Month in RRW" to all faculty, purchased radio spots on local public radio stations, advertised in the programs of the professional arts organizations, and published printed materials such as posters and flyers that advertised individual events in a timely manner.

Another key component was the association of RRW with a university program called "Path/Aviate" that awarded housing credits to students who attended specific events approved by that group, a division of Student Housing. These housing credits enabled students to have more control over where their campus housing would be located in the coming year. By carefully selecting RRW events that resonated with the criteria of "Path/Aviate" (their mission statement emphasized "*a focus on integrated, applied and transformative education*" and included as learning goals "*the holistically-focused, intended results of what you hope to learn during your time as a UD student*"), the opportunity for experiential learning through attendance of events outside of the normal classroom routine ensured that many of those events were well-attended.

Event Organization

Each year that UD offered RRW, we created a main theme: by choosing a topic that was broad and inclusive, professors in many disciplines found it to be adaptable to their courses, ongoing university programs, and university mission priorities. By selecting and identifying specific themes and associated artistic works, the activities and events in RRW spoke to multiple criteria as articulated in the Habits of Inquiry and Reflection that inform the CAP.[16] Professors then had the freedom to create their learning outcomes utilizing the perspectives and intersections of their own area of academic expertise to satisfy the goals of both the RRW and the CAP. The selected themes (and the accompanying First-Year Arts Immersion experience) included "Revolution and Change" (Stravinsky's music for *Le Sacre du Printemps*), "Faith and Reason" (the operatic version of *Dead Man Walking*), and "It's Your Nature" (Prokofiev's ballet, *Romeo and Juliet*), which also supported the creation of the university's Hanley Sustainability Institute.

Typically, there would be numerous supporting and contextual events scheduled to draw attention and interest to the upcoming performances. As an example, to prepare for the opera performance of *Dead Man Walking*, we held on-campus concerts featuring the music of the opera's composer, Jake Heggie, and brought him to campus for a residency consisting of symposia, workshops, and master-classes. We also worked with the University Speaker Series to bring Sister Helen Prejean to campus for a week, during which she spoke to classes, student organizations, faculty groups, and campus ministry organizations, as well as community groups. Concurrently, we scheduled panel discussions with jurists, advocacy groups, and other community activist organizations, while facilitating an exhibition at the Dayton Art Institute of a special work focusing on the death penalty, *The Last Supper*, Julie Green's compelling collection of paintings depicting the final meals of prisoners on Death Row.

In order to sustain an immersive experience, we developed multiple events occurring throughout the academic year. We carefully planned these events to avoid other major campus activities, such as Homecoming and major sports events and dates that were scheduled by and for campus organizations, such as concerts, exhibits, and plays. We avoided scheduling these events during evenings and weekends, and instead, worked to link various campus activities thematically to RRW, often resulting in an increase in attendance because of required participation by humanities classes. During the three years that we offered RRW, the schedule included over 400 events, ranging from 120 to 160 each year.[17]

We created faculty opportunities that were specifically focused on RRW activities. One successful venture was Campus Cultural Connections, in which professors from multiple disciplines presented their research and insights on a specific topic related to the annual RRW theme. The intent was to demonstrate how scholars in different fields reacted to a specific topic and how their unique insights provided creative and alternative perspectives focusing on a given subject. They were offered during regular weekly class times as an alternative and addition to the class schedule. For example, in conjunction with an exhibit at the University Library that included first editions of major literary and scientific works, three professors from the Departments of English, Sociology, Anthropology and Social Work, and Music offered a session on "The Lord of the Rings" (both the book and film versions), which examined the use and misuse of power, the aspects of the Quest theme, and the prevalence of music and contemporary settings of the lyrics in the text. We offered five or six of these Connections each semester.

RRW included events designed for the faculty as well, enriching campus conversations by scheduling activities such as panel discussions during an annual faculty day that celebrated research. These panel discussions featured prominent recognized scholars from the faculty and followed a keynote address by a guest lecturer: the topic of one of these panels, featuring four of the university endowed chairs, was "Faith Confronting Reason." By including a concluding reception as part of this event, we were able to stimulate interest and encourage attendance from a broad cross-section of faculty from across the campus.

Challenges

There were numerous obstacles to overcome when organizing and facilitating the RRW program. As with most universities, UD has a deeply ingrained campus culture, one that features many beloved traditions and calendar-dependent events. By adding the RRW events to this mix, we were attempting to create another experience that would become part of the campus culture. Also, because of the number of events scheduled, finding appropriate spaces on campus for RRW-focused activities required advance planning and a detailed knowledge of the facilities scheduling process.

Negotiating an already-crowded academic, social, and community schedule presented a logistical challenge, both on and off campus. Coordinating the schedule with the community arts groups had to be started well in advance due to professional commitments in engaging artists, developing a concert schedule for season subscribers, adhering to the contracts of ensemble artists, and determining the use of the performing arts center. We worked two years in advance planning thematic concepts, meaning that we were already working on the second and third year of RRW before we had inaugurated the first season. We also avoided main events in the athletic schedule, deciding that it would be unwise to organize events during major sports activities. Finally, we encouraged faculty to plan their events far ahead and include RRW in their syllabi. (One measure of the success and acceptance of RRW was the inclusion of the Arts Immersion Experience event on the main university calendar, drawing attention to the large number of students, faculty, and staff involved in the planning, execution, and participation in this yearly event.)

Adding RRW to the faculty culture presented a challenge. Initially, some faculty did not want to take the time to explore the opportunities of this initiative and either ignored it or dismissed it as a unidimensional and overly focused event that competed with their own class priorities and activities. Inevitably, there were some faculty and staff who perceived that an initiative of this size and breadth was in competition with their own events, although the stated emphasis and intent in organizing RRW was to demonstrate, emphasize, and support the rich offerings of the arts, language, and other humanities programs by student groups and faculty, and promote their contributions to the university. At the same time, every effort was made to reinforce the objective of creating an efficient and helpful network for communication about the importance of the arts and their relationship to the yearly RRW theme.

Finally, the logistics of transporting almost 2000 students to an off-campus venue for the Arts Immersion Experience event each year required detailed work and coordination from many different departments and academic units. Thankfully, a dedicated team of administrators and administrative assistants developed a smoothly running process that safely and efficiently delivered the students and participating faculty to the performance venue every year via buses, often coordinating with downtown restaurants for pre-concert meals and organizing post-concert talks with artists and others involved in the production. Thus, complicated logistical issues did not prevent us from providing a useful and enlightening method of engaging students who were experiencing the orchestra, opera, or ballet for the first time and had questions about what they had just seen and heard.

Outcomes and Conclusions

The impact of RRW was far-reaching and resonated throughout many departments and programs of the university. Positive outcomes included the connections established between various academic units that had, in the past, hosted events with little recognition by others on campus. By drawing attention to specific events and creating curricular associations, faculty were able to share the results of their research with a broad constituency. When I met with faculty to help with the development of their presentations, I asked, "Can you explain the importance of your research in a way that is understandable to a broad and diverse audience?" So, while not minimizing the significance of their work, I did encourage faculty to seek clarity and simplicity in their presentations, an approach that was successful in reaching a broad cross-section of students and faculty, and providing insight into subjects outside of the individual fields of study.

RRW encouraged faculty to think beyond their traditional methods of presenting materials and accept new collaborative models. It also inspired them to seek connections and breadth in perspectives and establish relationships with colleagues in other programs, informing them about parallel or complimentary lines of interest, research, and study. RRW created a process for the development of large-scale campus-wide initiatives by demonstrating the effectiveness of detailed organizational planning, collaborating with existing community resources, developing effective marketing and promotion strategies, allowing faculty to supplement their syllabi through outside-the-box course offerings, modeling curricular innovation, and presenting engaging programming. In one case, RRW facilitated a program called, "A Visual Feast," proposed by a member of the Department of Philosophy. It brought together members of the Departments of Art and Music, as well as the faculty and students of the UD Honors Program, all of whom gathered at the Dayton Art Institute for a late morning brunch that included a series of short lectures about specific works in the Institute collection, a gallery walk, and culminated with a concert by the university orchestra. All of the events of the Visual Feast schedule were focused on the specific theme of RRW, so that the artworks being discussed reflected different perspectives on a common theme, as did the buffet menu selections and the musical repertoire of the orchestra concert.

RRW also encouraged grass-roots activism by faculty to initiate and present supplemental course events that focused on contemporary issues and current thought. By giving faculty an outlet and providing support to create and fund panel discussions, symposia, and festival events, they could take advantage of the marketing and communication network that RRW offered and reach a broader audience for their activities.

In order to allow faculty the opportunity to have input in the selection of a yearly RRW theme, a committee was created by the Dean of the College of Arts and Sciences that was comprised of key personnel from the DPAA, Department Chairs from the Humanities, and a faculty member-at-large, whose job was to serve as a facilitator between the academic and the community groups, in effect serving as a "cultural translator" for the two different organizations. This committee was named the TAP Committee (for "Themes and Performances") and allowed faculty a forum to suggest ideas for future RRW themes individually, in faculty meetings, and in Humanities symposia, which were then shared with the DPAA, allowing them to think creatively several years in advance about programming for the Arts Immersion Experience event that would enhance, reinforce, and complement the chosen themes. As of this writing, plans are already underway for the scheduling of several more years of this collaborative programming, resulting in a distinctive synergy between the academic community and the local performing arts resources.

Through creating and facilitating this initiative, many of the objectives and mission of the Graul Chair were realized, including:

- the creation of a common shared intellectual experience reinforced by multiple events, classes, and activities,

- the communication of the importance and impact of the arts,
- the connections shared in multiple and diverse academic areas,
- the possibilities for creative and innovative curricular development when presented in a unified, collaborative, and organized manner,
- the development of contextual offerings that widened and deeply engaged the participants in the immersive arts experience,
- the creation of a support network for a broad and diverse population of empowered and energized faculty who received encouragement, publicity, and forums for their research,
- the increased visibility of the various campus arts units and organizations, and ultimately
- the recognition of UD's contributions to the enrichment of the cultural and intellectual life of the community.

Future programming possibilities include the establishment of continuing sophomore, junior, and senior arts immersion experiences with various supporting activities and continuing to emphasize the advantages of this complementary campus and community sharing of resources. Although it does require a significant amount of time, work, creativity, vision, and a dedicated faculty with administrative support, the campus community is richer for maintaining and continuing to develop and improve this initiative. As a reflection of the university's commitment to the concept of community, the ultimate recipients who benefit from the RRW project are the students and their future involvement in the arts in their own communities.

When approached in an organized, comprehensive, and inclusive manner, creating a common intellectual experience such as RRW can have a long-lasting, positive, and significant impact on the intellectual and creative development of a large group of students. It is an immersive experience in which they can share collectively, while at the same time, because of the breadth and the diversity of offerings, experience the connections with other academic areas, and form lasting beneficial impressions of the creative and performing arts.

Notes

1. Hart Research Associates, "Recent Trends in General Education Design, Learning Outcomes, and Teaching Approaches."
2. George D. Kuh and Carol Geary Schneider, *High-Impact Educational Practices: What They Are, Who Has Access to Them, and Why They Matter*, 9.

3. Deryl K. Hatch, Gloria Crisp, Katherine Wesley, "What's in a Name? The Challenge and Utility of Defining Promising and High-Impact Practices," 15.
4. For a good discussion of such a curricular effort, see Anne J. Herrington and Martha L. A. Stassen, "Intersections of Writing, Reflection, and Integration."
5. Randy Bass, "Disrupting Ourselves: The Problem of Learning in Higher Education," 6.
6. "General Education Maps & Markers."
7. Paul L. Gaston, *General Education Transformed: How We Can, Why We Must*, v.
8. Gaston, *General Education Transformed*, vi.
9. According to a 2015 survey of AAC&U institutions on general education trends, two in three (67%) administrators say their institutions are placing more emphasis on integration of knowledge, skills, and application in their general education program. "Recent Trends in General Education Design, Learning Outcomes, and Teaching Approaches," 10.
10. https://COPLAC.org.
11. These statistics, and those in the paragraph below, were obtained through an unscientific survey of the current course catalogs for the institutions in each list.
12. See, for example, Melissa Gerritsen, Russell Carpenter, Jennifer Fairchild, "Enhancing High-Impact Educational Practice through an ePortfolio Bootcamp Model."
13. See, for example, Victoria Arnold, Chez Redmond, Jacqueline Mansker, "Revitalizing the Fieldtrip: Field-Based Experiential Learning at the College Level."
14. Sandie G. Nadelson and Louis S. Nadelson, "In Search of the Right Book: Considerations in Common Read Book Selection," 60.
15. Kristen Ferguson, Natalya Brown, and Linda Piper, "Tensions and Issues in Selecting a Book for a University Common Book Program," 59.
16. For the seven Habits of Inquiry and Reflection of the Common Academic Program, see "Common Academic Program."
17. For examples of the series and events for the 2014–2015 program, see "Rites/Rights/Writes, 2014–15."

Bibliography

Arnold, Victoria, Chez Redmond, and Jacqueline Mansker. 2016. Revitalizing the Fieldtrip: Field-Based Experiential Learning at the College Level. *Journal of Transformative Learning*.

Bass, Randy. 2012. Disrupting Ourselves: The Problem of Learning in Higher Education. *EDUCAUSE Review* 47 (2): 1–12.

Common Academic Program. https://www.udayton.edu/provost/cap/.

Ferguson, Kristen, Natalya Brown, and Linda Piper. 2016. Tensions and Issues in Selecting a Book for a University Common Book Program. *Currents in Teaching & Learning* 7 (2): 58–69.

Gaston, Paul L. 2015. *General Education Transformed: How We Can, Why We Must*. Washington, DC: Association of American Colleges and Universities.

General Education Maps & Markers. *Association for American Colleges and Universities*. https://www.aacu.org/gems. Accessed 11 Aug 2017.

Gerritsen, Melissa, Russell Carpenter, and Jennifer Fairchild. Enhancing High-Impact Educational Practice Through an ePortfolio Bootcamp Model. http://encompass.eku.edu/swps/2016/graduate/25/. Accessed 13 Aug 2017.

Hart Research Associates. Recent Trends in General Education Design, Learning Outcomes, and Teaching Approaches. Association of American Colleges and Universities. https://www.aacu.org/sites/default/files/files/LEAP/2015_Survey_Report2_GEtrends.pdf. Accessed 11 Aug 2017.

Hatch, Deryl K., Gloria Crisp, and Katherine Wesley. 2016. What's in a Name? The Challenge and Utility of Defining Promising and High-Impact Practices. *New Directions for Community Colleges* 175: 9–17.

Herrington, Anne J., and Martha L.A. Stassen. 2016. Intersections of Writing, Reflection, and Integration. *Across the Disciplines* 13. https://wac.colostate.edu/atd/hip/herrington_stassen2016.cfm. Accessed 13 Aug 2017.

Kuh, George D., and Carol Geary Schneider. 2008. *High-Impact Educational Practices: What They Are, Who Has Access to Them, and Why They Matter*. Washington, DC: Association of American Colleges and Universities.

Nadelson, Sandie G., and Louis S. Nadelson. 2012. In Search of the Right Book: Considerations in Common Read Book Selection. *Journal of College Reading and Learning* 43 (1): 60–66. https://eric.ed.gov/?id=EJ1001042. Accessed 13 Aug 2017.

Rites/Rights/Writes. 2014–2015. https://www.udayton.edu/artssciences/endowed-chair/graul/rrw-2014-15/index.php.

CHAPTER 4

Learning Communities

Learning communities can take a variety of forms, but most commonly the moniker refers to a group of students taking two or more courses together, generally across disciplines. In the most intentional and effective learning communities, the content of those courses are linked in some way. Some learning communities may simply have a theme that is approached from two different disciplinary perspectives. At the other end of the spectrum are learning communities in which the courses are team-taught by faculty from the various disciplines, and content, assignments, and pedagogies are shared, creating essentially an interdisciplinary course taught across two or more class periods. More involved living-learning communities place those students in the same residence halls, raising the opportunities for group work, study groups, and extra-curricular course-related activities. According to the National Resource Center for Learning Communities at the Washington Center at the Evergreen State University, learning communities must at least consist of:

- Strategically defined cohorts of students taking two or more courses together, or sharing a residence hall experience and taking at least one course together
- Robust collaborative partnerships between student and academic affairs

- Explicitly designed opportunities to practice integrative and/or interdisciplinary learning[1]

Many colleges use learning communities as a central element of their First-Year Experience, some pairing academic courses with orientation-type seminars, others pairing general education courses, and still others incorporating introductory courses in the students' declared majors. But learning communities are increasingly being used as part of Sophomore-Year Experiences and within majors, and living-learning communities are frequently used with students at the sophomore year and above.

Historically, colleges and universities have seen learning communities as vehicles for increasing retention and persistence, especially for first-year students, since the peer bonding and support facilitated in even the simplest of learning communities increase the likelihood that students will succeed academically in the courses and return to school the following semester.[2] However, as Emily Lardner and Gillies Malnarich of the National Resource Center for Learning Communities note, time and energy should be spent on learning communities beyond simple co-enrollment, because "[t]he camaraderie of co-enrollment may help students stay in school longer, but learning communities can offer more: curricular coherence; integrative, high-quality learning; collaborative knowledge-construction; and skills and knowledge relevant to living in a complex, messy, diverse world."[3] Aside from the positive impact on persistence, learning communities are especially valuable for first-year students for other reasons. The interdisciplinary nature and integrative pedagogy of learning communities can guide students away from the mentality of "siloed" unconnected disciplines fostered by university and curricular structures. Getting in the habit of connecting information and problem-solving across disciplines in their first year helps students to make all of their learning opportunities high impact. The integration of content, pedagogy, and co-curricular programs in learning communities contributes to the time students spend on the course material, cross-disciplinary understanding and application of concepts, and the personal connections made with fellow students and faculty, all of which make learning communities one of the most high-impact practices (HIPs) when constructed and taught with intention.[4]

The performing arts disciplines are a constant source of learning communities embedded within our departments. These naturally occurring learning communities are imbued with the characteristics of knowledge integration, extended contact hours, and personal connections for majors and non-majors engaged in performance. Any performance is a learning process where all collaborators learn as a collective. These same performance communities of students and faculty often collaborate on more than one project, applying what they learned in one performance to the next, and creating a learning community that spans courses and performance projects over semesters and years.

Outside of our departments, learning communities are the HIPs where the performing arts are most often included by faculty in other disciplines and by administrators encouraging the implementation of HIPs. In order to prepare their students to be members of the creative class, and as "innovation," "out-of-the-box thinking," and "creativity" gain traction as the learning outcomes most prized by the business world, colleges are looking for ways to bring pedagogies of the arts to more traditional disciplines. One productive method of inspiring students to apply creative techniques to problem-solving is to pair an arts course with a course from another discipline. These types of pairings are also seen as ways to increase any of the several types of student engagement, which a 2014 study showed was the "outcome most associated with Learning Community programs across institutional types," with a large majority of institutions looking at student engagement as a significant focus of their assessment efforts.[5] According to another study that looked at the connections between learning communities and student engagement, "learning communities appear to be particularly well suited to promoting active and collaborative learning and student–faculty interaction. Learning community participation also appears to be effective in promoting student interaction with diverse peers. These forms of engagement appear to be most effective in promoting students' affective development."[6] The ubiquity of these practices in the performing arts, as well as the arts' strengths in affective learning, makes the performing arts particularly valuable to learning communities and vice versa. The translation of humanities or science artifacts and concepts through performing arts pedagogies requires considerable time-on-task and collaborative work, and results, when done well, in increased understanding by students of the non-arts topic and greater engagement with the learning process.

The commonly pursued student engagement goals of learning communities—extensive student–faculty interaction, collaboration with peers, and active learning—are achieved through the embodied learning that is a part of so many performing arts courses, and learning communities offer performing arts faculty a fertile territory for developing somatic pedagogies. As Sandoval and Mino note in their case study of their own adolescent psychology/theatre learning community, "With an explicit emphasis on community building, interdisciplinary integration, collaborative learning, and integrative assessment, learning communities seem ideally situated to foster embodied learning."[7] They emphasize that the embodying of knowledge experienced in the learning community did not just inform students' understanding of the psychology material, but also helped students to apply psychological concepts to their acting techniques as well.

Similarly, the two case studies in this chapter both take embodied learning well past the simple application of somatic exercises in individual assignments into the totality of the learning community experience. Brian LaDuca describes a living-learning community that uses dramatic structures to teach creative problem-solving to students of diverse disciplines in order to prepare them for the contemporary job market. One of the central subjects of focus in the courses LaDuca describes is the self, examined in a scaffolded series of exercises designed to help students break down barriers to creativity and to learn to associate themselves with the social issue being presented through dramatic structure. This emphasis on empathy and affective sensibility is key to the efficacy of embodied learning. Confidence in one's own creativity, as articulated by Robyn Tudor, "begins to emerge when students voluntarily start engaging in a fully embodied and experiential way with individual tasks and group projects that are designed to target subjective self-awareness and encourage self-determination."[8] Creative expression is also central to the learning community described by Blake Stevens and Bill Manaris. In their community, students with no significant coding or musical composition experience write and perform several types of musical composition on laptop computers. The projects enable students to create music that would be impossible (at their skill level) on traditional instruments and also turn computer coding into a collaborative exercise, providing them with experiences in both disciplines at a level rarely achieved so quickly in either subject area alone. Both of these case studies, while ambitious, provide inspiring role models for institutions seeking to create learning communities that use performing arts subjects and pedagogies to inform other disciplines and contribute to students' creativity skills acquisition.

Call to action:

- Administrators of college-wide initiatives like First-Year Experiences and living-learning communities need to include the performing arts as foundational disciplines in these endeavors. In addition to the arts' ability to increase student engagement, they offer pedagogical tools uniquely suited to the pursuit of the creativity and innovation skills that are the goals of such collaborative learning experiences. Aside from contributing courses to learning community initiatives, performing arts faculty can run training sessions on active and embodied learning techniques, and provide assessment methods for such assignments.

- The tendency of faculty looking for learning community partners is to approach disciplines with which they are most familiar and with which they share theoretical approaches to course content. Performing arts faculty must reach out to faculty in other departments who might not see obvious linkages between the disciplines, in order to form connections and demonstrate the value of performing arts pedagogies and ways of knowing for all disciplines. It is not uncommon for performing arts faculty, especially theatre faculty, to worry that they are just being used as "service courses" to help students become better engaged with course material in other disciplines. We need to accept that that might be the case in the beginning of interdisciplinary partnerships and take the opportunity to educate our colleagues on the depth and breadth of both our subject matter and pedagogies.
- Performing arts departments should develop learning communities with their own majors in intentional ways, to better prepare them for life after college. While the use of artistic products and pedagogies to deepen connections to science or philosophy topics may be the easiest connection to spot, interdisciplinary learning of the type pursued in learning communities benefits arts subject matter as well. Students of the performing arts may be foremost among those students who see general education as "hoops to jump through" and irrelevant to their interests. Partly due to their passion for their major, and partly due to the long history of dismissal of the arts by other university disciplines, performing arts students often fail to make connections between their courses, missing out on potential applications of their arts knowledge that could serve them well if they don't pursue careers in the arts after college. Learning communities that connect their artistic work to the theories and methods of other disciplines can help arts majors to better articulate their own artistic practice and to make cognitive connections between their courses, both within and outside of their major.

Connecting Music and Computer Science: An Interdisciplinary Learning Community for First-Year University Students

Bill Manaris
College of Charleston
Charleston, SC, USA

Blake Stevens
College of Charleston
Charleston, SC, USA

Art and science were inseparable in the times of Pythagoras, Plato, and Aristotle. However, in modern times, they are diametrically separated within institutional education. While this division may have helped better organize and clarify epistemological organization of knowledge, it has also produced artificial silos that hide shared underlying logic and connections between such disciplines and practices. For instance, as is the case in our report, music and computing share (among other things) deep connections between algorithmic processes and musical processes and structures. These connections have become more explicit with the introduction of modern computing devices during the twentieth century.[9] Accordingly, various educational activities have emerged which try to reintroduce these connections within academe, in a way fixing this artificial rift that has existed between arts and sciences.[10]

We report our experiences in offering a First-Year learning community combining music and computing at the College of Charleston.[11] From fall 2010 to fall 2014, we offered five different instances of this learning community, under two different course titles (at different times): "Computer Music and the Quest for Beauty" (initially), and "Introduction to Computer Music and Aesthetics: Programming Music, Performing Computers" (later). This learning community provided an opportunity to draw together computing and music—two disciplines separated by the artificial division between arts and sciences mentioned above.

This effort combined an introductory course in computer programming ("Computers, Music, and Art," CITA 180) initially with a course in music history and style ("Music Appreciation," MUSC 131) and later with a course in music fundamentals and aesthetics ("Music Fundamentals,"

MUSC 146). As the learning community evolved, it became apparent that the demands of active, creative music-making afforded by the coding environment required more focused training in music theory and practice. The shift to conceiving the music course as an introduction to music theory did not, however, eliminate the study of the development of musical styles across history. As a result, the music course became a hybrid of theory, history, and aesthetics designed to introduce students to a basic, just-in-time knowledge of theoretical concepts, as well as issues related to style and aesthetics. These just-in-time topics were chosen to guide students in selecting models for adaptation and emulation in the musical artifacts they created through coding. These resultant artifacts included transcription projects, creative modeling of musical styles, and beginning compositional exercises/etudes.

Combining computer programming with music has the advantage of providing "high-impact," "authentic" learning experiences related to music.[12] Traditionally, introductory computer science courses focus mainly on programming syntax (e.g., Python) and algorithmic fundamentals (e.g., sequence, selection, iteration, and modularization/abstraction). Moreover, such courses emphasize numerical applications of computing, which can push away students who are more artistically inclined. The engagement with musical creation and expression may help motivate students to master these algorithmic fundamentals. Similarly, from a music education perspective, combining music with computer programming allows the introduction of active and creative learning experiences earlier than is often possible with traditional instruments. The computing environment provides students with opportunities to acquire experience in designing and implementing musical ideas on a computer, which is treated in this context as a musical instrument shared by all students (i.e., a common instrument). This simplifies teaching pertinent concepts, as it minimizes the need to support and translate between different traditional musical instruments (e.g., piano, guitar, and flute). All students become proficient on the new common instrument (e.g., the computer). This method allows theoretical and notational issues to be introduced in practice, through exercises in transcription, rearrangement, composition, and performance. Our approach has allowed us to introduce these concepts to students of differing abilities and backgrounds, and to integrate important music and computing knowledge that is not easily accessible in introductory courses into a cohesive whole, following an integrated, natural progression of understanding and skills.

An unexpected outcome of combining these two related disciplines is the introduction of more advanced material earlier in the curriculum.

The learning community has focused on a core cluster of essential learning outcomes for higher education (as identified by the Association of American Colleges and Universities [AAC&U]) that are characteristic of "high-impact practices," including inquiry and analysis of concepts in computing and music, creative thinking demonstrated through coding and musical modeling, and collaborative problem-solving.[13] Most significantly, the community is explicitly oriented around a "big question," namely, the question of "musical beauty," whether in its first title ("Computer Music and the Quest for Beauty") or revised title ("Introduction to Computer Music and Aesthetics: Programming Music, Performing Computers"). The question of what constitutes musical beauty has been addressed in multiple ways. Drawing upon material related to traditional music appreciation courses, this question is examined through a historical narrative of how forms of music have developed and have been challenged or extended with the emergence of electronic and computer music in the twentieth and twenty-first centuries. Exploring research in computer science and acoustics, the question is examined through a study of Zipf's law and its implications for understanding musical coherence and patterning.[14]

The learning community also involves extensive collaboration among students, including pair-programming projects conducted within the classroom. These projects conceive classroom encounters as a "workshop" and outside-of-class work as collaborations on more extended compositional modeling projects that culminate in class presentations and demonstrations of creative work. In these collaborative projects (in which the pairings change with different projects), students work with peers whose musical skills and backgrounds, as well as programming experience and competencies, may differ from their own. The goal in these collaborative projects is to synthesize knowledge about musical style and practices with dynamic coding skills, whether manifested in compositional projects or musical performances using the computer as the primary instrument.

The use of technology to foster collaboration and reinforce the learning outcome of developing written communication skills extends outside of class to a common course wiki for student notes; extra credit is offered to students in the computer science half of the learning community to update the wiki with the day's class notes. Studies show that use of such a shared-notes mechanism improves student understanding and overall course performance.[15]

Selected Projects

In this section we outline several projects in the learning community that exemplify the synthesis of computer science and musical instruction through authentic and high-impact learning experiences. The first is a small-scale project that represents the type of scaffolding assignment that introduces and reinforces the basic skills—in this case, fluency in reading musical notation—necessary to build to more advanced projects. The other projects illustrate two contrasting approaches to a final project that involved public exhibition and performance.

Transforming Bach

Literacy in standard musical notation is merged with musical representation in the programming language introduced in the course (JythonMusic).[16] After an introduction to both the conventions of standard notation and the representation of pitch and rhythm in the programming language, students applied this knowledge by transcribing short melodic excerpts in JythonMusic to test this knowledge. Of the exercises and homework assignments that reinforce these skills, one of the most effective ones has involved students listening to selected transcriptions for Moog synthesizer by Wendy Carlos from her landmark 1968 album *Switched-On Bach*,[17] and then developing their own creative work in response.

Students were given a score packet with a selection of individual pieces from J. S. Bach's *Well-Tempered Clavier* and *Goldberg Variations*, with recordings posted on a course webpage. The project involved choosing one movement and arranging this piece for the JythonMusic environment (see Fig. 4.1). Students were presented with three different approaches to this project:

- *Transcription*: transferring a piece of music from one instrumental medium to another—in traditional practice, for example, from violin to lute, guitar, or piano. This is the most "literal" form of adaptation, although the transfer of the work from the piano to the medium of the computer (with its wide range of sounds) will nonetheless entail creative thought.
- *Arrangement*: adaptation or development of an existing work that preserves a clear, perceptible correspondence to the original work, although features such as voicing, register, timbre, and instrumentation are more significantly altered than in a transcription.
- *Recomposition*: transformation or appropriation of elements of an existing work to create a new work; with new parts or voices, rhythms

```
 1 # JS_Bach.Canon_1.GoldbergGround.BWV1087.py
 2 #
 3 # This program (re)creates J.S. Bach's Canon No. 1 of the Fourteen on
 4 # the Goldberg Ground.
 5 #
 6 # This canon is constructed using the Goldberg ground as the subject
 7 # (soggetto) combined with the retrograde of itself.
 8 #
 9
10 from music import *
11
12 # how many times to repeat the theme
13 times = 6
14
15 # define the data structure
16 score  = Score("J.S. Bach, Canon 1, Goldberg Ground (BWV1087)", 100)
17 part   = Part()
18 voice1 = Phrase(0.0)
19
20 # create musical material (soggetto)
21 pitches = [G3, F3, E3, D3, B2, C3, D3, G2]
22 rhythms = [QN, QN, QN, QN, QN, QN, QN, QN]
23 voice1.addNoteList(pitches, rhythms)
24
25 # create 2nd voice
26 voice2 = voice1.copy()
27 Mod.retrograde(voice2)    # follower is retrograde of leader
28
29 # combine musical material
30 part.addPhrase(voice1)
31 part.addPhrase(voice2)
32 score.addPart(part)
33
34 # repeat canon as desired
35 Mod.repeat(score, times)
36
37 # play score and write it to a MIDI file
38 Play.midi(score)
39 Write.midi(score, "JS_Bach.Canon_1.GoldbergGround.BWV1087.mid")
```

Fig. 4.1 A sample of a JythonMusic program transcribing J.S. Bach's Canon No. 1 of the Fourteen Canons on the Goldberg Ground (see http://bit.ly/bachCanon1)

(including percussion), basslines, and freely composed music added by the composer, the original work now functions as a "template" or "scaffolding" on which a new work or performance is built, or as a mine of musical "material" to be exploited. This technique is related to John Oswald's concept of "plunderphonics," the sampling of audio recordings to create sound collages.

These three levels of creative adaptation allowed students with prior musical background and compositional interests to create independent works based on tonal materials from Bach, while beginning music students were able to create successful transcriptions of Bach in a new medium, demonstrating knowledge of both notational conventions and a new programming language. This project idea also allowed the two faculty members to find an early common ground to explore the intersection of their respective fields (musicology and computer science), while exploring new ways of collaborating in future offerings of the learning community, informed by a better understanding of each other's disciplines.

Laptop Orchestra Performance of Terry Riley's "In C"
The second creative project that emerged from this collaboration took place during the fall 2010 offering of this learning community. This project was assigned in lieu of a comprehensive written final exam and involved a laptop orchestra performance (see Fig. 4.2).

Laptop orchestras became popular in university settings after the Princeton Laptop Orchestra (also known as PLOrK) was introduced at Princeton University in the mid-2000s.[18] One of the main advantages of laptop orchestras is that they make computing tasks more communal and socially relevant, which is something that appeals to students not usually

Fig. 4.2 A Laptop Orchestra Performance of Terry Riley's "In C" (see video—http://bit.ly/charlestonLaptopOrchestra)

attracted to computing. Members of a laptop orchestra program their computer in real time to perform musical tasks in conjunction and coordination with other members, usually guided by a conductor (in our case, one of the faculty members).

In addition to providing new types of motivation for learning how to program, such projects offer invaluable opportunities for musical performance and social interaction and collaboration not usually seen in music or other university courses. Additionally, while programming has traditionally been treated as a solo activity in computing pedagogy, when seen in this context, it becomes a valuable social as well as musical skill. It is the synthesis of the two bodies of knowledge (music and computing) that bring this unexpected, gestalt outcome to life.

This ensemble activity came at the tail end of the course, complementing other solo and smaller group projects during the semester. Even though we experimented with such a large ensemble experience only once, and only after students had mastered enough concepts through earlier activities, the learning opportunities discussed by Mudd still apply:

> Ensemble playing forms the backbone of transferable skills development in higher education music courses, and demonstrates how laptop ensembles, as well as being musically engaging projects in their own right, can be a useful way of integrating such skill development into more technologically oriented music degrees. The fact that such ensembles have few established modes of practice allows them to be particularly open to student engagement in a variety of roles and can help to promote an active learning environment.[19]

One possibility that we may explore in the future is to develop a learning community that focuses exclusively on a laptop orchestra platform to deliver additional educational material from both computing and music, while satisfying curricular objectives in both degree areas (computer science and music).

The fall 2010 experience centered on a live coding performance of "In C." This is a well-known work of early minimalism composed by Terry Riley in 1964. The piece consists of 53 melodic patterns to be played in sequence by different musicians, with the only constraint that, once a musician has moved on to a new pattern, they are not allowed to return to an earlier one. Musicians are allowed to repeat a pattern as many times as they like, but, once a musician moves on to a next pattern, other musicians usually follow to provide a more cohesive movement through the different phases of the piece. Musicians are encouraged to listen to what their neighbors are doing, as well as the whole ensemble, to help shape and enhance the musical outcome. This results in a performance of indeterminate length and concurrencies.

In preparation for the performance, we had students pre-code the 53 different patterns of the piece in whichever timbre (of the computer's default 128 MIDI instruments) they chose and demonstrate that they could transcribe them accurately. Additionally, we made available three recordings of the piece: Terry Riley's first recording (1968), a recording by Bang on a Can (2001), and one by Ars Nova Copenhagen/Percurama Percussion Ensemble (2006).

During the performance, students were required to write the necessary code to generate these different patterns in real time. Since precise coordination was difficult with the computer instruments, we omitted the eighth-note pulse on high Cs that is a standard (yet optional) part of the piece's performance. Nevertheless, our experience confirmed Riley's observation that during a performance "some quite fantastic shapes will arise and disintegrate as the group moves through the piece when it is properly played" (1989). Since this performance, we have explored a coding pattern based on temporal recursion,[20] which utilizes a loop function that plays a phrase once and then schedules itself to repeat. The laptop performance successfully realized the core set of outcomes that guided the learning community, particularly through its focus on creative coding and music-making through a collaborative (and public) experience.

Visual Soundscapes
This project was part of the fall 2011 offering of the learning community. It involved creating musical pieces from material found in images. While the process of deriving music from images, or images loosely guiding the composition of music, has been explored by composers such as Sergei Rachmaninoff and Claude Debussy,[21] it is the introduction of a digital media representation and ways that this representation can be automatically processed by a computer (through computer code written by the students) that invites vast new opportunities for creative realizations and outcomes. This is by far one of the most advanced, engaging, and inspiring projects that emerged from offering this learning community.

This project, like the laptop performance of "In C," was undertaken in lieu of a final exam. Students were asked to produce a sonification of visual data from photographs, paintings, and other images. Working alone or in pairs, students were instructed to select beautiful or otherwise compelling images and then design a set of musical parameters through which these images could be transformed into sound. Musical parameters included pitch and scale, dynamics, timbre, and instrumentation—concepts that the students had already been introduced to during the semester (or were introduced to just-in-time, as needed per project). Students were encouraged to draw inspiration from a range of musical models, including selected works of the minimalist composer Arvo Pärt and examples of jazz, rock, serialism, and aleatory music.

In terms of algorithmic process, students were free to select different parts of the image for specific musical functions. Not all parts of the images were necessarily sonified, yet most of the sound emerged from numeric data (pixels) inside these images. Changes in sound correspond to a scanning of pixels in the image from left-to-right, up-to-down, center-to-corners, or diagonally—all choices available to students based on their judgment of the desired properties of sonification. In some of the resulting projects, sound came from the averaged regions of the image, and in others, complex sequencing rules were used.

These projects synthesized visual, musical, and algorithmic processes. While the students did most of the work on their own (in terms of selecting an image or images and making certain musical decisions), they were given some assistance (in terms of code examples, and, most importantly, music composition guidance) by the two professors. In the end, visual, musical, and algorithmic processes became intertwined as equal aesthetic partners—none subservient to others. This outcome was something we did not initially expect, but in retrospect, it is something that should naturally emerge for the project to be successful. In other words, the visual, aural, and algorithmic became one. Here are three notable examples:

"Daintree Drones"
The piece "Daintree Drones" was created by Kenneth Hanson (see Fig. 4.3). It utilizes an original image (drawn by the student), which is scanned from left to right, capturing small vertical stripes (areas of pixels). These pixels are separated into five areas, each contributing a new note created by averaging the luminosity of the enclosed pixels. These notes are played concurrently generating a chord. As scanning (and averaging of pixels to generate the chord) proceeds from left to right, a musical piece is created. Of course, the mapping between image values and notes has been

Fig. 4.3 "Daintree Drones" by Kenneth Hanson—sonification of digital image by computer programming (see https://vimeo.com/64110119)

done very carefully to ensure that the outcome is harmonious and aesthetically intended. The piece is rendered using six FM and dynamic filter synthesis instruments (provided by JythonMusic).

"Lugna"
The piece "Lugna" was created by John Thevos and Katherine May (see Fig. 4.4). This piece follows a similar approach to the previous piece, except as the image is scanned from left to right, only five pixels per column are captured (i.e., by tracing five horizontal lines across the image). By using only a single pixel (as opposed to an area of pixels) times 5, the piece lasts longer and thus explores more varied harmonic material. The piece is rendered using three PAD (GM #89), one PIANO (GM #0), and one RHODES (GM #4) MIDI instruments. These harmonic and instrumental choices generate an ethereal, melancholic musical soundscape that corresponds well with the image's visual aesthetic.

"Manhattan Solstice"
Finally, Caroline Freeman (née Bowman) utilizes a photo by music composer (and photographer) Robinson McClellan to create the piece "Manhattan Solstice" (see Fig. 4.5). This piece is inspired by the phenom-

Fig. 4.4 "Lugna" by John Thevos and Katherine May—sonification of digital image by computer programming (see https://vimeo.com/64109534)

Fig. 4.5 "Manhattan Solstice" by Caroline Freeman (née Bowman)—sonification of digital image by computer programming (see https://vimeo.com/64101616). Photo courtesy of Robinson McClellan, Rutgers University

enon known as "Manhattanhenge" (or Manhattan Solstice), where, twice a year, the setting sun is aligned with the east-to-west streets in Manhattan, NY. The piece utilizes a reduced pitch set (0, 4, 7), that is, a major triad, two pixel scan lines, and the more esoteric MIDI instruments CRYSTAL (MIDI no. 98) and HELICOPTER (MIDI no. 125). The piece uses the same process as the previous example, although the musical mappings here are designed to evoke the chaotic, heavily populated, technology-laden, mechanical urban landscape and soundscape of a modern megalopolis like New York City.

The selected projects were combined with projects from a parallel standalone course in the computer science department for a month-long exhibition at the campus library from April 6 to May 7, 2012. This collection of projects, titled "Visual Soundscapes," captured an exploration and synthesis of twenty-first-century media: the merging of the visual, the aural, and the algorithmic.[22] The complete student sonification examples from this exhibition are available on Vimeo at https://vimeo.com/cofccita.

Evaluation

In addition to the various examples provided above, which demonstrate the depth and quality of material produced and synthesized learning achieved by the different student cohorts, during fall 2014, we administered a student survey to assess the effectiveness, from the students' perspective, of our teaching approach and the tools developed and used in the learning community.

The survey questions measured attitudes about the musicality of the programming approach used in class (e.g., "How well can musical ideas be represented in a computer programming language?" and "The musical outcomes I achieve with JythonMusic are similar to those I achieve with more traditional methods of music making"). This survey was administered on the very last day of class, after the final project presentations were completed. Earlier in the semester (first day of class), we had discovered through a different survey that our student cohort consisted of equal numbers of students with prior musical or programming knowledge (but not both). So, in a way, this equal distribution of pre-existing knowledge (which was not a prerequisite for this community) served as an equalizer in the cohort.

This post-survey has been described in detail elsewhere[23]; herein, we summarize its results.

In tabulating the results, we found that there was little variation in the student answers between music students and computer students, indicating that, by the end of the semester, this community learning experience was not influenced by the earlier, pre-existing knowledge (of music or programming) that students may have had coming into the course.

In the results below, percentages indicate the average measurement across all relevant questions for a particular measured attribute, characteristic, or issue[24]:

- The students were very confident (97%) that creating music with code is a good method for music composition, and that musical ideas can be represented well in a computer programming language.
- The students believed (>90%) that being able to interactively run and edit code facilitates live performance.
- The students believed (>90%) that using musical tasks was an effective motivator to learn computer programming and also that making music by coding was enjoyable.
- The students were relatively confident (71%) that the musical outcomes they can achieve with the programming environment used in the course (JythonMusic) are similar to those with more traditional methods of music-making. Of course, this is to be expected, considering that programming a computer is a far more time-consuming task than playing a musical instrument directly. However (and this is something we have not evaluated through survey, but only through observation), students, upon completion of this course, are capable of producing very advanced musical outcomes, which to do through a traditional musical instrument would require many years of study in performance (for that particular instrument). So, in a way, learning how to code musical tasks is a more efficient (but possibly less nuanced) method for performing music; supplementing this coding approach with musical controllers like Ableton Push may help tremendously with nuance and expressiveness.
- The students felt confident (81%) that they would likely continue making music through code beyond the class. This positive attitude likely resulted from the intensive exposure (six hours) to musical activities that fostered positive and supportive experiences. In comparison with attitudes assessed in a similar course in the college's honors program designed for juniors and seniors, our experience in this learning community suggests that offering such experiences earlier and at more length in an academic curriculum is likely to produce stronger learning outcomes in both computer science and music degree programs.[25]

Conclusions

We have described the results and experiences from teaching a First-Year learning community synthesizing knowledge and learning outcomes in introductory music and computer science courses. This community is part of a larger academic endeavor at the College of Charleston in creating a curriculum and undergraduate bachelor of arts in computing in the arts (see http://cita.cofc.edu).

This and similar learning communities elsewhere[26] offer wonderful opportunities for creative interplay and productive learning experiences between computing, music, and art, which combine diverse, yet interrelated, complementary courses in these fields. In our case, although the original courses are traditionally offered within their own academic silos (i.e., within different university schools or departments), when "forced" to co-exist within the same classroom, they encourage an exploration of potential overlapping between them, and the ways that each body of knowledge can inform, enhance, and advance the other. This collaboration opens the door for new creative and inspiring gestalt learning experiences for the students, as well as (unexpectedly, at first, but perhaps not surprisingly, after the fact!) for the professors. The incorporation of coding into introductory music courses opens a new path of reimagining these courses, asking students to take on more active roles as makers of music, whether in transcribing and creatively adapting the music of Bach, realizing a minimalist composition in a collaborative ensemble, or creating original works through the sonification of visual media. These projects, as well as the more elementary scaffolding exercises that led to them, would be difficult or impossible to realize in a traditional music fundamentals or music appreciation course, whose students would not possess a common instrument capable of powerful musical expression (the computer) and fluency in a shared set of languages (music theory and coding).

Therefore, we expect to offer similar learning communities and other related courses in the future, both within and outside of the CITA program, as (a) it is clear that students benefit tremendously from synthesizing these two bodies of knowledge (music and computer science); (b) this will further improve our approach and learning materials; and (c) such courses expose and engage more cohorts of students in this very positive learning experience.

Acknowledgments

The authors would like to thank the following: Professor of Studio Art Jarod Charzewski, for coordinating the "Visual Soundscapes" exhibition; Claire Fund and James Williams at Addlestone Library, for offering their most prominent space for a month; students Daniel Anderson, Marissa Croop, Caroline Freeman (née Bowman), Jordan Freeman, Forrest Hammond, Kenneth Hanson, Hudson Jones, Elizabeth Koury, Katherine May, Sam McCants, Stephen Rainey, John Thevos, and Dylan Walsh for participating in this exhibit; and the National Science Foundation (DUE-1044861) for providing partial funding for this work.

SOCIAL INNOVATION THROUGH PURPOSE, PERFORMANCE, AND STORY

Brian LaDuca
University of Dayton
Dayton, OH, USA

A well-made play is defined as "a play constructed according to a predetermined pattern and aiming at neatness of plot and theatrical effectiveness but often being mechanical and stereotyped." This fixed pattern has origins in Aristotle's Tragic Plot Structure: *Inciting Incident, Plot Reversal, Denouement*. The narrative format evolved through the late 1800s with explorations by such literary dignitaries as Henrik Ibsen and George Bernard Shaw. The structure began to grow in depth beyond the "mechanical and stereotypical" to have a greater focus on the human condition, shifting from the impersonal, expected structure of a well-made play to its next evolution, the problem-play. Shaw's problem-play is a story that puts a person or people in conflict with an institution, confronting a contemporary social question.[27] Ibsen would find synergies between the well-made play and Shaw's problem-play design by qualifying it as a human tragedy story, a story investing in that moment "[when a person] stands in a tight place ... [and] cannot go forwards or backwards."[28] The Institute of Applied Creativity for Transformation (IACT) at the University of Dayton is a living-learning program that transforms the well-made play into collaborative, transdisciplinary humanity-centered education through a radical creative curriculum leveraging arts and innovation processes and practices to render unique, transdisciplinary experiential learning. This learning transforms the well-made play design, specifically Ibsen and Shaw's evolution of well-made into problem-play focusing on the human condition, into a pedagogical structure for introducing students to the creative competencies that today's job market demands, while applying those same skills to the students' diverse disciplines of study, with a special focus on developing a personal vision statement, or purpose-based learning design, that is additive to their academic pursuits.

In addition, famed anthropologist Victor Turner's four-part social drama theory (*Breach, Crisis, Redressive Action, Reintegration*) provides a twenty-first century framework to elevate the well-made and problem-play structure into today's student living experience. If the problem-play provides familiarity in story structure, Turner's theory provides a more dynamic, rapid, and forceful process during a contemporary time of global crisis. At the IACT, applied creative learning demands new idea creation for action across all disciplines of study. The institute places students into that "tight" place Shaw's narrative format introduced and then challenges the student's ability to move backward or forward by overlaying Turner's dramatic framework. Turner's definition of social drama is an eruption from the level surface of ongoing social life. He focuses on the interactions, transactions, reciprocities, and customs of life that define regular, orderly sequences of behavior.[29] This evolution of the problem-play is the exact, real-life action the students lean into when experiencing an applied creative pedagogy. The IACT's unique ecosystem offers a novel living/learning environment for students that not only supports and thrives on the HIP's living-learning community of encouraged integration of learning across courses and challenging the "big questions" of life but also creates a framework for action and education where students discover potential solutions and ideas for the big questions that can be immediately realized through the empathetic, collaborative *Ideation-Disruption-Aha* (IDA) pedagogical design directly influenced by Aristotle, Shaw, and Turner. This narrative three-step process defined as IDA (pronounced idea) focuses on the student outcomes of critical perspective, creative confidence, and innovative application as they apply to the students' specific disciplines or expertise.

Similar to Turner's four-part theory and the direct inspirational framework to the IACT's IDA pedagogy, Shaw's problem-play formula is divided into three sections: *Exposition, Situation, Unraveling. Exposition* depends upon a key piece of information kept from some characters, but known to others (and to the audience). Most of the story takes place before the action of the play begins, making the beginning of the play a late point of attack. *Situation* explains actions that precede the opening scene, and generates the audience's sympathy for the hero (or heroes) over their rival (or rivals). With the *Unraveling*, the plot moves forward in a chain of actions that use minor reversals of fortune to create suspense.[30] The pace builds toward a climactic obligatory scene, in which the hero triumphs. A dénouement follows, in which all remaining plot points are unraveled and resolved.

The IDA pedagogy begins with the "I" in IDA; *Ideation* (or Shaw's *Exposition*) introduces the development of critical perspective focusing on what is and what can be for that specific class with the goal of broadening it in creative, analytical, and innovative ways. Students negotiate and collect the session *content* or data in the room. The content can be made up of all dimensions including sight, space, sound, and emotion. Students are challenged by the *ambiguity* or what they do not know about the content presented, and then the final step in ideation is the *tension* or how they feel and what emotional and physical obstacles they might encounter with the ambiguity of the content. The second step of the process is *Disruption*, or the "D" in IDA, aligning with Shaw's *Situation*, which uses the students' building critical perspective to develop the creative confidence to see the broad and diverse set of solutions in front of them and chase solutions that they haven't totally figured out yet. Students seek ways to disturb, make more conscious, and awaken other "avenues" for ideas and solutions. This process includes a combination of *empathy* and *collaboration* wherein value-driven learning and shared experiences provide a pivot in students' thinking, resulting in the humanization of collaborative interests and ideas. The final step of the process is the *Aha*, or the "A" in IDA, similar to *Unraveling* where participants begin the fearless practice of seeing the world in complex ways and experimenting with improbable materials in seeking imaginative, unexpected, and innovative solutions for multiple outcomes. In this step, the participants generate new *knowledge* and identify what they can transform from the original content for a result that is an unexpected outcome in their presented challenge or original ideas.

The narrative journey of an IACT session is never dependent on a hierarchical front of class lecture or rudimentary and repetitive lab work. More specifically, the narrative, play-influenced structure puts both educators and students in the same proverbial story based on the session's theme at the given point within the semester. No longer does a student know what to expect as they enter the room. Are they the characters? Are they the narrator, antagonist, protagonist? The outcome of the session becomes not about simply telling the student what he or she needs to learn but becomes a narrative design of problem-solving together using various disciplinary tools to reveal the *Aha* of the session, an *Aha* directly mirroring the denouement of Shaw's or Ibsen's problem-play formula and encompassing an honest resolution of both failure and success akin to the back end of Turner's theory where repairs—formal or informal—are enacted; and if the repairs work, the group concept returns to normal, but if the repairs fail, the group concept breaks apart.[31] Collaborative problem-solving with innovative learning through a human narrative thus empowers the story of the human condition and perhaps tragedy as a new process for humanity-centered learning, thus educating the whole student preparing them for the twenty-first century workplace evolution.

Shaw's and Turner's dramatic theories are unique tools that have had great effect on engendering the applied creative learning models across the academic silos of higher education. Those in the performing arts and film communities understand narrative play and film structures but may not recognize that the majority of citizens who study or practice outside of the arts are unfamiliar with these structures as processes for potential real-life solutions to real-life problems. As Dan McAdams, chair of psychology at Northwestern, has written, "The stories we construct to make sense of our lives are fundamentally about our struggle to reconcile who we imagine we were, are, and might be in our head and bodies with who we were, are, and might be in the social contexts of family, community, the workplace, ethnicity, religion, gender, social class, and culture writ large. The self comes to terms with society through narrative identity."[32] When information, problems, or decision-making are funneled through a human narrative form, individuals unfamiliar with the historical, theatrical application of the problem-play form but familiar with a narrative structure, begin to grow in critical, creative, and innovative confidence. A similar example is when mathematicians are able to present their problems in a visual manner. In that occurrence, left brain learners can find relations and new knowledge in numerical problems that take on visual shape and story. Thus, when the actions that make us human are authentically framed as valued, innovative learning tools through actionable storytelling, students and educators alike are more likely to explore alternative solutions as confidence builds in a journey they recognize as occurring every day.

The IACT's narrative and performative redesign of critical and creative learning in higher education has come in direct response to the critical change of workforce development in the twenty-first century. In a July 2016 article in Adobe for Education, author Tacy Trowbridge outlined recent findings from the compensation data provider PayScale published in its 2016 Workforce-Skills Preparedness Report: "The report details the responses of almost 64,000 hiring managers across a wide range of industries who were asked about the 'skills gap'—the disconnect between the skills students have when they graduate from college and the skills companies need." Trowbridge highlighted three specific points:

- 60% of managers said new graduates do not have the critical-thinking and problem-solving skills necessary for the job.
- 46% said new graduates lack the necessary communication skills.
- 36% reported new graduates have inadequate interpersonal and teamwork skills.

In the article, Trowbridge asks educational institutions how they intend to help students close the skills gap. She states, "it's clear to us that they need to go beyond teaching traditional skills and make fostering creativity and developing digital skills a priority in the classroom. Many of the skills current grads lack are associated with creativity, from critical thinking to communication to collaboration."[33]

A recent AAC&U journal article on Creativity and Innovation by Fernando Lozano and Amanda Sabicer stated,

> efforts to enhance creativity and innovation are changing the educational landscape of the United States. These efforts can take many names and forms—clinics, design thinking, entrepreneurial accelerators. But [Lozano and Sabicer] argue here that campus interventions alone are not sufficient. ... Enhanced creativity should be fostered and guided toward answering 'real-life' problems; it should affect the very communities where our schools exist, even as its development prepares students for life after graduation. ... The main idea is that creativity is not fostered in isolation; rather, creativity is best enhanced when it is part of a collective and diverse ecosystem.[34]

The ecosystem and mindset of applied creativity stem from transdisciplinary learning (the unity of intellectual frameworks beyond the disciplinary perspectives) and humanity-centered design. Other national models for creative confidence focus on human-centered design such as IDEO,[35] wherein design starts with the people they are designing for and ends with new solutions that are tailor made to suit those needs. Our model of humanity-centered design is built to provide creative design for humankind; that is, humans as a community and the acts that make up the community. The Catholic and Marianist Philosophy of Community Living at the University of Dayton[36] recognizes community living as an essential learning experience; the IACT makes this principle of community living an academic act. In essence, everyone has a story and every person has a collection of acts that make up their humanity. When combined into a narrative format for transformative disciplinary outcomes, new types of teachers and learners are developed.

All IACT students seeking creative learning must take the ACT I course *Creative Confidence Through Critical Perspective* where students are introduced to applied creative theory and critical thinking through the IACT transdisciplinary sessions focused on developing inquiry, reflection, and confidence through critical and creative experimentation. This 14-week course is set up in two sections of 35 students each and is tri-taught weekly to elevate and apply the transdisciplinary models upon which the IACT is built. Tri-Teaching is a progressive collaborative teaching design that disrupts the "he said, she said" of team teaching while encouraging diverse perspectives to partner around a core concept in the problem-play-influenced session. It is within these three educators of various disciplines and expertise where we truly see a transdisciplinary creation of a unified intellectual framework beyond the individual disciplinary perspectives. In these weekly 50-minute sessions the problem-play design is implemented and is transforming the HIP's common intellectual experience and collaborative assignments and projects into a continuous, connected storyline that is both familiar to the student and full of human purpose, success, and failure. These HIPs make up the humanity-centered design of the IACT and its institutional mission (Table 4.1).

In the fall of 2015, during week ten of the semester focused on the theme of bringing to life the implicit and explicit multitudes that challenge our daily climate and the exploration of our human desires for spirituality, energy, freedoms, and change, the transdisciplinary team of educators (Engineering Innovation, Student Athlete Advising, Residence Life) focused their intellectual frameworks on an outcome of exploring the imposter syndrome and the anxiety when one's resources have been completely stripped away. This session was the first session of a four-week mini-section entitled FEAR that presented an opportunity for students "to do

Table 4.1 Fall 2016 ACT I schedule providing scaffolding and top-level definitions of the three-part themes that supported the overarching outcomes of the semester

Part 1 of 3—SENSSATIONALIZE	*Life often presents us with what appears to be binary choices. Is it really that simple?*
Session 1.0	Applied Creativity, Theatre, Dance and Performance Tech, Military History
Question	Define subject vs. subjected & agent vs. agency
Experience	A series of movement based, strategic selections to build on identity and depth of person.
Goal	Understanding and recognizing the sometimes necessary binary in our lives
Session 2.0	Applied Creativity, Cultural Arts Mgmt., Marketing
Question	How do we find collective refuge with multiple identities that embody fear driven by media?
Experience	Establish a framework that goes beyond just merely tolerance to understanding for collective refuge and safety.
Goal	Enable students to identify who they can trust as a primary source and safety structure for themselves.
Session 3.0	Applied Creativity, Human Rights, Career Services
Question	Can you maintain personal security in a publicly insecure space?
Experience	Rapid fire binary process of questions and answer that builds confidence then pushes students to consider the tensions that exist between their choices in deciding how to invest their tax dollars
Goal	Understanding that the search for more security does not always make you more secure.
Part 2 of 3—CONTROL	*Psychological or physical restraint is perceived … or real, acknowledged … or dismissed, beneficial … or not.*
Session 1.0	Applied Creativity, Theatre, Dance and Performance Tech, Aerospace Engineering
Question	How do you (students) navigate the balance of being under control to (the illusion of) being in control?
Experience	An experiential model that examines this balance through the Serenity Prayer.
Goal	Give students the necessary "wisdom" to navigate the difference between knowing what they can and cannot control.
Session 2.0	Applied Creativity, Art Education, Mechanical Engineering
Question	Does False Empathy Create Active Construction of Power?

Experience	Deconstructing discomfort to disable assumed empathy
Goal	Re-engineering shared concepts to empower true empathy
Session 3.0	**Applied Creativity, Greek Life, Multidisciplinary Arts**
Question	What is your personal stake in gaining control?
Experience	Navigating the prospect of protest as an investment-risk.
Goal	Identified process to regain control through ownership and release.
Part 3 of 3—RELEASE	When striving through tantrums and struggles, we lose hope, we fail to forgive. Will we celebrate and see the beauty?
Session 1.0	**Applied Creativity, Bioengineering + Engineering Wellness, Biology**
Question	What is the fare to ride the healthy bus?
Experience	A Pandemic inspired session that puts the class into engineered groups to solve a food borne cookie dough pandemic!!
Goal	To put empathy into action by capitalizing on the students' new group diversity and awareness of each other
Session 2.0	**Applied Creativity, English, Graphic Design**
Question	How is spiritual energy exchanged between people for collective freedom?
Experience	Establish a framework that goes beyond just merely tolerance to understanding for collective refuge and safety.
Goal	Being able to identify what personal freedom is—and how your freedom can help someone else.
Session 3.0	**Applied Creativity, Health & Sport Sciences, Religious Studies**
Question	Recognize cycles of life and utilize this knowledge and understanding in order to maintain stability in the face of change.
Experience	Looking at turning points after "releasing" wherein students will reframe muscle balance/fatigue as life balance/fatigue in order to stabilize their growth after a moment of renewal.
Goal	To recognize that the concept of stability has a range and in order to maintain renewal one most always work toward a productive "tomorrow"

Areas in gray represent the disciplines within the Tri-Teaching Transdisciplinary Cohorts battle creatively against one of the most powerful emotions that holds us back from ourselves and from each other."[37] As the students experienced well-made sessions in previous weeks that challenged them through transdisciplinary frameworks focused on the thirst for desire and proceeding capitalistic consumption of that desire, this specific session's story design was as follows:

- Question: Am I _____ enough?
- Experience: Silent session where students explored internal perceptions versus actualities through visual immersion, mask work, and real-life emergency situation and story.
- Goal: Making visible what keeps you from being you and does that personal realization keep others around you from becoming their true whole self?

The *Ideation* for this session started the moment the students entered the room. The rolling tables were completely removed, the lights were low, and a projector was set up on the floor showing a slideshow of a number of images. Students entered, left their cell phones in a bin and silence was requested. They were then directed to sit on the floor, in the corner of the room. As students gathered they were instructed to begin responding to the slideshow of images being shown. These images were a myriad of content they had engaged with thus far in the fall semester including images around desire, climate issues of all kinds, success, failure, depleting resources and other juxtaposed, emotionally charged visuals. As they watched this slideshow silently, they wrote on the whiteboard wall responses to the following questions:

WHO AM I
WHAT DEFINES ME
MESSAGES THAT INFLUENCE WHO YOU ARE OR WANT TO BE

After 20 minutes the slideshow was turned off and the session moved into *Disruption*. Two of the educators began to lay out clear, transparent masks on the floor as another educator began reading the details from the 2015 Umpqua Community College school shooting in Oregon where, according to reports,[38] the shooter demanded students respond to his question about what they believed in prior to shooting. This scenario was delivered peacefully, highlighting the goals of the disruption and the demand for empathy in the face of highly charged, authentic decision-

Fig. 4.6 Mask-making at the Institute of Applied Creativity for Transformation

making when challenged to be yourself. As the details were read, the actual, printed out images from the ideation slideshow were laid around the room with the masks. Students were then asked to first grab a mask and put it on and then charged to begin ripping parts of the images that are present and glue these images to their mask (Fig. 4.6). The prompts for choosing images were:

> *Who are you when no one is around?*
> *Who are you to you?*
> *You put a mask on every day to present to others. But who are you to you, when no one is looking, watching, evaluating?*

Upon completion of their masks, each student was asked to find a partner and sit on the floor with that other individual, face to face, and still in silence. They were tasked to study each other's mask and then they each were given a small notebook and a pen. During the final 20 minutes, the students used methods from Simon Sinek's *Start With Why* book as an iterative interrogative technique exploring the cause-and-effect of their relationships with the visuals on their respective masks. In this IACT disruptive process, only two questions were asked in an intentionally slow and methodical repetitive style allowing the students in the room to both think and respond. The two questions were:

Why do you define yourself in this way?
Why did you make the choice to put this image on your mask?

The students began alternating writing the one word or phrase in their books and one at a time, still in silence, show their responses to their partners. One educator, again, read the Oregon Shooter story and posed the final question, *What Matters Most?* In the *Aha* of the narrative journey, each partner, one at a time, looked at their partner's mask and after learning about what defined and represented their partners during *Start With Why*, took the one image that best represents the answer to "What Matters Most" off of their partner's mask. They then opened up the partner's book and placed the image among the words that were written down during the interrogation. This silent and intimate journey closed with the students understanding that the mask they are currently wearing was a symbol of the images that make up their second face or imposter syndrome. That this is the mask they tend to wear in the face of fear and their image placed in their book is what absolutely matters most. To have that image presented to them by another individual provided a space of confidence for continued sharing of one's true self (Fig. 4.7).

Beginning in 2017–2018 there will be 100 students experiencing all levels of the IACT learning models starting with 70 in the ACT I course

Fig. 4.7 Mask-making at the Institute of Applied Creativity for Transformation

in the fall of 2017 and 30 upperclassmen pursuing the IACT undergraduate certificate in applied creativity for transformation.

In December 2016, a pre- and post-survey was given to the 70 students who completed the fall ACT I semester using Grant Wiggins' creativity assessment tool.[39] Using the 1–6 scale the 70 students, on average, identified their work at the beginning of the semester as being a 3, or "The work is somewhat creative. The ideas/materials/methods used show signs of imagination and personal style." Those same 70 students identified their work after the semester as a 5, or "The work is highly creative. The ideas/materials/methods used are imaginative and effective. There is attention to detail. A clear and confident voice and style are present" with the majority highlighting "Novel approaches/moves/directions/ideas/perspectives were used to good effect" and "There is an effective blend of personal style and technical knowledge" as specific impacts to their creative confidence.

In closing, the IACT living-learning program and the maturing ACT pedagogy and curriculum are radical HIPs of collaborative learning. Learning to work and solve problems in the company of others is quintessential to the development and design of a theatrical performance and is a key transferrable within each week of the ACT course. The sharpening of one's own understanding by listening seriously to the insights of others, especially those with different backgrounds and life experiences, is exactly the collection of actions that drive the humanity-centered design of this institute.

Notes

1. "Defining Features," *The National Resource Center for Learning Communities*.
2. For some representative studies and summaries of research on Learning Communities, see Anne Goodsell Love, "The Growth and Current State of Learning Communities in Higher Education"; Tiffany Cambridge-Williams, Adam Winsler, Anastasia Kitsantas, and Elizabeth Bernard, "University 100 Orientation Courses and Living-Learning Communities Boost Academic Retention and Graduation via Enhanced Self-Efficacy and Self-Regulated Learning"; Gene Popiolek, Ricka Fine, and Valerie Eilman, "Learning Communities, Academic Performance, Attrition, and Retention: A Four-Year Study."
3. Emily Lardner and Gillies Malnarich, "A New Era in Learning-Community Work: Why the Pedagogy of Intentional Integration Matters."

4. Some research on the positive impact of learning communities on various aspects of student learning and acclimation to college can be found in the NSSE publication "Experiences That Matter: Enhancing Student Learning and Success, Annual Report 2007."
5. Emily Lardner, "What Campuses Assess When They Assess Their Learning Community Programs: Selected Findings from a National Survey of Learning Community Programs," 6. For the various types of student engagement as measured by the National Survey of Student Engagement (NSSE), see "NSSE/Engagement Indicators."
6. Gary R. Pike, George D. Kuh, and Alexander C. McCormick, "An Investigation of the Contingent Relationships between Learning Community Participation and Student Engagement," 314.
7. Patricia G. Sandoval and Jack J. Mino, "The Play's the Thing: Embodying Moments of Integration Live, on Stage," 1.
8. Robyn Tudor, "The Pedagogy of Creativity: Understanding Higher Order Capability Development in Design and Arts Education."
9. See Iannis Xenakis, *Formalized Music: Thought and Mathematics in Composition*.
10. See Bamberger, Jeanne Shapiro, *The Development of Musical Intelligence I: Strategies for Representing Simple Rhythms*; Andrew R. Brown and Steve C. Dillon, "Networked Improvisational Musical Environments: Learning through online collaborative music making"; Bill Manaris and Andrew R. Brown, *Making Music with Computers: Creative Programming in Python*.
11. Funding for this work was provided in part by the National Science Foundation (DUE-1044861).
12. David Williamson Shaffer and Mitchel Resnick, "'Thick' Authenticity: New Media and Authentic Learning"; Felipe Otondo, "Using spatial sound as an interdisciplinary teaching tool."
13. George D. Kuh and Carol Geary Schneider, *High-Impact Educational Practices: What They Are, Who Has Access to Them, and Why They Matter*.
14. Bill Manaris, Juan Romero, Penousal Machado, Dwight Krehbiel, Timothy Hirzel, Walter Pharr, and Robert B. Davis, "Zipf's Law, Music Classification, and Aesthetics."
15. Melissa E. O'Neill, "Automated Use of a Wiki for Collaborative Lecture Notes."
16. JythonMusic is an environment for music making and creative activities based on the programming language Python (see http://jythonmusic.org).
17. Louis Niebur, "'Switched-On Bach'–Wendy Carlos (1968)."
18. Daniel Trueman, Perry Cook, Scott Smallwood, and Ge Wang, "PLOrk: The Princeton Laptop Orchestra, Year 1"; Daniel Trueman, "Why a laptop orchestra?"

19. Tom Mudd, "Developing transferable skills through engagement with higher education laptop ensembles."
20. Andrew Sorensen, "The Many Faces of a Temporal Recursion."
21. Peter Vergo, *The Music of Painting: Music, Modernism and the Visual Arts from the Romantics to John Cage.*
22. Nandini McCauley, "Computing in the Arts Exhibition: Visual Soundscapes."
23. Bill Manaris, Blake Stevens, and Andrew R. Brown, "JythonMusic: An environment for teaching algorithmic music composition, dynamic coding and musical performativity."
24. Again, see Manaris et al. "JythonMusic: An environment for teaching algorithmic music composition, dynamic coding and musical performativity," for the specific questions asked.
25. See Manaris et al. "JythonMusic: An environment for teaching algorithmic music composition, dynamic coding and musical performativity," 49–51.
26. For example, see Brown and Dillon, "Networked Improvisational Musical Environments"; Tom Mudd, "Developing transferable skills through engagement with higher education laptop ensembles"; Shaffer and Resnick, "'Thick' Authenticity"; Trueman "Why a laptop orchestra?"; Trueman et al. "PLOrk"; Ge Wang and Perry Cook. "ChucK: A Concurrent, On-the-fly, Audio Programming Language."
27. E.J. West, *Shaw on Theatre*, 59.
28. Raymond Williams, *Drama from Ibsen to Brecht*, 37.
29. Victor Turner, *On the Edge of the Bush: Anthropology as Experience*, 196–197.
30. Stephen Stanton, *Camille and Other Plays*, xiv–xv.
31. Elizabeth Bell, "Social Dramas and Cultural Performances: All the President's Women."
32. Dan P. McAdams, "Personal Narrative and the Life Story," 242–243.
33. Tacy Trowbridge, "Closing the Skills Gap: Why Creativity is Essential to Students' Workplace Success."
34. Fernando Lozano and Amanda Sabicer, "Creativity and Innovation: Building Ecosystems to Support Risk Taking, Resiliency, and Collaboration."
35. *Ideo.org.*
36. "The Catholic and Marianist Philosophy of Community Living at the University of Dayton."
37. Maggie Fiegl, "FEAR Makes its Way into ArtStreet's IAN Installation Series."
38. Julie Turkewitz, "Oregon Gunman Smiled, Then Fired, Student Says."
39. Grant Wiggins, "On Assessing for Creativity: Yes You Can, and Yes You Should."

Bibliography

Assayag, Gerard, Hans G. Feichtinger, and José-Francisco Rodrigues, eds. 2002. *Mathematics and Music: A Diderot Mathematical Forum*. Berlin: Springer.

Bamberger, Jeanne Shapiro. 1975. *The Development of Musical Intelligence I: Strategies for Representing Simple Rhythms*. Cambridge, MA: Massachusetts Institute of Technology.

Bell, Elizabeth. 2006. Social Dramas and Cultural Performances: All the President's Women. *Liminalities: A Journal of Performance Studies* 2 (1). http://liminalities.net/2-1/sdcp/sdcp-print.htm. Accessed 12 Apr 2017.

Blackwell, Alan, and Nick Collins. 2005. The Programming Language as a Musical Instrument. *Proceedings of Psychology of Programming Interest Group* 12: 120–130.

Brown, Andrew R., and Steve C. Dillon. 2007. Networked Improvisational Musical Environments: Learning Through Online Collaborative Music Making. In *Music Education with Digital Technology*, ed. J. Finney and P. Burnard, 96–106. London: Continuum.

Cambridge-Williams, Tiffany, Adam Winsler, Anastasia Kitsantas, and Elizabeth Bernard. 2013. University 100 Orientation Courses and Living-Learning Communities Boost Academic Retention and Graduation via Enhanced Self-Efficacy and Self-Regulated Learning. *Journal of College Student Retention: Research, Theory & Practice* 15 (2): 243–268. https://doi.org/10.2190/CS.15.2.f.

Collins, Nick, Alex McLean, Julian Rohrhuber, and Adrian Ward. 2003. Live Coding in Laptop Performance. *Organised Sound* 8 (3): 321–330.

Defining Features. *The National Resource Center for Learning Communities*. http://wacenter.evergreen.edu/new-era-lcs/definingfeatures.html. Accessed 29 July 2017.

Experiences That Matter: Enhancing Student Learning and Success, Annual Report 2007. National Survey of Student Engagement. http://nsse.indiana.edu/NSSE_2007_Annual_Report/docs/withhold/NSSE_2007_Annual_Report.pdf. Accessed 19 July 2017.

Fiegl, Maggie. 2013. FEAR Makes Its Way into ArtStreet's IAN Installation Series. *Arts at UD* (blog). *University of Dayton*, October 23. https://udayton.edu/blogs/arts/15-10-23-fear.php.

Ideo.org. http://www.designkit.org/human-centered-design. Accessed 8 Feb 2017.

Kuh, George D., and Carol Geary Schneider. 2008. *High-Impact Educational Practices: What They Are, Who Has Access to Them, and Why They Matter*. Washington, DC: Association of American Colleges and Universities.

Lardner, Emily. 2014. What Campuses Assess When They Assess Their Learning Community Programs: Selected Findings from a National Survey of Learning

Community Programs. *Learning Communities Research and Practice* 2 (2): Article 2: 1–19. https://eric.ed.gov/?id=EJ1112491.

Lardner, Emily, and Gillies Malnarich. 2008. A New Era in Learning-Community Work: Why the Pedagogy of Intentional Integration Matters. *Change: The Magazine of Higher Learning* 40 (4): 30–37. https://doi.org/10.3200/CHNG.40.4.30-37.

Love, Anne Goodsell. 2012. The Growth and Current State of Learning Communities in Higher Education. *New Directions for Teaching and Learning* 2012 (132): 5–18. https://doi.org/10.1002/tl.20032.

Lozano, Fernando and Amanda Sabicer. 2016. Creativity and Innovation: Building Ecosystems to Support Risk Taking, Resiliency, and Collaboration. *AACU Liberal Education* 102 (2). https://www.aacu.org/liberaleducation/2016/spring/lozano.

Manaris, Bill, and Andrew R. Brown. 2014. *Making Music with Computers: Creative Programming in Python*. Boca Raton, London, and New York: CRC Press.

Manaris, Bill, Juan Romero, Penousal Machado, Dwight Krehbiel, Timothy Hirzel, Walter Pharr, and Robert B. Davis. 2005. Zipf's Law, Music Classification, and Aesthetics. *Computer Music Journal* 29 (1): 55–69.

Manaris, Bill, Blake Stevens, and Andrew R. Brown. 2016. JythonMusic: An Environment for Teaching Algorithmic Music Composition, Dynamic Coding and Musical Performativity. *Journal of Music, Technology & Education* 9 (1): 33–56.

McAdams, Dan P. 2008. Personal Narratives and the Life Story. In *Handbook of Personality: Theory and Research*, ed. Lawrence A. Pervin and Oliver P. John, 3rd ed., 242–262. Elsevier. https://www.sesp.northwestern.edu/docs/publications/1698511162490a0d856d825.pdf. Accessed 7 Feb 2017.

McCauley, Nandini. Computing in the Arts Exhibition: Visual Soundscapes. *College of Charleston School of the Arts* (blog). https://blogs.cofc.edu/sota/2012/04/05/cita. Accessed 5 May 2017.

Mudd, Tom. 2012. Developing Transferable Skills Through Engagement with Higher Education Laptop Ensembles. *Journal of Music, Technology & Education* 5 (1): 29–41.

Niebur, Louis. 2005. 'Switched-On Bach'–Wendy Carlos (1968). In *National Recording Preservation Board Documents*. Library of Congress. https://www.loc.gov/programs/static/national-recording-preservation-board/documents/Switched-OnBach-Niebur.pdf. Accessed 5 May 2017.

NSSE/Engagement Indicators. *National Survey of Student Engagement*. http://nsse.indiana.edu/html/engagement_indicators.cfm. Accessed 19 July 2017.

O'Neill, Melissa E. 2005. Automated Use of a Wiki for Collaborative Lecture Notes. Proceedings of the 36th SIGCSE Technical Symposium on Computer Science Education, 267–71.

Otondo, Felipe. 2013. Using Spatial Sound as an Interdisciplinary Teaching Tool. *Journal of Music, Technology & Education* 6 (2): 179–190.

Pike, Gary R., George D. Kuh, and Alexander C. McCormick. 2011. An Investigation of the Contingent Relationships Between Learning Community Participation and Student Engagement. *Research in Higher Education* 52 (3): 300–322. https://doi.org/10.1007/s11162-010-9192-1.

Popiolek, Gene, Ricka Fine, and Valerie Eilman. 2013. Learning Communities, Academic Performance, Attrition, and Retention: A Four-Year Study. *Community College Journal of Research and Practice* 37 (11): 828–838. https://doi.org/10.1080/10668921003744926.

Riley, Terry. 1989. *In C.* Score and Performing Directions. N.p: Celestial Harmonies.

Sandoval, Patricia G., and Jack J. Mino. 2013. The Play's the Thing: Embodying Moments of Integration Live, On Stage. *Learning Communities Research and Practice* 1 (2): Article 2: 1–21. http://washingtoncenter.evergreen.edu/lcrp-journal/vol1/iss2/2/.

Shaffer, David Williamson, and Mitchel Resnick. 1999. 'Thick' Authenticity: New Media and Authentic Learning. *Journal of Interactive Learning Research* 10 (2): 195–215.

Sorensen, Andrew. 2013. The Many Faces of a Temporal Recursion. http://extempore.moso.com.au/temporal_recursion.html. Accessed 3 May 2015.

Stanton, Stephen. 1956. *Camille and Other Plays*. New York: Hill & Wang.

The Catholic and Marianist Philosophy of Community Living at the University of Dayton. *UDayton.edu*. https://udayton.edu/provost/_resources/docs/CM_Philosophy_7.07.pdf. Accessed 7 Feb 2017.

Trowbridge, Tacy. 2016. Closing the Skills Gap: Why Creativity Is Essential to Students' Workplace Success. Adobe For Education (blog), July 27. http://blogs.adobe.com/education/2016/07/27/closing-the-skills-gap-why-creativity-is-essential-to-students-workplace-success/.

Trueman, Dan. 2007. Why a Laptop Orchestra? *Organised Sound* 12 (2): 171–179.

Trueman, Daniel, Perry Cook, Scott Smallwood, and Ge Wang. 2006. PLOrk: The Princeton Laptop Orchestra, Year 1. Proceedings of the International Computer Music Conference, 443–50.

Tudor, Robyn. 2008. The Pedagogy of Creativity: Understanding Higher Order Capability Development in Design and Arts Education. Proceedings of the 4th International Barcelona Conference on Higher Education (4th: 2008), Vol. 4—Higher Education, Arts and Creativity. http://hdl.handle.net/2099/5756.

Turkewitz, Julie. 2015. Oregon Gunman Smiled, Then Fired, Student Says. *The New York Times*, October 9. https://search.proquest.com/docview/1721317485?accountid=9959.

Turner, V.W., and E.L.B. Turner. 1985. *On the Edge of the Bush: Anthropology as Experience*. Tucson, AZ: University of Arizona Press.

Vergo, Peter. 2010. *The Music of Painting: Music, Modernism and the Visual Arts from the Romantics to John Cage*. London and New York: Phaidon.

Wang, Ge, and Perry Cook. 2003. ChucK: A Concurrent, On-the-fly, Audio Programming Language. Proceedings of the 2003 International Computer Music Conference, 219–226.

West, E.J. 1959. *Shaw on Theatre*. New York: Hill & Wang.

Wiggins, Grant. On Assessing for Creativity: Yes You Can, and Yes You Should. *GrantWiggins.wordpress.com* (blog). https://grantwiggins.wordpress.com/2012/02/03/on-assessing-for-creativity-yes-you-can-and-yes-you-should/. Accessed Oct 2016.

Williams, Raymond. 1973. *Drama from Ibsen to Brecht*. 2nd Rev. ed. Harmondsworth: Penguin.

Xenakis, Iannis. 1971. *Formalized Music: Thought and Mathematics in Composition*. 2nd ed. Bloomington and London: University of Indiana Press.

CHAPTER 5

Writing-Intensive Courses

There's no question that quality writing is at the very top of lists of desired student learning outcomes. The ability to express ideas clearly, whether they are one's own or those of an employer, is crucial for almost any career path. Writing of the type that qualifies as a high-impact practice is not simple composition, and it doesn't mean that all faculty must teach grammar. As Kuh describes them, effective writing-intensive courses "emphasize writing at all levels of instruction and across the curriculum, including final-year projects. Students are encouraged to produce and revise various forms of writing for different audiences in different disciplines."[1] Most importantly, writing-intensive courses involve writing in the discipline—following up first-year composition courses that teach general academic discourse with courses that have students practice the forms of writing for particular discourse communities. Whether or not a student is majoring in the discipline of a particular course, a critical aspect of learning the content and ways of thinking of that discipline involves practicing its modes of writing.

High-impact writing is not about volume. Writing lots of pages for a class without revision or a well-structured assignment that considers audience will not result in meaningful writing. High-impact writing is also not (exclusively) about showing what has been learned or even about writing as a method for reasoning. In their study of many types of writing assignments across several institutions in the United States, Michele Eodice, Anne Ellen Geller, and Neal Lerner discovered that "meaningful writing

© The Author(s) 2018
M. Hayford, S. Kattwinkel (eds.), *Performing Arts as High-Impact Practice*, The Arts in Higher Education,
https://doi.org/10.1007/978-3-319-72944-2_5

projects offer students opportunities for agency; for engagement with instructors, peers, and materials; and for learning that connects to previous experiences and passions and to future aspirations and identities."[2] High-impact writing connects students to their disciplines in ways that other practices do not. Eodice, Geller, and Lerner note that several studies have shown that "writing is essential to the ways students form identities as fledgling members of their disciplines."[3]

Aside from those characteristics that make writing assignments meaningful, they can take any format that has significance for the discipline. Following the work of James Britton and others, Dan Melzer divides writing into four categories: expressive—reflective writing for oneself, poetic—artistic writing, transactional—either informative or persuasive, and exploratory—expressive writing for a public audience.[4] All of these categories have specific applications in the performing arts. Our students are often quite gifted at reflective writing—they are comfortable sharing their opinions and, as artists, accustomed to self-examination. Poetic writing appears most commonly as playwriting, but may also include poetic responses to performances or writing as a method of idea clarification in the process of composition, design, or choreography. Transactional and exploratory writing most closely resemble the types of academic writing that students tend to associate with scholarship, and may be difficult to relate to artistic passion for performing arts students. As Ann Nugent put it in an article on teaching writing to dancers in the UK, "[d]oing and seeing are activities using different kinds of energy, and those who want to release their energy in the studio and on the stage often feel crushed—even dulled—by what they think of as the 'static' activity needed for seeing, thinking, and writing."[5] Additionally, many forms of performance may defy representation in the written word, especially for students trying to describe or analyze it, rather than just express an opinion about it. Writing about post-modern dance, Julie Malnig says that students often feel that it "seems to connote some 'secret language' for which they feel they lack a code."[6] Nevertheless, the ability to describe and explain art—which is often defined by its very opposition to logocentrism—is necessary for criticism, reviewing, grant applications, manifestos, and multiple other functions crucial to the creation and exploration of the performing arts.

In the performing arts, as in other disciplines, writing often bridges Melzer's four categories. Disciplinary writing in the performing arts is often multi-modal in format, and nearly always in intention. Writing about the performing arts generally refers not to other written artifacts but to bodies in motion, images, and sounds. Third-person address feels awkward, and objectivity can be counterproductive. As Paul Bonin-Rodriguez notes, in the performing arts, even grant writing, budget narratives, and so on must have "evoked and advocated for the artist's project, process, and/or body of work"[7] in order to be successful. This type of writing hones certain writing skills not necessarily emphasized in traditional composition courses, where writing generally involves responding to other writing like literature or research on contemporary issues. Some characteristics of writing in the performing arts that have wider applications include:

1. Immediacy. Writing about performance demands immediacy because the artifact to which one is responding is often not available for viewing more than once. Students must quickly process and analyze their own responses before the memory of the event is gone. That rehearses attention and focus. That immediacy reflects real-world writing situations, where employees must often respond to events quickly, turning out thoughtful written responses without the opportunity to consult the inciting event multiple times.
2. Corporeality. Writing about performance has a corporeal aspect to it absent from much traditional compositional practice. In responding to moving, working bodies, the writer must incorporate their own bodily experience as well. In addition to thinking about something they have read, the performance writer must take into account their own senses—their experience of accessing the performance, their personal physical and sense-based responses, and the responses of those around them. This bodily involvement in the subject of writing connects both the event and the writer to the community and keeps the writer focused on the wider public, rather than just on one voice of authority they might expect to read their work. Even when one does the work of a playwright—alone with one's own thoughts—the writer must always consider that the end result will involve other bodies and other interpretations, once again connecting the work to the wider community in a way that reflects the types of writing most commonly performed in the working world.
3. Public dissemination. Writing assignments in performing arts courses often involve writing for public consumption. Program notes for music and dance concerts and theatre performances, as well as audience guides and dramaturgical material, demand a concise and accessible form that is not always called for in traditional

academic writing. Traditions of performance writing, like manifestos and performance criticism, are imbued with the expectation of response and must therefore anticipate questions and arguments. The arts are perhaps most like the sciences in this way that all writing is conceived as part of a larger conversation about entities that find their first expression outside the world of words.

The case studies in this chapter present writing assignments that deal directly with the problem of representing the non-verbal in writing and with the challenge of writing for a non-academic audience. K. Dawn Grapes writes about assignments for music majors that employ all the standard skills of academic writing—research, bibliography, critical analysis, and so on—in the construction of program notes designed to be both informational and exploratory. She describes how such practical assignments can get students past the anxiety often prompted by traditional academic research papers. James Brock details his discovery that the act of performance could help creative writing students to find their own voices and move beyond the "modeling" on traditional formats in which many students become trapped. Common to both of these projects is scaffolding—either through a series of related assignments or through frequent revision—and clear rubrics that help students to visualize the many important and intertwining elements of a writing project. Each of these case studies should be useful to both arts faculty working with majors at advanced levels of study and to faculty working with non-majors who are looking for practical ways to engage students in the process of honing their writing skills.

Call to action:

- Administrators must recognize that performing arts faculty have something to contribute to writing skills taught as part of general education. The many forms of writing that are an endemic part of the working lives of performing artists can be useful as models for other faculty looking to expand the forms of writing that their students use to master basic writing skills.
- Performing arts faculty, who are accustomed to expressing themselves in corporeal and other non-logocentric formats, must incorporate writing into all levels of courses in the major. Although some may view intensive writing as something reserved for the history or theory courses in the discipline, in fact everyone who works in the

performing arts must be able to express their ideas in writing, both for professional and public audiences. Writing should be taught in all formats relevant to the discipline, through scaffolded and revised assignments.
- Writing about the arts must be taught to non-performing arts students, in introductory and survey courses. When faculty concentrate solely on other modes of expression, students don't learn how to express their opinions about the art that they see. Writing about art is a crucial element of our goal of cultivating informed audience members, as well as artistic and cultural literacy.

Program Notes in the Classroom

K. Dawn Grapes
Colorado State University
Fort Collins, CO, USA

Writing is difficult for many students, but writing about music is especially so, for the practice requires an author to translate impressions of an aural medium into written words. Academic musical writing is often presented in the same forms found in other humanities fields. In the music history classroom, writing assignments include semester research papers, book reports, and reading reflections, among others. One type of writing unique to the music world, however, is the creation of program notes, those informative essays commonly found in concert program booklets. Program notes typically feature composer biographies, cultural contextualization of musical compositions, and musical analysis. In an age when creativity in teaching is not only encouraged, but expected, incorporating program notes assignments in writing-intensive courses, both for music majors and non-majors, is an approachable, adaptable, and useful precursor to the traditional semester-long academic research paper. Writing quality program notes requires making good source choices, understanding an audience, practicing honed research skills, applying bibliographic principles, and working toward meticulous prose. While all of these objectives are also linked to traditional academic writing forms, program notes seem to hold fewer stigmas for students, perhaps because of the narrative writing style often employed. As such, program notes can be used in writing-intensive courses as an alternative writing genre that requires both critical and creative thinking within written communication. While it is somewhat surprising that writing well-crafted program notes is a skill not often considered within the traditional higher education music curriculum, its incorporation into both music and non-music courses provides opportunities to reinforce fundamental undergraduate writing expectations.

An Experiment to Improve Research Writing

At Colorado State University, Music History I and Music History II are required junior-level bachelor of music core courses marked to add depth and integration to five categories of university "Foundations and Perspective" core curriculum classes (biological/physical sciences, arts/humanities, social/behavioral sciences, historical perspectives, global and cultural awareness).[8] As such, these music history courses are expected to build upon applied critical thinking and writing skills gained in extra-departmental courses completed in students' first three years of study. Two of the course learning objectives for Music History I and II include: Students will "write about music in a knowledgeable manner, incorporating personal analysis and reputable sources"; and "conduct research about an approved topic through appropriate resources and present findings in a manner that subscribes precisely to a prescribed manual of style." Traditionally, instructors of these courses meet these objectives by requiring a semester research paper. In such a project, students demonstrate previously gained knowledge and perspective, and are expected to synthesize tenets of extra-departmental classes with their own applied and academic musical training. Over a number of semesters of my own teaching, it became apparent that many students, in spite of completing required general writing composition courses, are unprepared to write a full-length research paper conforming to the conventions of academic music writing. Addressing "how to write" in class puts additional strain on an already limited amount of time to teach expected historical content, yet adding planned drafts and assignments outside of class to address proper source selection, style guide expectations, and paper organization are not always successful.

As I was writing a set of program notes for a regional professional music ensemble one spring, it occurred to me that my research and writing process followed much of the same methodology that I would use when writing a conventional academic article. Perhaps, then, this type of exercise would be useful in helping students move beyond some of their writing apprehension, if presented as research in a different guise. In my Music

History I survey course the following semester, I created a project consisting of a series of six short program notes writing assignments, each based on specific repertoire and composers studied in class. Expectations for application of research skills and writing quality increased sequentially for each set of notes. Through every successive assignment, students moved along a spectrum from simple information-collation to thesis organization. Though program notes normally do not include footnotes or bibliographies, both were incorporated to allow for citation practice and to shape the students' research methodologies. I began the semester with a short in-class introduction to program notes. During this session, we discussed writing for a general, educated audience and outlined the most common organizational approach of first providing information on a composer, then setting a piece of music in its proper historical setting, and finally (after listening multiple times to the composition) describing for the listener any especially relevant musical choices the composer made.[9] Students searched for program notes online, which were then used to assess authors' strengths and weaknesses in writing, evidence of sources consulted, and maintenance of reader interest. Afterward, students began weekly or bi-weekly program note assignments with the following instructions and follow-up questions:

Assignment 1: Write program notes for the two pieces listed. Your goal: to create unique, personalized program notes for an educated, general audience that are truly your own. Notes should **not** simply restate the words of others. Avoid quotes, unless from a primary source, and make sure everything is paraphrased in your own language and cited properly. Use one approved library resource (*Grove Music Online* recommended) and your textbook for background research. Include citations that conform to the examples provided in a bibliography at the end of your paper. You may use additional sources if you wish, but they must have a named author and each item must be cited. Check the paper-writing checklist before you turn in your work! 500-word minimum.

Post-assignment discussion questions: For what purpose(s) are textbooks and encyclopedias most appropriate? Why might they *not* be the best choice for academic research projects? How do you determine the quality of a source? In what ways should a writer consider his or her audience when preparing program notes?

Assignment 2: Prepare program notes as in assignment one. This time, however, you are to gather research from one approved library resource (*Grove Music Online* recommended) and at least one other named-author source *besides your textbook* for your research. Apply any feedback from assignment one to assignment two, including citation format corrections. Include a bibliography at the end of your paper. You may use additional sources if you wish, but they must have a named author and you must cite all sources. 500-word minimum.

Post-assignment discussion questions: Why are bibliographic citations important? What is the difference between a primary and a secondary source? How can writers provide a personal voice when presenting information from only secondary sources?

Assignments 3: Prepare program notes as before, but this time use **at least three** named-author sources (*not* your textbook) for your research. At least one source should be a book from the university library. As always, include a bibliography at the end of your paper. You may use additional sources if you wish, but they must have a named author and you must cite all sources. Also include Chicago Style footnotes, as discussed in class. Check the paper-writing checklist before you turn in your work! 500-word minimum.

Post-assignment discussion questions: How do footnotes aid a reader in ways that a final source list will not? What is plagiarism? How might it appear in program notes, either intentionally or unintentionally? How does one determine general knowledge versus ideas that should be attributed to a specific author?

Assignments 4 and 5: Prepare program notes chosen from the approved list of compositions as in assignment three. Pay special attention to the quality of sources used for your research. Consult at least four named-author sources including books, academic journal articles, scholarly music scores, dissertations, or other library database sources. In your writing, give special attention to your own personal aural and score analysis. Add footnotes as needed and be meticulous in your citation formats. Include a properly formatted bibliography of all sources used. 750-word minimum.

Post-assignment discussion questions: What is a thesis statement? What makes a good thesis statement? Would the promise of peer editing change your process? Which types of sources are most useful in researching and analyzing subjects of program notes? Why is it important to follow prescribed style guidelines exactly?

Assignment 6: Pick one major work by a late Baroque composer on which to write an in-depth program note of at least 1000 words. Make this the best, most personally inspired program note you have ever written.

- Pay attention to grammar and spelling.
- Include footnotes as appropriate (at least one per paragraph).

- Include an introduction with an incorporated thesis statement and a conclusion (do not repeat parts of your introduction in your conclusion).
- Include historical background information gained from secondary sources and musical information gained from YOUR OWN listening and score analysis.
- Use at least six *named author* sources. Textbook and general encyclopedia entries are no longer appropriate sources. Look especially for books and articles specifically about your composer and/or piece.
- Double-check the paper-writing checklist before you turn in your work!

Each assignment was due on Friday and graded and returned by Wednesday so that students received feedback for incorporation into each subsequent assignment. Specific issues such as source selection and formatting were detailed in full instructions available through the university's online course management system. The one forbidden research source was previously published program notes, for two reasons: they usually do not include citations; and plagiarism, based on another program note writer's organization, is especially tempting. As outlined above, each week the class spent a short amount of time on a research and/or writing concept to make future assignments more meaningful and quality-oriented. A provided paper-writing checklist served as style guide, with sections pertaining to expectations for formatting, writing conventions, musical example and figure insertions, editing, bibliographic citations, and footnotes (in this case conforming to *The Chicago Manual of Style*).

Assessment and Results

For assessment, the same rubric was used for each assignment. Categories on the rubric included: depth of content (with subcategories: synthesis of primary and secondary sources and individual analysis); organization; source quality; writing components (grammar, spelling, clarity, overall writing style, application of writing checklist); and citation skills. Expectations for each category, however, were increasingly rigorous as the semester moved forward. Collecting and grading papers through an online course management system was helpful in tracking previous feedback given and kept students accountable for continued growth. Because of raised expectations for each sequential assignment, average numerical scores actually went down from a 90 on the first assignment to 82 on the last, even though instructor-perceived quality of the work rose. Had the final standard been maintained from the start, most of the early submissions would have fallen into the 65 to 70 range. The payoff for students came when they applied the techniques they had worked on in miniature to a longer paper due at semester end. In fact, the results were remarkable in comparison to papers students had submitted in previous semesters. The final longer, more traditional research paper centered on a piece of music of each student's choice, incorporating all the skills used in earlier program notes assignments. In their final research papers, not only did students show a better understanding of standard writing styles within the arts community, but they also successfully demonstrated knowledge of style guide usage, presented well-crafted individualized arguments, and exhibited marked improvement in their own personal writing acumens. In the course evaluation survey administered at the end of the semester, multiple students singled out the program notes assignments for comment. One stated that she preferred a single longer paper, but others were uniformly positive in their assessment. Examples of specific comments included "I did very much prefer the program notes as to what we did last year" (student retaking course), and "Program notes are better than a final research paper." The main drawback of the project was the amount of instructor time it took to provide individual weekly feedback to 35 students. While it might seem unreasonable to devote so much assessment time to a larger class, in-class peer review or fewer assignments might make the task more manageable.

Proposed Adaptations for Non-Music Classrooms

In this case, the instructor gave students specific topical options for each assignment based upon course content (i.e., composers and compositions actively studied in class), but instructors of non-music courses might guide students to select musical pieces upon which to write program notes based on subjects relevant to the given course. For example, there are many art music compositions inspired by historical, political, and social events: the musical choices of compositions by Dmitri Shostakovich and Sergei Prokofiev were, by necessity, restrained by or written in reaction to Soviet policy; Ludwig van Beethoven's Third Symphony is linked to the rise in power of Napoleon; George Crumb, Ned Rorem, and Roger Sessions, among other composers, wrote music reflecting on or inspired by the Vietnam conflict; and many works were composed to commemorate

9/11, including pieces by well-known contemporary composers such as John Adams, John Corigliano, Joan Tower, and Steve Reich. Both choral and instrumental music have direct ties to literature and poetry. *Faust* is a common theme in nineteenth-century works, such as those by Hector Berlioz, Franz Schubert, and Franz Liszt, and Claude Debussy and Arnold Schoenberg wrote works inspired by French and German Symbolist poets, respectively. Works such as Modest Mussorgsky's *Pictures at an Exhibition* and Ottorino Respighi's *Trittico Botticelliano* tie directly to specific pieces of visual art, and the early electronic music of twentieth-century art music composers illuminate cutting-edge mathematical and scientific concepts of their time. And while program notes are usually provided for concerts and recitals of Western art music, there is no reason that students cannot write program notes for songs or compositions that fall outside the art music world—works that fit more securely into popular, commercial, movie, jazz, or world music categories.

The purpose of multiple assignments in this case study was to introduce specific skills sequentially to build toward a more successful research paper. A single program note assignment, however, could be used in courses as a low stakes, accessible research essay that serves as practice for a larger, more in-depth paper, or for consideration of writing for a specific audience. For writing-intensive courses with the objective of introducing many types of writing, program notes certainly offer an opportunity for students to write from a perspective they may never before have considered, one that can be tailored to many different audiences across a diversified curriculum.

Performing the Australian Crawl

James Brock
Florida Gulf Coast University
Fort Myers, FL, USA

The cake is surprisingly cool, spongy, beneath the thick icing as I paw out a large handful. I think of the mud pie fights of my childhood, all the while Tiffany is still rattling on about her stupid dress, her platinum tiara, her country-club birthday. So I let her have it, a thick glomp of chocolate cake strikes her shoulder.

An associate dean stops by this scene in the middle of the campus green, where twelve students and a professor are throwing chocolate cake at a student, a trans woman of color, wearing clown white on her face, dressed in a sequined evening grown, all the while she is ranting nonsense. Worse, from the dean's perspective, an audience of other students has gathered around to watch. I see the dean, give her a nod, and I take another handful of the cake—it's a privilege of being a cis-hetero, white, male full professor, after all—and throw another glob at Tiffany. She's not rattled a bit, and she continues to rage on about her BMW. I am so proud of Tiffany that tears are coming to my eyes.

"This," I shout, "this is a voice!"

* * *

In my 35 years of teaching creative writing and English composition courses, I have a long, conflicted relationship with "voice," that authentic style and perspective students are supposed to have innately, that I am to affirm and assist in its discovery. For me it had become something of a dreary task: especially in my creative writing classes, where their "unique" voices typically become less distinguished as the semester wears on, or worse, their unique voice is a matter of an unthinking habit rather than an imaginative, intellectual, critical, and spiritual engagement. However, I have discovered over the last ten years that the discipline of the performing arts, specifically with live theatre, that "voice" is not some buried, repressed authentic self to be unearthed through practice and revision and workshops and reading, but that it is a living, contrary, elastic set of choices to be *used*, performed, and then released. This discipline reminded me that "voice" is also a verb.

One of the foundational mantras in composition and creative writing pedagogy over the last 40 years has been "Find your voice," an empowering, student-centered, process-oriented corrective to models-based and rules-bound instruction. Building on Peter Elbow's arguments in his seminal *Writing Without Teachers* (first published in 1973), the emphasis of this approach focused on engaging students in the active processes of writing: pre-drafting, free-writing, revising, peer-reviewing, conferencing, final drafting, and then post-product self-evaluation. It is a wonderfully liberating approach, especially for those of us who were first teaching composition at the beginning of the 80s in progressive English programs. Everyone has a style, everyone has a voice—it's not about teaching rules that lead to silence, timidity, and obedience—and the point of writing was the process itself, of self-discovery, of finding your voice.

Of course, this idea of voice, an authentic, self-created "style," has fared poorly under theoretical scrutiny, and is now generally derided as a quaint, dated notion that fails to acknowledge how the self, let alone the voice, is a complicated, contradicting, and unstable social construct. Elbow himself appreciates this liability in his retrospective essay, "Voice in Writing Again." Even so, despite this rational critique against "voice," Elbow argues that the idea of "voice" continues to have currency in public discourse: "yet voice stays alive, even in the most 'naïve' forms that have been most powerfully critiqued."[10] To be sure, "voice" remains alive and well especially in the teaching of creative writing because it's a useful metaphor that reifies agency and process in the practice of writing.

Those of us in creative writing, however, recognize that Elbow lifted his essentialist ideas about voice from creative writing pedagogy, as developed in the 60s and 70s as graduate creative programs were first burgeoning. Central to this pedagogy was the poet William Stafford's seminal short essay, "Writing the Australian Crawl," in which he noted just how easily and naturally his six-year-old daughter talked, quoting her:

> We'd have a old car, the kind that gets flat tires, but inside would be wolfskin on the seats and warm fur on the steering wheel, and wolf fur on all the buttons. And we'd live in a ranch house made out of logs with a loft where you sleep, and you'd walk a little ways and there'd be the farm with the horses. We'd drive to town, and we'd have flat tires, and be sort of old.[11]

Why shouldn't writing be so immediate, transparent, clear, and authentic? And from this initial point, Stafford proffers a thrilling alternative to model-based writing, something quite alive about writing that is free of self-consciousness:

> When I write, grammar is my enemy; the materials of my craft come at me in a succession of emergencies in which my feelings are ambivalent; I do not have any commitments, just opportunities. Not the learning of methods, not the broadening of culture, not even the preserving of civilization (there may be greater things than civilizations), but a kind of dizzying struggle with the Now-ness of experience, that is my involvement in writing.[12]

Inherent in this perspective is a profound affirmation: that within us, every one of us, is this authentic voice in concert with the Now. Unfortunately, our genuine voice has been beaten down by education, by social pressure, by conformity. And so it's a question of an old Romantic leap to childhood freedom and autonomy, where we silence those judging and correcting voices, and we tune in to ourselves.

In creative writing, especially, are books that celebrate the finding of one's own voice: Natalie Goldberg, Charles Johnson, Anne Lamont, Kelli Russell Agodon and Susan Rich, Dean Young, Mark Doty, and Kim Addonizio have written some of my favorites. But in the end, even after all that celebration of the authentic, the individual, the empowering, I still found that my students, especially my upper-level students, continue to model their writing. That's to be expected. They read a lot of poetry, and they will quickly test and adopt the tricks of their new favorite poet. That's also a valuable and necessary process of discovery, and it certainly forces them to negotiate what they do "naturally" with some other foreign approach—some modeling, I would argue, is a necessary thing. But what I notice is that the static quality of how a poem is produced, permanently on paper or on a web site, sanctioned by publication and taught in a classroom, reinforces a kind of modeling that is ultimately derivative and not generative. In short, as a semester typically progresses, my students produced poems that looked more and more alike: variations of the poets we read, colored by my guidance and shaped by the workshops, group conferences, and writing activities, through all the revision. As a print medium, a poem is an object, a thing, and as such, it begs to be appropriated, copied, and reproduced. And no matter how much a teacher valorizes a student's own odd and off voice, there's that codification which occurs when they read a poem in print in *Poetry* magazine. This is what a "real" poem looks like successfully voiced. At this point, there's no going back to the students being six-year-olds, to using a wild, errant voice. I've learned I can't make that happen in a traditional writing classroom.

Fortunately, poetry's tradition is an oral one, and conventionally, to get students to develop their voices is to have them read and recite their poetry out loud. Indeed, voicing your poem is often a recommendation as a part of the revision process: how does your poem "sound"? And this tradition gives the poetry instructor the opportunity to introduce performance as another means to produce and display a poem. It's not on the page, and it becomes a communal act, a very powerful phenomenon evident in the spoken word movement of the last three decades. But even in this use of performance, where students were attempting to find their own physical voices, that same problem of modeling persisted; in fact, it became worse in my own experiences.

The problem is that our exposure to spoken word poetry is typically not a "live" exposure, but a recording of a live performance, usually through YouTube. A performance like Saul Williams' "Coded Language" for the Def Poetry Jam program on HBO in 2004 becomes the template. But these performances were fashioned after the poetry slam movement of Marc Smith and his slams at the Green Mill Tavern in Chicago in the 1980s. Here, performances are judged by a panel, not unlike what we have seen on *American Idol*, and the winners and their styles are sanctioned, deified, and then become normative. Once captured on film or digitalized, the performances are as static, then, as the poem published on the page. Of course, the slam poets were influenced by the recordings of John Giorno in the 1960s and the beat writers of the 1950s, who were influenced by recordings and broadcasts by Dylan Thomas, Langston Hughes, and Edna St. Vincent Millay. Copies of copies of copies of recorded performances with some generational shift in elocution and rhythm. In any event, while the individual performers in a spoken word event will have varying competency, their style of presentation is distressingly uniform.

For several years I would end a semester with the students performing an open mic, relying on videos and recordings of spoken word poets as exemplars. The students would also share their own favorites. What I noticed was just how bored I became after the third or fourth performer: the same gestures, the same posturing, the same voicing, the same speed, the same dramatic closing stop. It was almost as dreadful as going to an academic poetry reading where one has to endure the dreaded poetry drone-voice. After a semester of helping students develop their own physical voices, I could only think what a failure, on my part, to witness poem after poem so homogenously presented.

The problem was the act of recording. As students imagined or developed their own performances, they would be playing and replaying those recorded performances. And they themselves would record their performances as well, as a way to hear their own voice (as unpleasant as that is for most of us) and then reshape their performance, as if they were revising a poem. They felt successful if their work sounded *like* a piece done by Taylor Mali, or T. Miller, or Sarah Kay, or Lauren Zuniga, or Elizabeth Acevedo. They often did.

My mistake was in not recognizing just how a recorded performance could be so powerful, coercive, defining. I forgot about my teenaged friends in Idaho imitating Jimi Hendrix, playing guitar solos with their teeth. How can you expect to find your own voice before Hendrix's loud, blazing fire? You're going to want to copy and ride that flame.

Perhaps because I'm married to a dancer—whose work has been captured on film only one time—or perhaps because I have been involved in theatre for the last ten years, it dawned on me that my mistake was that I was using recordings as exemplars, not live performance, something wholly temporal, ephemeral, and inconsequential. Messy, imperfect, and momentary experience. Stafford's "now-ness." And more importantly, I realized that the point to my pedagogy wasn't really about "finding your own voice," but using it as a living, imperfect, immediate, and changeable instrument. It is the discipline of the performing arts, and more specifically live theatre and its inherent embrace of the momentary, that provide an intellectual and academic and pragmatic approach that would be free of modeling, whether on the page or through the recording.

* * *

To this end, I set up a month-long final assignment for my poetry writing students: The students would have to perform the text of a poem as a piece of theatre in collaboration with at least one other student. As I designed the requirements for the activity, I kept it simple, borrowing from what I observed of theatre students in producing their own showcases and one-act productions. The greatest resistance, initially, was with the aspect of collaboration, as typically, writing poetry is a solitary craft. What eased some of the resistance was framing the activity as a theatrical production. Students understood theatre requires directors, playwrights, actors, stage crew, costumers, designers—theatre, they understood, wasn't a solo gig. The grading rubric included separate elements of stagecraft, costuming, props, reinforcing the necessity for engaged collaboration, as students would typically break down duties in accord with their individual inclination and skill sets. The two "writerly" elements I insisted on also came directly from theatre: the poetry-text had to be a fluid construction serving the production and that the characters in the theatrical production had to be personas. The poem, then, became a working script, which students understood in terms of filmmaking, making the idea of drafting and revising seem more purposeful. They understood that the poem-script would remain in flux depending on the realties and dictates and limits of the performance. In insisting that the characters in the poem-play be personas, I wanted to avoid having a highly confessional, personal poem being used as a subject for display. All the same, I would say that many of the productions indeed had deep personal value for the students.

I wanted students to speak with their real voices, using their bodies, to move, to inhabit, in service of building a character. I borrowed greatly from my acting professor colleagues on a wide range of physical activities to promote both a sense of security and safety (where they would not be judged) and an ability to use the core of their bodies to move and project. Yes, it's a little odd to have students in a writing class walk in set patterns, making eye contact with each other, and say as slow as possible, "How now, you!, brown cow." But this activity made it clear to my students that a voice is a body, and is a physical thing. The moment of discovery is something like that for Dorothy in *The Wizard for Oz*, that the secret of returning to Kansas was with her all along. You see, as we played with the physical voice, and its squawks and squeaks and honks, the theoretical idea of the polyvocal became transparent. You discover you have many voices, many vocalizations: you're finding your *voices* by using them.

Likewise, because the script had to serve those voices, the revision process became practical and purposeful—it wasn't about the usual writerly problem of getting *le mot juste*, of painstaking exactness, but of experimentation and play, what the speaker could say, would say, and then, maybe not. Yes, in fiction writing classes, such character-driven dialogue exercises are fundamental. But with a theatre-informed approach to dialogue, speech exists without the other underlying elements of narrative writing: paragraphs of description, setting, scene, backstory. I also insisted on calling their work texts "script-poems," and so I made it clear that they were always performing a poem. Finally, the only modeling I engaged in was requiring students to attend a play or a student showcase at the university, just to be sure that they had some exposure to live theatre. And that exposure was to review basic stagecraft, mostly blocking and design, not to learn how to write a poem-script.

The final requirement to the assignment was that the performance could not take place in our classroom. This requirement, probably more than any other, shaped their script-poems in terms of their subject matter, where the choice of setting colored the poem and the production. Because our campus is mostly wetlands, several of the productions took on environmental themes, or the functionality of the location (a computer lab for one production and the astronomical observatory for another) shaped the content of the production. But the most interesting and far-reaching were the productions that were purposefully transgressive, making use of the setting and then devising the poem-script to subvert that setting. For instance, two students performed a tag-team cigarette smoking rant, each dressed as university administrators, standing outside the entryway of the Dean of Students' Offices, sharing a single cigarette—this on a smoke-free campus. One would take a drag and exhaled a line of poetry. With the exhale of poetry, the other actor took a drag of the cigarette, and then exhaled another line of poetry immediately after the other actor was finished. The exchange grew quicker and madder and dizzying, a foul cloud of second-hand smoke and bureaucracy.

But the most memorable performance was "Tiffany's Birthday Cake," where my transgendered woman-of-color student had her make-up removed by her partner, and then she applied clown white to her face, and was crowned with a silver tiara. A really bad and broken recording of "The Birthday Song" was playing on one of their phones, as the cake was delivered. At this moment, "Tiffany" spoke, at first a strange litany of gratitude, that at first was genuine, but then became more snarky, self-absorbed. "Tiffany's" partner led us to the cake, but there were no plates, no forks, no napkins, and then when "Tiffany" said a particularly obnoxious thing, her partner cupped a small handful of the cake and tossed it lightly at "Tiffany," striking her gown. It didn't take long for the audience to get in the act as well, and by the end of the performance, "Tiffany" was abundantly smeared with cake, until the performance closed with the distressing image of being "feathered and tarred."

After each performance, the actors would discuss the performance and the poem-script with the rest of the class. The actor who played "Tiffany" talked about her own transitioning, something she wrote about in other poems in first person. But in taking on this other voice and in physically inhabiting her was a revelatory process for her. "There's so much rejection I've carried with me. But here, I took on the skin of a woman I would never want to be. I spoke with her voice. And I felt her humiliation, what she had done to get people so angry at her. Like it felt true, real. I'm not her, but then I am."

* * *

Inherent in any performance is its own disappearance—perhaps all the more marvelous and beautiful because of the amount of work and rehearsal and collaboration that any good performance will require. Voice, then, as an action is just a part of that immateriality, and in this regard, it is where I see reconciliation between the post-structuralist and essentialist assumptions about voice and its "authenticity." A real voice, it now occurs to me, is that momentary physical utterance, but mercury-like, takes no final form, while taking almost every form possible. It's not about finding "your" voice—as if that's some definite, certain thing—but about finding voices, using them, all those breaths we take and then release.

NOTES

1. George D. Kuh and Carol Geary Schneider, *High-Impact Educational Practices: What They Are, Who has Access to Them, and Why They Matter*, 10.
2. Michele Eodice, Anne Ellen Geller, and Neal Lerner, *The Meaningful Writing Project: Learning, Teaching and Writing in Higher Education*, 4.
3. Eodice, Geller, and Lerner, *The Meaningful Writing Project*, 5.
4. Dan Melzer, "A Panoramic View of College Writing," Chapter 2.
5. Ann Nugent, "Extending Critical Voices Between the Lecture Room and the Dance Studio," 96.
6. Julie Malnig, ""But How Do I Write about Dance?": Thoughts on Teaching Criticism," 93.
7. Paul Bonin-Rodriguez, "The Staged Business of Artists in Public Practice: Writing for/about Art," 25.
8. "Colorado State University Academic Core Curriculum Report on Objectives and Criteria," 5–9. Also see https://curriculum.colostate.edu/aucc-foundations-and-perspectives/.
9. Michael Allsen, "Writing Concert Program Notes," 39–40. For one argument against using musical analysis within public program notes, see James M. Keller, "Program Notes," 39–40. For additional information on program notes writing, also see Jonathan Bellman, *A Short Guide;* Michele L. Henry and Laurel E. Zeiss, "Musicians as Authors"; Joseph Kerman, "The Art of the Program Note"; Fred Everett Maus, "Learning from 'Occasional' Writing"; Nigel Simeone, "Program Note"; and Richard Wingell, *Writing about Music.*
10. Peter Elbow, "Voice in Writing Again: Embracing Contraries," 171.
11. William Stafford, "Writing the Australian Crawl," 12.
12. Stafford, "Writing the Australian Crawl," 12.

BIBLIOGRAPHY

Allsen, Michael. Writing Concert Program Notes: A Guide for UWW Students. Revised November 2014. http://www.allsenmusic.com/NOTES/Writing Notes.html.
Bellman, Jonathan. 2007. *A Short Guide to Writing About Music.* New York: Pearson Longman.

Bonin-Rodriguez, Paul. 2014. The Staged Business of Artists in Public Practice: Writing for/About Art. *Theatre Topics* 24 (1): 25–37.

Colorado State University Academic Core Curriculum Report on Objectives and Criteria. Colorado State University. Revised October 2, 2007, 5–9.

Elbow, Peter. 1998. *Writing Without Teachers*. New York: Oxford University Press.

———. 2007. Voice in Writing Again: Embracing Contraries. *College English* 70 (2): 168–188.

Eodice, Michele, Anne Ellen Geller, and Neal Lerner. 2017. *The Meaningful Writing Project: Learning, Teaching and Writing in Higher Education*. Boulder: University Press of Colorado.

Henry, Michele L., and Laurel E. Zeiss. 2004. Musicians as Authors: Teaching the Art of Writing Program Notes. *College Music Symposium* 44: 121–132.

Keller, James M. 2000. Program Notes. *Chamber Music* 17 (4): 36–41, 57.

Kerman, Joseph. 2008. The Art of the Program Note. In *Opera and the Morbidity of Music*. New York: New York Review Books.

Kuh, George D., and Carol Geary Schneider. 2008. *High-Impact Educational Practices: What They Are, Who Has Access to Them, and Why They Matter*. Washington, DC: Association of American Colleges and Universities.

Malnig, Julie. 2009. "But How Do I Write About Dance?": Thoughts on Teaching Criticism. *Dance Research Journal* 41 (2): 91–95.

Maus, Fred Everett. 1997. Learning from 'Occasional' Writing. *Perspectives* 6 (2): 5–23.

Melzer, Dan. 2014. A Panoramic View of College Writing. In *Assignments Across the Curriculum: A National Study of College Writing*. Boulder: University Press of Colorado. GoogleBooks.

Nugent, Ann. 2009. Extending Critical Voices Between the Lecture Room and the Dance Studio. *Dance Research Journal* 41 (2): 95–98.

Simeone, Nigel. Programme Note. In *Grove Music Online*. http://www.oxfordmusiconline.com.

Stafford, William. 1964. Writing the Australian Crawl. *College Composition and Communication* 15 (1): 12–15.

Wingell, Richard. 2009. *Writing About Music*. 4th ed. Upper Saddle River, NJ: Pearson-Prentice Hall.

CHAPTER 6

Collaborative Assignments and Projects

Faculty in the performing arts take collaboration for granted. Long before it became a buzzword associated with effective pedagogy, performing artists have always relied upon collaborative creative processes to accomplish our work together. Even the solo artist is likely working with composers, choreographers, directors, and a technical theatre team to realize their performance. In the current climate where teamwork and collaboration are desired skill sets in many career paths, performing arts students accustomed to creating and performing in ensembles are positioned to effectively market these skills, unless, of course, they take these skills for granted too. It is our responsibility as educators to ensure that students are intentional about developing their collaborative skills and understand the transferability of those skills to all areas of their lives.

Most performing arts faculty are not explicit about the teaching of collaborative skills, as it is regarded as implicit in the performance and practical courses we teach. However, our students would be able to make more connections across the curriculum and apply their learning in the performing arts in other areas if performing arts educators were more savvy and explicit about framing and implementing collaborative teaching and learning theories.

Collaborative learning looks different in every context that it is deployed, and therefore it is difficult to provide one all-purpose definition. Pierre Dillenbourg proposes the following; "[t]he broadest (but unsatisfactory) definition of 'collaborative learning' is that it is a *situation* in which *two or more* people *learn* or attempt to learn something *together*. Each element of this definition can be interpreted in different ways. . .."[1] The terms *situation, learn,* and *together* are defined according to discipline, and therefore vary greatly. In the performing arts, the *situation* is often a performance featuring the performers *together* demonstrating what they have *learned*. Alternatively, the situation could be an applied performing arts practice or project rather than a performance, taking place in a practical setting rather than a performance venue.

The review of the literature on collaborative learning clarifies the various factors informing collaborative learning practice: collective problem solving, pedagogical practice, social interactions, and cognitive processes.[2] The best practices that have been identified for facilitating collaborative learning include making expectations clear, holding students accountable for regular interactions with their team, and attempting to group students so that asynchronous learning occurs (in which students of different knowledge backgrounds are on the same team). Dillenbourg reminds us that

> peers do not learn because they are two, but because they perform some activities which trigger specific learning mechanisms. This includes the activities/mechanisms performed individually, since individual cognition is not suppressed in peer interaction. But, in addition, the interaction among subjects generates extra activities (explanation, disagreement, mutual regulation, ...) which trigger extra cognitive mechanisms (knowledge elicitation, internalization, reduced cognitive load, ...). The field of collaborative learning is precisely about these activities and mechanisms.[3]

If we apply these cognitive processes in performing arts contexts, we can easily understand how performing ensembles learning choreography, a composition, or a script are negotiating the collaborative learning endeavor. In a context where original works are created, the creative team is approaching the collaborative process with even more at stake, with the "problem solving" culminating in the premiere of a new work.

Piet Van den Bossche et al. define "the learning behavior of the team" as a "social process of building mutually shared cognition," through "the interaction among members of the group and the characteristics of their discourse."[4] For performing arts students, this interaction is embodied and aural, the characteristics of the discourse may be non-verbal, intuitive, improvisatory, responsive to the real-time give and take, and invoking all the senses through the semiotics of performance, where the ensemble works cohesively to realize an artistic vision. This particular mode of collaborative learning might be described as highly potent. Potency is a useful term for talking about the "high" that performing creates in the performers, an elation felt when all the performing elements come together and the ensemble has successfully realized a collective artistic vision. Van den Bossche et al. note that group potency, or the acknowledgment among group members that they can be successful together, contributes to the efficacy of learning: "a high group potency belief strengthens the idea that investment will pay off and so encourages processes of learning."[5] In performing arts education, we are often preparing students for the public dissemination of performance, cultivating group potency, and seeking that performance "high," a cognitive and embodied response for both performers and audience that confirms effective collaborative learning has taken place.

In addition to group potency, other qualities of effective collaborative learning have been identified, such as interdependence, task cohesion, and psychological safety.[6] Interdependence and task cohesion are inherent in performance, wherein the performers and technicians value the role of each one in the ensemble. It is understood that the orchestra would be incomplete without one of the musicians needed for the composition, or the lift would not happen if the dancer does not bear his or her share of the weight. Psychological safety is needed for collaborative learning so that the individuals in the team know they can take risks, fail, and posit ideas that are not fully formed. Psychological safety allows all team members to contribute to the whole in a generative process without fear of being "wrong," and with trust that another team member may provide the cognitive load to make sense of a partial contribution. The ability of team members to take risks in any given creative process is dependent on the social dynamics of the creative team. As educators, it would serve our pedagogy to develop or implement explicit structures that encourage effective collaborative learning.[7]

Modeling collaboration for our students happens regularly within performing arts departments, where faculty work together on creative teams to bring a performance to the stage or deliver curriculum. Interdepartmental and interdisciplinary collaborations are also important to model for our students. Performing arts faculty collaborate with faculty in other disciplines in numerous creative ways, such as illuminating coursework with performance, mutual knowledge sharing about the context and content of a play, dance, or piece of music (which reaches any conceivable discipline), or applied performing arts projects with on campus and off campus community partners.

Creating opportunities for students to work on diverse teams, learning collaboratively with students in other disciplines, or community partners, will only further enhance their learning. Team teaching interdisciplinary courses can be a powerful collaborative learning practice for faculty and students alike, bringing students together to consider subjects in ways that wouldn't be possible within their academic silo alone. Technology is making collaborative learning more accessible than ever, erasing distance and creating virtual communities of learners that can use various digital media to co-create creative scholarship.[8] The performing arts are inherently collaborative, but it is time to be didactic about the benefits of teamwork that we largely take for granted.

The following case studies consider collaborative learning through practical performance experiences and innovative curricular means. Claire M. McDonald produced a new play festival at her institution and realized a strategy for creating multicultural collaboration that encouraged interdisciplinary creative processes. Angela Sweigart-Gallagher and Kristin Hunt examine their redesign and teaching of a performance practicum course with a focus on the ethical dimensions of student labor and the curricular framing of this experiential and collaborative project-based learning as a teaching strategy.

Call to action:

- Administrators need to provide professional development training for faculty in collaborative learning theories and pedagogy.
- Performing arts faculty need to seek out faculty development in collaborative learning theories and pedagogy to better articulate and accomplish the collaborative learning already taking place. Many universities offer special workshops on effective pedagogies, or request one on collaborative learning.
- Performing arts faculty need to remind administrators of this skill set in the performing arts, and as intentional practitioners performing arts faculty should offer workshops in collaborative learning to faculty in other disciplines.
- Performing arts faculty should consider adding courses or sections of courses that focus on collaboration, so that students learn these skills

with intention and reflection. And performing arts faculty should be explicit about naming the collaborative learning that is taking place, drawing students' attention to the skill sets they are gaining in teamwork and problem solving in groups.
- Performing arts faculty should team teach with faculty outside the performing arts to promote collaborative learning among asynchronous learners and to broaden the reach of performing arts pedagogies in the academy. Work across the silos and encourage your students to do the same.
- Performing arts faculty need to implement digital media in the curriculum where it makes sense to do so, and encourage collaborative learning on digital platforms that will broaden students' skill sets and creative communities. Think beyond the typical online learning management systems to include platforms and software that encourage collaborative composition, choreography, and theatre practices.

The Ampersand Festival: A Case Study in Theatre as High-Impact Educational Practice

Claire M. McDonald
University of St. Thomas
Houston, TX, USA

Ampersand, a festival of new, student-directed ten-minute plays was produced by the University of Saint Thomas (UST), Department of Fine Arts and Drama in Houston, Texas in April 2015. This project realized a strategy for creating multidisciplinary and multicultural connections between the theatre program and other departments employing high-impact educational practices including collaborative assignments, production company (cast, crew, and artistic leadership) as learning community, diversity/global learning, and capstone projects.[9] The vision of the *Ampersand* project is described well in Nancy Kindelan's *Artistic Literacy*:

> Learning occurs through carefully planned teaching and high-impact strategies in which teachers not only transmit information but also encourage student involvement and the active construction of knowledge—through critical and creative thinking, the exchange of ideas across the curriculum, and experiential projects. The interpretation of a play evolves over time: it is subject to

changing perceptions about self, others, relationships, historical ideas, and social awareness; it is enriched by interconnected thoughts and multiple theories, which often arise within a community of learners. Through the conceptual study of diverse plays, students become comfortable with ambiguity and change. Beyond promoting self-reflection, ethical reasoning, and the ability to identify, explore and negotiate inequities, theatre studies enhance interpersonal skills and the habits of mind, hand, and heart that students need to guide their professional lives after college and in the community.[10]

The goals of the project were ambitious: promote interdisciplinary conversations about theatre, encourage interdisciplinary involvement in the creative process using theatre pedagogy, create an avenue for town and gown exchange through the conduit of theatre in the liberal arts environment, foster buy-in of all stakeholders (the academy, the community, the corporate sponsor, and the administration), and generate original theatre with a broad spectrum of contributions from diverse aesthetic legacies. The anticipated outcome of the project was enhanced artistic literacy and particularly theatrical literacy of all stakeholders. If successful, the plan was to repeat the project for a new group of students in two years.

Conceived in April 2014, the initial impetus for the Ampersand project came from a desire to support new works coupled with a meaningful project for our group of talented student directors. Producing new works was not new to the department. Typically, those productions centered on a theme and a select group of local and regional playwrights submitted scripts. The Ampersand project sought to be more far-reaching and inclusive of many and diverse playwrights. The project abandoned the relative security of the umbrella theme and familiar playwrights and embraced everything and anything submitted. *Ampersand* generated the hoped for diversity of plays.

The call to playwrights went out in late August. Posting on the Dramatists' Guild site was key.

Submissions Now Open for UST Spring 2015 Evening of Ten-Minute Plays *AMPERSAND*
   Deadline: DECEMBER 1, 2014 (11:59 pm CST)
   The University of St. Thomas Drama Program announces a call for scripts to be produced as part of our spring 2015 evening of original, ten-minute plays, *AMPERSAND*. All works are welcome. Special consideration will be given to scripts which feature characters aged 18–28 years, have casts of 1–4 actors (favoring female characters), do not exceed 10 minutes, have simple production requirements and best suit our UST liberal arts tradition.

Writers Selected are Provided with:

- a fully staged production of the work directed by a senior UST directing student under the supervision of UST drama faculty.
- four public performances: April 22–25, 2015.
- a $100.00 honorarium.

A Complete Submission is Composed of Two Parts:

1. A cover sheet identifying you, your work and your contact information.
2. A single, 10 minute, original work (preferably not previously produced and c.10 pages), with your name or any identifying information removed. Send us your best.

We strongly encourage you to submit your cover sheet and script (in Word or PDF form) electronically.

Email/Postmark Deadline: DECEMBER 1, 2014 (11:59 pm CST) NO EXCEPTIONS

This call provided the interested playwrights with as much creative latitude as possible while informing them of university specific concerns that would influence the final selections. The response from playwrights was awe-inspiring. By the submission deadline, the initially anticipated 100 scripts had grown to 434. They came from countries around the globe including Australia, England, France, Canada and most of the United States including Hawaii. The global reach of the project exceeded expectations. The tremendous response to our competition and the global visibility it provided our little campus piqued the interest of the UST Performing and Fine Arts Society board members. They, together with a member of the university Institutional Advancement Office approached SHELL with a proposal to support the production with a $10,000 dollar grant in the fall of 2014. We would not discover the successful result of our bid until the following April.

All submitted work was read. The scripts were distributed "blind," with no author identification to bias the reader, to a select group of forty-four theatre savvy readers across the country. The readers, most of whom had no immediate ties to the university, each received ten scripts to rate. They also received guidelines to ensure consistency in the evaluations.

Guidelines to Readers for the UST **AMPERSAND** Festival of New Plays

1. After reading your set of plays please choose the two best works and rate them first and second.

2. Email your top two titles and their rating to mcdonald@stthom.edu by **JANUARY 11, 2015.**
3. If you feel that no play in your set is ready for production, you may so indicate.
4. If you receive a set of exceptional plays, you may extend your rating past two, i.e. 1–10

Keep the following in mind as you read:

We are seeking ten-minute (i.e. ten pages) plays **not** standard length one acts; **not** act one of a full-length play.

Special consideration will be given to scripts which feature characters aged 18–28 years, have casts of 1–4 actors (favoring female characters), do not exceed 10 minutes, have simple production requirements and best suit our UST liberal arts tradition.

The playwrights were provided this information because:

- We will be casting primarily college-aged actors.
- We are a small department with a limited actor pool size.
- We have more female than male actors in our pool.
- The eight to ten scripts chosen for the production will be performed as a single evening and no one play can overwhelm the others technically.
- This is a Catholic college. Some content and language are problematic on our stages. If in doubt, err on the conservative side.

In all cases, an exceptional work should be recognized as exceptional even if it fails to follow the guidelines.

Please note: Playwrights were instructed to send a blind copy of their script and an informational cover sheet. Not all playwrights follow directions well. If you receive a script that includes the playwright's name and you have personal knowledge of the writer, please inform me and I will assign that script to another reader.

I cannot thank you all enough. Feel free to send any questions my way.

The top selections from each reader were recombined with others and a second more elite group of theatre professionals was assembled to further refine the group of plays. When the number of plays was reduced to twenty, they were presented to the group of ten student directors selected to participate in the directing course. Each director read all twenty plays and chose the piece they felt called to direct. The vetting process conducted by the student directors at this point was critical. They had to collaborate with each other and compromise when more than one director chose the same piece. There were also thoughtful and probing conversations about the content of the works and their appropriateness to the venue. Original play selections changed during this phase but all choices still came from the group of twenty finalists. The playwrights remained unknown to the directors during this process.

After the ten winning plays had been selected, it was revealed that a UST student playwright's work had made the semi-final cut but had not been selected by a student director for production. The drama faculty agreed that the significance of a student writer who had progressed so far through the competitive vetting process had earned the opportunity to have his play produced. Former UST drama majors turned theatre professionals were engaged to direct and perform in it as guest artists.

The final selections represented a diverse group of plays, styles, and opportunities. As a group, the playwrights brought an impressive array of talents to the production. They included an Emmy nominated television writer, many significant award winners, a Canadian, an MFA playwriting graduate student, an alumna of UST drama, and a current UST student.

In February, the student directors held campus-wide auditions for their plays. The call went out to the entire student body in the bi-weekly UST student email blitz and was advertised with flyers around campus for several weeks prior to auditions in an attempt to attract as diverse a group of students across as many majors as possible.

> CALLING ALL UST ACTORS
> Come audition for *AMPERSAND*, an evening of new, UST student-directed ten-minute plays.
> TUESDAY, FEBRUARY 24th from 5:00 to 7:00 pm in JONES THEATRE
> Why YOU should audition:
>
> There are roles for 30 actors (men and women)! Each play has two to four actors.
> Rehearsals for ten-minute plays require much less time than long plays.
> It is fun to be in a brand new play. Be the first to create these characters!
> No prior stage experience is required.
> You've always wanted to act.
> IT'S FUN!
>
> For more information call or email Prof. Claire McDonald.

This call was designed to attract students who might otherwise feel that the drama program was not open to them. The student directors campaigned among their friends and classmates in other fields to encourage them to participate. The turnout of students to the auditions was gratifyingly substantial but, even after initial call backs for specific shows, an additional open audition was scheduled for the following week. The directors collaborated in the casting process working to cast the best talent in each show while offering as many aspiring performers as possible an opportunity to participate. Some actors, particularly male, were double cast. Still, twenty-two UST student actors and two UST drama student alumni were cast. Additional students were involved in the technical aspects of the production. The statistics for University and community involvement in the project were impressive.[11]

UST Participants

43 students from 14 majors across all four UST schools
Arts and Sciences; School of Business; School of Education; School of Nursing
10 student directors
1 student playwright
22 student actors
13 student technicians
4 alumni
2 drama faculty
Office of Advancement
UST Performing Arts Society Board
UST Office of Marketing and Communications

Community Partners

434 playwrights from around the globe (USA, Canada, England, France, Australia)
50 play readers
1 visiting designer
SHELL $10,000.00 grant
400 audience members

Majors of UST students involved in the Ampersand production

Drama—12
Communication—6

Biology—4
Education—4
English—3
Math—2
Accounting—2
General Business—2
History—2
Theology—1
Psychology—1
Political Science—1
Liberal Arts—1
Nursing—1

After casting, the student directors managed all elements of rehearsal and production with guidance from me. They held production meetings and actively participated in designing and building sets, lights, sound, costumes, props, makeup. Unaware at this time that the bid for external sponsorship would be successful, no professional extra-departmental technical or design assistance was engaged with the single exception of a local professional lighting designer. The student directors all agreed that this intense involvement taught them not only about how to create theatrical art but also much about collaboration, management, and team leadership.

The rehearsal process commenced after the mid-term break and lasted four and a half weeks. Until the technical rehearsals began a week prior to opening, each of the eleven plays rehearsed separately with its director. As the plays evolved, the directors conferred about the practical and theatrical considerations for each piece and an order for the production emerged. During the final week of technical rehearsals the eleven pieces coalesced into a unified whole. All of the actors assisted with the scene changes between pieces. Each "stagehand" outfitted with an apron imprinted with an ampersand, an inexpensive gray beard and a pointed paper hat emerged in the semi-darkness between scenes onto the black box stage to effect the change. Since there had been no attempt to unify the evening thematically, these somewhat mysterious "gnomes" drew the audience ever closer to the final piece *There's No Place Like Gnome* which, as the single student written work, had been given a place of honor at the conclusion of the evening. Throughout the rehearsal process, the directors continued to meet with me at their regular course time to discuss their progress and continue to explore directing theory. I also attended individual play rehearsals at regular intervals to provide feedback for the directors. I gave this feedback outside of the rehearsal time to avoid undermining the student director's authority and to allow each to process which aspects of the feedback they wished to share with their casts.

The student directors shared the responsibility for marketing and publicizing the production. Their grassroots efforts across campus with word-of-mouth, flyers, Facebook posts, and student body email blasts were invaluable. The university office of Marketing Communications collaborated with the program to spread the word to the wider Houston audience. The combined effort resulted in four sold out performances. Jones Theatre seats ninety-six but, with the strategic addition of extra chairs, the theatre accommodated 100. The intimate nature of the theatre was ideal for this production. Audience members reported having a visceral, poignant, and personal experience. Many marveled at the variety and quality of the performances. This was high praise for the many novice actors, but these kinds of reactions are typical in small theatre spaces. The humanity of the performers was what was so compelling. This occurs frequently when the performers are close enough to the audience to reach out and touch. Communication is inevitable.

The audience members submitted feedback to the directors in the form of a ranking card included inside the program.

PLEASE HELP US EVALUATE OUR WORK.
Take a moment to rate the plays. Award your favorite play #1
and so on. Even a few ratings would be helpful to us.
Drop your evaluation in the "coffee" box on the lobby table.
Thanks!
Ampersand Festival Plays
ACT I

____*Goodbye Breakfast* Jessy Lauren Smith   Director Kathleen Smith
____*Surprise* Mark Harvey Levine   Director Sophie Vigil
____*Dancing in the Elevator* Dorothea Cahan   Director Marika Karastamatis
____*Corporate* Ross Donatelli   Director Shawna Hardy
____*Engagement Chicken* Cheryl D. Duffin   Director Alex Brokmeyer
____*Egg* Mark Jensen   Director Amelia Templeton

ACT II

____*Magic Hour* Jack Karp   Director Jesús Ramos
____*The Interview* Michael Somes   Director Andres Santos
____*Close Encounter* Robin Pond   Director Mason Burruss
____*Stat!* Ron Burch   Director Theresa Weatherford
____*There's No Place Like Gnome* Daniel Gartland   Director Chris Tennison

Final critique sessions with the directors both individually and together in class incorporated audience feedback and rankings. The four audiences generated sufficient response to produce statistically valid and constructive conversations about effective directing. This elevated the group discussion well above the personal level. The student directors examined their strengths and weaknesses in an unbiased fashion. Myself, other drama faculty members, the audiences, the student actors in the casts, and the directors all contributed to the evaluation.

Setting UST drama program specific outcomes aside, linking essential learner outcomes as identified by George Kuh with similarly identified high-impact educational practices leads to the most universally useful assessment of the Ampersand project and its applicability in other venues. The Ampersand project was successful in addressing each of the four essential learning outcomes with each of four high-impact educational practices.[12]

Theatre is, by its very nature, a collaborative art form. Live theatre is inherently strengthened by the contributions of the many. Months prior to the convening of the directing course, a global collaboration of over 400 playwrights submitted their work for consideration. The fifty readers who read and vetted the scripts were a second collaboration. The most significant, measurable collaboration commenced as the student directors received the final twenty scripts. As each read every script, the directors remained in communication about the scripts that best worked for them. The entire group discussed each choice. Compromises occurred in the instances where first choices overlapped. Serious discussion occurred as when it became clear that one of the script choices could be offensive to our Muslim student population. After auditions, the student directors had to come to agreements on casting and, particularly, double casting of actors in the pool. Once cast, the directors had to coordinate a rehearsal schedule that would allow each to have sufficient rehearsal time in the available rehearsal spaces. The group decided on the layout for the fixed scenic units after considering the scenic demands of each piece. In addition to the directors collaborating with each other, each director guided the actors cast in their play specifically focusing on what each actor brought to the production from their fields of study. Ultimately, all the directors, casts, and technical support staff came together to complete the final product. The entire semester involved groups working to solve production problems by gathering the best ideas and putting them into practice. A successful performance emerged from individual discipline motivated by the common good, trial and permissible error, creative solutions, listening, and reacting collaboratively.

A theatrical production company in an academic institution is a learning community. The "big question"[13] in keeping with the UST mission is and always has been what aspect of universal truth can this production reveal? The over 900 university participants and community partners involved in this project represented numerous constituent perspectives that contributed to the unique creation. This learning community formed around a concept initially supported by the contributing playwrights followed by the play readers who were tangential, but critical, to the central university learning community. The drama faculty, select university staff, and the UST Performing and Fine Arts Society were the next to join the community as the superstructure for the core of the community, the students. The directors, actors, and student technicians breathed life into the project. They all had the option of reaching out to the playwrights to discuss changes. In this way, the community looped back on itself. Finally, the students invited the outside community as audience to evaluate the success of the project. All core learning community constituents engaged with the "question," contributed critical and creative thinking, were actively involved, and demonstrated this learning throughout the performances.

The wide scope and global reach of the Ampersand project required the student participants to "explore cultures, life experiences and worldviews different from their own."[14] This exploration began with the vetting process for the many scripts as each piece was assessed for its artistic and social merits. It continued with the casting and rehearsal process. UST is a 68% ethnically diverse student group. The university has been designated a Hispanic Serving Institution and 44% of the freshman class are first generation college students. The student body is over 50% female. The cast and crew of the Ampersand project represented over ten distinct cultural groups. The scripts themselves were primarily interpersonal relationship stories involving two to eight actors but, viewed together, became a fascinating experience in multicultural harmony.

The Ampersand project was the capstone experience for the student directors. They brought all aspects of the UST degree program into their work. They were required to draw on all they knew about acting technique, vocal production, movement, stagecraft, design, technical theatre, playwriting, and theatre history. Their work was then set before the public audience for evaluation. For small liberal arts drama generalist programs such as the one at UST, directing is a superb capstone experience. All of the ten student directors pursued professional work in the theatre as actors, theatre arts teachers, a stage manager, a stage carpenter, and a box office manager after graduation. Although there is only anecdotal evidence, involvement in the Ampersand project appears to have been a significant influencing factor in career choice. The knowledge, skills, personal discipline, and ability to integrate evident in their productions carried forward into the marketplace.

At the time of this writing *Ampersand 2.0* is cast and ready to go into rehearsal with ten new directors and plays. Repeatability is an undeniable indicator of program viability. Lessons learned during the first project are being applied. Although exciting, 434 plays was too large a number to vet. By shortening the play submission window, the number of plays submitted was reduced to seventy. This considerably reduced the number of play readers needed. Fortunately, plays still arrived from around the globe. It was critical to the project that its international and multicultural impact remain intact. Not surprisingly, it was not possible to attract another $10,000 grant but the $100 honorarium for each playwright continues. It ensures high-quality scripts and demonstrates support for writers. An original hope for the project to attract more plays by and about women is more fully realized in the second iteration. Both projects involved plays with more female characters than male and the second project will produce more plays written by women, five scripts versus two in the first project. The second production will also include a script written by a UST student. Finally, much of the assessment for the first project is anecdotal. To remedy this, a strategy to collect more concrete data to support the value of theatre as high-impact educational practice is being developed.

The lasting impact of high-impact practice on the individual learner is clear. Here is a short biography from the program notes of *Ampersand*.

> Daniel Gartland is a current University of St Thomas student majoring in liberal arts. He was introduced to playwriting last year and found another outlet for his imaginative mind. When he transferred from Austin Community College, where he studied video game design, he never imagined the new direction his studies would take him. He has been inspired by his professors, and found his voice, no small task for someone with Asperger Syndrome and who, just a few short years ago while at boarding school in Connecticut at The Woodhall School, found conversing a challenge.[15]

Daniel not only found his voice participating in the Ampersand Festival, it is loud and clear.

An Ethical Balancing Act: Student Labor and Project-Based Learning

Angela Sweigart-Gallagher
Saint Lawrence University
Canton, NY, USA

Kristin Hunt
Arizona State University
Phoenix, AZ, USA

On many university campuses, faculty struggle to carve out space for excellent teaching even as competing forces urge us to mechanize, streamline, and make our teaching more efficient. In response to these competing values, faculty have innovated, developing models like community-engaged learning and peer-led team learning. We work hard to find ways to justify investing in our teaching, particularly in the performing arts, in a system that often privileges metrics and deliverables over time, care, and the intangibles of learning, values once considered common sense and now often deeply mistrusted in a world in which education is a major front in a larger cultural war. The arts in particular face institutional pressure to speak to these metrics, and we often justify investments in teaching by touting second-order impacts, including increased publication, community connection, and economic efficiency. For instance, community-engaged learning benefits local stakeholders and increases a university's standing within its community,[16] while practice-based learning leverages student labor to efficiently build and run the university theatrical production apparatus. But the necessity of student labor to these outcomes introduces ethical challenges. Faculty warn against the "student as customer" model of education, and for good reasons.[17] But we should guard against another insidious economic model: the student as unacknowledged laborer. Many pedagogical innovations lauded among educators as high-impact teaching strategies also leverage student labor for the benefit of the institution as a whole. As faculty members in a tripartite department of Communication, Media, and Theatre (CMT) at Northeastern Illinois University, we experienced the competing demands of pedagogical excellence and logistical and fiscal efficiency first hand, especially in managing the department's mainstage theatrical productions in the face of shrinking school budgets and a state financial crisis. Many students within the CMT major saw themselves primarily as documentarians, journalists, or communication scholars rather than theatre artists, but the department's mainstage productions depended on student labor from all of its majors to function. Our concern about creating an ethical balance between student labor and high-impact teaching practices led us to reimagine the department's Theatre Practicum course in the summer of 2015.

In this required course for all CMT majors, students either attended shop hours each week or worked as run crew or stage managers for productions. Students frequently complained to their advisors that they felt taken advantage of as "free labor" due to this requirement. As part of a tripartite department, many students didn't consider themselves "theatre people." Faculty struggled to address this concern that the course was more focused on theatrical labor than student learning priorities, including the following justification in a course syllabus: "This course will provide students with lifelong skills needed to repair their future homes/apartments." Even we, who implicitly believed in the benefits of practical theatrical training, could hardly call this rationale compelling. So, in the summer of 2015, we redesigned the course to address the concern that students ought to not primarily function as laborers in their learning environments, reworking course procedures and objectives toward an ethical and high-impact teaching and learning practice. In this redesign, we drew an ethical distinction between learners and laborers, a practice we consider critical especially for theatre programs housed in multidisciplinary departments, but which may also serve as a best practice for stand-alone theatre majors. In the case study, we address the ethical, fiscal, and pedagogical dimensions of student labor practices in university theatrical production and analyze the design, implementation, and assessment of our course in terms of student learning outcomes, impact on the student community, and student engagement in production on campus.

Laborers or Learners: Rethinking Student Roles in Production

In reimagining the course, we knew we had to address the value of student labor, which seemed locked in a catch-22. Student labor had clear financial value to the department and university. We could not, for example, replace student labor with paid faculty or staff. And yet, student labor was not considered particularly valuable in terms of its quality, or even its visibility. For instance, as recently as 2012, practicum workers appeared in season programs only as "practicum students." Crediting students by class title, rather than by name, further diminished their labor's perceived prestige and value. Furthermore, faculty often treated student labor as unreliable or of little value. This attitude showed in the types of labor students typically performed, such as cleaning the dressing room or taking out trash. Faculty regularly scheduled complex construction projects or "artistic" tasks such as painting the deck or recording light cues during times when no students were present. When students participated in high-value tasks, they were often Talent Scholars who received tuition remission in exchange for a certain number of hours of work per course credit, making them in essence paid workers. The argument for this approach hinged on efficiency. Unfortunately, this efficiency-oriented model effectively shut practicum students out of tasks critical to a key practice-based learning benefit: developing capacity to "work and solve problems in the company of others."[18]

Significant structural challenges within the program made it difficult for faculty to imagine our practicum students as competent, reliable, and valuable collaborative workers. First and foremost, the course had no prerequisites. Students often had no idea how to identify or use the tools in the scene shop, and they had varying degrees of comfort and experience with sewing, painting, or other craft skills. Furthermore, some majors' inability to imagine themselves in theatre often led them to put the course off until they were juniors or seniors, making timely training investments impractical.

Longstanding interpretations of how faculty labor operated presented another significant structural challenge. Because faculty contracts treated production as part of an instructor's teaching load, rather than as a separate responsibility, building and implementation of design elements took place across the multiple sections of the course within class meeting times, which were limited to regular increments of 1.5 hours two days per week. In total, we had approximately 3 hours of class time four days per week devoted to the production of two mainstage shows per semester. These dynamics of student and faculty labor coalesced, leading to both faculty burnout and student frustration.

We used the summer session as a laboratory for reevaluating both sides of the labor equation and reimagining the course's relationship with production. Our central revision focused on integrating students more fully into the creative process. One of our major concerns was the degree to which students felt ownership of the production. We knew from our previous experiences as directors that student enjoyment and development of new skills was directly proportional to their feeling that their work was integral to the success of the show. In other words, we suspected that students didn't object to the *amount* of labor asked of them. Rather, our students desired more engaging types of labor. Specifically, they desired to do work that was manifestly of value, both to their learning goals and to the program and production.

In order to create opportunities for more engaging work, we restructured the syllabus to provide students with the tools they needed to collaboratively conceive, execute, run, and close a show. These goals are reflected in the course learning objectives, which included developing the skills to:

- Read a text for design cues and information.
- Conduct design research and communicate that research verbally and visually to directors and other collaborators.
- Apply fundamental construction and technical standards in the field to the execution of the group's design elements.
- Collaborate effectively in a dynamic production environment.
- Assess and respond to directorial, actor, and audience needs pertinent to assigned design areas.

In order to meet these objectives, we reframed course content around a series of collaborative design projects that led students through the design process from research to concept to construction. We served as lead designers, providing scaffolding ideas on which our student designers could build and expand. The director attended class periodically to participate in design meetings and give students feedback.

Arts-Led Pedagogy: Key Features of Instructional Design

Due to its focus on leveraging the economic benefits of student production work, earlier versions of the course had positioned students largely as interchangeable laborers, contributing a predetermined amount of work units in the form of hours in exchange for a passing grade in the course. This model assumed that learning follows as a corollary of labor itself, and prioritized labor as the primary value driving instructional design. However, our skepticism of this concept, paired with our ethical concern that students ought to be fundamentally differentiated from laborers, necessitated starting from learning itself rather than labor. We speculated that, by focusing first on students as learners, we could deepen students' senses of commitment to the project at hand and thus increase their investment in the skills they acquired in service of our common production goal. In other words, we would invert the prior order; labor would be a necessary corollary of learning. With this notion in mind, we implemented two interrelated strategies to drive our learner-centered lesson planning: a relational approach to instructional design and an arts-led approach to course management and pedagogical practice. Furthermore, we tied course learning outcomes to the skill of collaboration, which allowed us to connect our instructional design and pedagogical practice to a key theatrical skill with wide relevance to other fields and knowledge domains.

First, in order to ensure that the design of our in-class sessions cohered with a learning-focused rather than a labor-focused model, we adopted a relational approach to lesson planning. Our aim was to place learning first, and with it, the essential relational qualities of in-person learning environments. Our model paid special attention to two relational models in particular, treating student–student relationships as collaborators within creative teams (rather than members of a work crew) and student–instructor relationships as mentor–mentee (rather than supervisor–laborer). These two adjustments to the class model shifted students' senses of themselves from laborers to artists, raising students' awareness of their own learning opportunities and skill development but also increasing student investment in the stakes of their contribution to the work of the course and the classroom community. Where the prior instructional design minimized this kind of interaction and maximized shop hours, our design prioritized students' sense of themselves as creative collaborators, necessitating specific adjustments to our lesson planning. We balanced skill-building workshop sessions with team-driven design meetings in which the entire class collaborated to respond to design ideas, building skills in critical feedback while also developing a strong sense of the design approach as learner-driven. Instructors functioned as both facilitators of these meetings, helping teams negotiate divergent ideas and soliciting feedback from the show's director, and as mentors, offering alternative ideas for implementation of design concepts and providing practical support in purchasing, research and development, and labor management.

Second, in order to maintain a clear focus on students as learners rather than laborers, we adopted an arts-led approach to course management and pedagogical practice. In our analysis of prior course incarnations, we noted a pedagogical practice that was focused strongly on efficiency. But, we reasoned, learning itself is, in terms of labor practices, highly inefficient, a fact that continues to reshape our economy as employers increasingly attempt to outsource more and more of what was once costly on-the-job training to colleges and universities, changing their curricula accordingly. The arts, however, often operate outside the confines of efficiency, providing a space for activities often crowded out of efficiency-driven enterprises: contemplation, excess, beauty, revision, reiteration, happy accidents, and leaps of faith. These values, we felt, were central to the joy of theatrical creation. Our relational instructional model insisted that, rather than the most efficient path forward, in which we as experienced artists designed the show and directed our students to realize our vision quickly and cleanly, we ought to follow the richest path forward for maximizing student engagement with the creative process, which would in turn drive their development of skills needed to conceive and implement a collaborative design. Thus we positioned artistic values as the core principles that would drive individual course management decisions and our overall pedagogical approach. This arts-led approach meant that, when faced with thorny decisions about pedagogical problems, we began with aesthetic priorities rather than with efficiency-based ones.

Our arts-led approach dovetailed with the relational value that drove our lesson planning. This approach required us to develop a collaborative relationship with each student as well as attend to the relational qualities of each student team. For instance, early in the design process one student revealed a strong talent for drawing, while another demonstrated an interest in making musical instruments from found objects and another evinced strong critical feedback skills. These three students became team leaders for the paint crew, music crew, and properties crew respectively, allowing them to mentor other students while also asserting a strong artistic vision that drove their individual areas. Meanwhile, we balanced developing these students' individual artistic perspectives with giving each student team member space to make their own aesthetic contributions, from materials selection to refinements of scenic design to lead design responsibilities for specific props and costumes. This approach required vigilance on our parts in identifying and developing students' areas of primary aesthetic interest, teaching and assessing collaborative creative skills, and streamlining design and production choices to allow the time and space within the course to hold team meetings, review individual design ideas, and mentor team contributions to bring them in line with a holistic design concept for the entire production. Again driven by a relational and arts-led approach, we devoted the final 30 minutes of each course day to sharing accomplishments and plans among different teams, asking each member to share their aesthetic successes and challenges for the session and allowing students from all teams to provide suggestions and feedback to their peers, sacrificing more shop hours in favor of fostering a collaborative environment and a unified design.

Outcomes: Visibility, Engagement, and Happiness of Student Learner-Laborers

Our attempts to shift from a labor-based to a learner-based model yielded several positive outcomes. First, student labor became more visible within the class and to the broader campus community. Second, the course generated greater student buy-in that resulted in a rise in student volunteerism. Finally, student evaluations indicated a high level of satisfaction with the course.

As we began revising the course, we aimed to increase the visibility of students and their labor. As we discussed above, student labor was clearly integral to production, but individual student contributions seemed undervalued. In our revised model, almost every student exercised primary creative control over at least one element of the production (a musical instrument, a prop, a costume, etc.). In a simple gesture to acknowledge this work, we listed each student by name in our program with a specific design or construction credit. These individual program credits sent our students a signal that their work was valued and specific and made the value of student labor more explicit to the university and department.

We also perceived an increase in student buy-in and in student participation in theatre overall. We noted that most of our students appeared enthusiastically engaged in their work, which countered the prior class narrative about disinterested students hiding backstage during work hours. Students genuinely devoted themselves to making the show a success. We watched students fret over how the director would receive a decision they had made about a scenic element, and celebrate when it was approved or enthusiastically rework an idea in response to peer or directorial feedback. One student spent hours building wing elements and, after participating in a conversation with the director during dress rehearsal, agreed they didn't work and needed to be cut. This same student arrived early to shop hours the next day to finish removing the elements even though she had already fulfilled her shop hours. This student had grumbled about the notion of shop hours at our first meeting, but now she wanted to make sure her wings were successful, and she donated her time because she wanted them "to be done right." Multiple students demonstrated similar commitment, further suggesting they were engaged in the production. Even when they were not required to be there, they came; they volunteered their time. Rather than the model of compulsory labor enforced by the power of a grade, these students came to see their work as of intrinsic value to them as learners and creators. This enhanced student buy-in lasted beyond the confines of the single summer semester. Several students from our summer session grew more involved in the university theatre. Most notably, a student who spent much of his energy on creating an articulated wing and taking the lead on props design enlisted as a Special Skill Scholar the following year. In the new role, he was paid through tuition remission to work in the shop and lead student crews.

Despite the intensity of the summer session and the fact that they put in shop hours outside of class time, students responded to the course enthusiastically. When asked to identify positive aspects of the course and/or the instruction, students wrote:

> "I really liked that this course had a hands on approach to the design aspect of the theatre."
> "Pure perfection and a well-thought out class. I loved the setup and learned a lot!"
> "The overall process and time of putting a play together. It was an amazing experience to work on different parts and see it come together at the end."

Another student wrote that the best aspects of the course were, "The hands-on experience, the great feedback, the overall community that was formed during the course of putting the show together." Indeed, the class was a community, an ensemble, and the end result was a production that we were all proud to call our own.

While we consider the class a proof of concept, the model was not without its challenges. The revised course required that faculty be strong collaborators, communicators, and planners. Although we frequently discussed how our model could be executed with one instructor, the course hinged on two co-teachers helming multiple design areas. Therefore, applications to different settings or with different faculty would need to address whether all areas of design would be collaboratively designed with students. We found that some design areas (such as set, props, and costumes) were easier to collaborate on with students than others (lighting), but this experience may be specific to our own areas of expertise and the specific production. Given that the course deliberately leaves space for students as co-designers, we found that faculty must be able to provide structure while leaving plenty of room for student input, which requires a considerable amount of planning and flexibility when the design process leads the group in new directions.

We felt the class was successful, but still have the following questions: How can we apply an ethical approach to student labor within a traditional semester or a more traditional theatre program? What types of productions best suit this high-impact model? What long-term effect might this reimagined course have for the program? And finally, what steps can we take to ensure such a model is sustainable?

Both of us have since moved on to other universities, and have consequently had the opportunity to think about how to apply this model in new settings. The approach we devised hinged on students collaborating with faculty and one another on design challenges, and this aspect is transferable to many other contexts. For example, at Arizona State University, Kristin collaborated with undergraduate and graduate students to design food elements for an edible production of Shakespeare's *Titus Andronicus* in spring 2017. Angie plans to teach a course with a colleague at St. Lawrence University in fall 2018 called "DIY Theatre" that will provide opportunities for students to collaborate with faculty on design and performance elements. In each case, treating students first as learners and collaborators within the context of high-impact teaching and learning practices helps us achieve an ethical approach to balancing pedagogical excellence with the practical demands of production.

Notes

1. Pierre Dillenbourg, "What Do You Mean by Collaborative Learning?," 1.
2. For an example on social interaction see Amy Soller, "Supporting Social Interaction in an Intelligent Collaborative Learning System."
3. Dillenbourg, "What Do You Mean by Collaborative Learning?," 5.
4. Piet Van den Bossche, Wim H. Gijselaers, Mien Segers, and Paul A. Kirschner, "Social and Cognitive Factors Driving Teamwork in Collaborative Learning Environments Team Learning Beliefs and Behaviors," 495.
5. Van den Bossche et al., "Social and Cognitive Factors," 515.
6. Van den Bossche et al., "Social and Cognitive Factors," 514.

7. See figure 2 in Amy Soller for the conversation skill taxonomy, an excellent tool to assist faculty in this process.
8. Ideas about revising theatre curriculum to include collaboration and technology can be found in Peter Zazzali and Jeanne Klein, "Toward Revising Undergraduate Theatre Education."
9. George D. Kuh and Carol Geary Schneider, *High-Impact Educational Practices: What They Are, Who Has Access to Them, and Why They Matter*, 9–11.
10. Nancy Kindelan, *Artistic Literacy*, 136.
11. The University of St. Thomas has a 2016–2017 student population of 3312 including 1814 undergraduates and 1498 graduate students. Thirty-five undergraduate majors are offered. The drama program faculty includes two fulltime and one adjunct member. More UST facts can be found at www.stthom.edu under the "About Us" tab.
12. Kuh and Schneider, *High-Impact Educational Practices*, 4, 9–11.
13. Kuh and Schneider, *High-Impact Educational Practices*, 6.
14. Kuh and Schneider, *High-Impact Educational Practices*, 10.
15. This passage was included in the *Ampersand* program notes edited by Claire McDonald, April 2015.
16. Janet Eyler, Dwight E. Giles, Christine M. Stenson, and Charlene J. Gray. *At a Glance: What We Know About the Effects of Service-Learning on College Students, Faculty, Institutions and Communities, 1993–2000*.
17. William Keep, "Business in Higher Education," and Nate Kreuter, "Customer Mentality."
18. Kuh and Schneider, *High-Impact Educational Practices*, 10.

Bibliography

Dillenbourg, Pierre. 1999. What Do You Mean by Collaborative Learning? In *Collaborative-Learning: Cognitive and Computational Approaches*, ed. P. Dillenbourg, 1–19. Oxford: Elsevier.

Eyler, Janet, Dwight E. Giles, Christine M. Stenson, and Charlene J. Gray. 2001. *At a Glance: What We Know About the Effects of Service-Learning on College Students, Faculty, Institutions and Communities, 1993–2000*. Nashville, TN: Vanderbilt University.

Keep, William. 2012. The Worrisome Ascendance of Business in Higher Education. *The Chronicle of Higher Education*, June 21. http://www.chronicle.com/article/The-Worrisome-Ascendance-of/132501/. Accessed 24 June 2017.

Kindelan, Nancy. 2014. *Artistic Literacy: Theatre Studies and a Contemporary Liberal Education*. New York: Palgrave Macmillan.

Kreuter, Nate. 2014. Customer Mentality. *Inside Higher Ed*, February 27. https://www.insidehighered.com/views/2014/02/27/essay-critiques-how-student-customer-idea-erodes-key-values-higher-education. Accessed 24 June 2017.

Kuh, George D., and Carol Geary Schneider. 2008. *High-Impact Educational Practices: What They Are, Who Has Access to Them, and Why They Matter.* Washington, DC: Association of American Colleges and Universities.

Soller, Amy. 2001. Supporting Social Interaction in an Intelligent Collaborative Learning System. *International Journal of Artificial Intelligence in Education (IJAIED)* 12: 40–62.

Van den Bossche, Piet, Wim H. Gijselaers, Mien Segers, and Paul A. Kirschner. 2006. Social and Cognitive Factors Driving Teamwork in Collaborative Learning Environments: Team Learning Beliefs and Behaviors. *Small Group Research* 37 (5): 490–521.

Zazzali, Peter, and Jeanne Klein. 2015. Toward Revising Undergraduate Theatre Education. *Theatre Topics* 25 (3): 261–276.

CHAPTER 7

Undergraduate Research

Since the founding of the University of Berlin in 1810, undergraduate research has been identified as paramount to a quality education. The university embraced the tenets of Friedrich August Wolf who asserted "research and discovery, not initiation into a closed body of knowledge, the primary goal of an academic philologist."[1] This German approach to education was not unanimously embraced, but by the time the Sigma Xi fraternity was founded in 1886, their members were identified at Cornell as "Companions in Zealous Research," and inquiry-based education had a stronghold in the United States.[2] Other significant events on the timeline of undergraduate research are National Science Foundation's (NSF) 1953 conference on undergraduate education, and Massachusetts Institute for Technology's (MIT) establishment of the Undergraduate Research Opportunities Program in 1969.[3]

Throughout the twentieth century and through the present, undergraduate research persists in being most readily identified with the sciences, for obvious reasons: the nature of collaborative laboratory work, the accessible dissemination of scientific research, and the urgency of scientific research to public health. The performing arts have always served as a site of inquiry alongside the sciences, but without the same validation in the way of funding, state sponsorship, and public recognition. Understanding creative activity as research is still contested ground, even among artists. To promote the move toward STEAM,[4] administrators and faculty need to advocate for the understanding of creative activity as research, and performing arts students involved in that creation need to value their efforts as research.

Undergraduates participating in the performing arts need to be acknowledged for their contributions to the institution's research profile. Ensembles and individuals that create plays, choreography, and compositions *are* conducting undergraduate research and we need to educate our peers in other disciplines that this is the case. This is important for equity reasons, as the perception of what "counts" as undergraduate research relates to the distribution of grant funds on and off campus. Devised original theatre performance, or original choreography and music composition are the most easily recognizable examples of undergraduate research by traditional metrics, but all theatre, dance, and music performances involve research by the entire creative team. Performances that may be understood as interpretations of already scripted, choreographed, or composed works require not only research in the theoretical sense but also "laboratory" research of trial and error, and problem-solving to identify what methods work best. Those of us in the academic performing arts fields have not found common ground in articulating how we're *always* engaging in undergraduate research with students.

The Council on Undergraduate Research (CUR) is a national non-profit founded in 1978 by chemists at liberal arts colleges to share the research they were conducting with undergraduate students. Since its founding, CUR has grown to 11,000 members at over 900 colleges, universities, and associations, representing many more disciplines beyond chemistry. Of CUR's 12 divisions, the "Arts & Humanities" is one, and the arts are represented at the annual National Conference of Undergraduate Research (NCUR), CUR's signature event with participation from around 4000 attendees annually. The NCUR's first gathering was in 1987. Happily, the performing arts are represented at the NCUR, with special dedicated sessions to showcase undergraduates' performances. At NCUR's 31st annual conference in 2017, 24 students presented in the "performing arts sessions." There are also presentations of performing arts scholarship in the more traditional format of "oral sessions," and in 2017 there were 54 of these offerings representing theatre/drama, dance, and music.[5] The NCUR publishes select juried papers from the proceedings, and NCUR's 2016 published proceedings include only two performing arts papers (one ethnography about dance from a sociological perspective, and another about environmental protest music) out of 233 published papers, and all are uploaded in pdf format, not allowing other media formats that may be more conducive to publishing the research of performing arts scholars.[6] While the inclusion of the performing arts at the NCUR is to be applauded, we still have a long way to go to address the relative disproportionate underrepresentation of the performing arts at the conference. The marked lack of performing arts at the NCUR can be explained by several factors affecting the understanding and dissemination of creative activity as research within and outside of our performing arts fields. The NCUR defines undergraduate research and its benefits on its website:

> An inquiry or investigation conducted by an undergraduate student that makes an original intellectual or creative contribution to the discipline.

What are the Benefits of Undergraduate Research?

- Enhances student learning through mentoring relationships with faculty
- Increases retention
- Increases enrollment in graduate education and provides effective career preparation
- Develops critical thinking, creativity, problem-solving, and intellectual independence
- Develops an understanding of research methodology
- Promotes an innovation-oriented culture[7]

Certainly the performing arts disciplines achieve all of the above. The NCUR is paying attention to the performing arts as evidenced by their advisory team of faculty specifically tasked with the planning of performing sessions for the conference. Additionally, the performing arts presenters are explicitly targeted in the invitation to students in the conference program to submit their work for publishing in the proceedings:

> One benefit of presenting at NCUR is the opportunity for students to publish their work in the conference proceedings, produced annually by the University of North Carolina at Asheville and distributed to institutions across the nation. All student presenters at the conference (*including students in the performing/visual arts*) [italics ours] are invited to submit manuscripts for review by the Proceedings board.[8]

This explicit invitation to performing arts presenters serves as a reminder to the students and faculty in the performing arts that we are underrepresented in such proceedings, and while it is welcomed encouragement to be called out explicitly, it is a red flag indicating our work still to do in preparing our students to articulate their creative activity as research. Why are students of the performing arts not presenting or publishing their work at the NCUR (and smaller conferences on undergraduate research) in the same numbers as students in STEM or humanities fields? Why are only 24 performing arts presentations in performance format, compared to 54 "oral sessions" in the performing arts, and of these only 2 published (among the many hundreds of presentations at the NCUR)? In answer to these questions, we must begin with the false dichotomy between theory and practice that exists within the performing arts fields. This fission persists even as particular fields have been founded on the premise that it must be collapsed in order to assert practice as theory and theory as practice (see, e.g., performance studies), and many scholars are creating work that performs research in the face of the long-standing and still fraught divides in the understanding and dissemination of our creative activity as scholarship.

This divide is mirrored in the very categories that the NCUR uses to identify the presentations: Dance Choreography and Performance, Dance History and Theory, Music, Music Performance, Theatre/Drama, Theatre/Drama Performance. This divide between theory and practice is evident in most academic performing arts curriculums, so certainly the NCUR is not responsible for this dichotomy, but merely reflecting back the proposals submitted. Even within the performing arts, there is debate among practitioners and theoreticians that are not resolved, as to what should "count" as research in our field. Those who call for a breakdown between theory and practice are most likely expected to teach in curricula that service this false dichotomy, with theory and writing classes offered as the "critical thinking" part of the major, discrete from the performance or practice courses.

The evolution of performing arts disciplines and curricula is moving toward a broad understanding of creative activity as research, but until we arrive at a "post-course" design that does away with the fallacy that all there is to learn about either theory or practice is to be taught in courses designated as such, then we are failing to educate our students about the breadth of their creative activity as research.[9] Undergraduates in the performing arts are underrepresented at such conferences because most performing arts faculty are bifurcated with their own training and how they engage in the curricula they teach. Terminal degrees in the performing arts promote this divide (DM, DMA, PHD, MFA) with each indicating a focus on theory or practice, and even in those programs that ostensibly understand performance as research, performance is often not recognized as scholarship and a written dissertation is ultimately required for the completion of study. Combine these disciplinary specializations with the difficulty of capturing and disseminating live performance media (whether through rights prohibitions, or lack of resources to attain high-quality documentation of performance on film) and we have the tricky roadblocks to broad acceptance of performance as research.

Within the performing arts fields there is not a problem with understanding theory and practice as two discrete categories with merit. However, too many refuse to understand theory and practice as a relational dialectic that in some cases collapses so as to be rendered an impractical distinction. This is a result of fear and territorialism, not an absence of creative activity asserting itself in the gray area of the theory/practice continuum. The performing arts fields are far more diverse and messy on this pole than our curricula, programs, or departments in the United States currently accommodate (with exceptions, see Northwestern Performance Studies, New York University (NYU) Tisch, and Arizona State University (ASU) Herberger for a few examples of interdisciplinary curricula that collapses the theory/practice divide). It is worth noting that the embrace of performance as research is not so uneasy in the United Kingdom, Canada, New Zealand, Australia, and numerous others countries where the higher education landscape in the performing arts does not suffer from the fraught divides between theory and practice that plague United States performing arts students and faculty.[10]

The University of Dayton has diversified their undergraduate research showcase day beyond poster presentations and traditional oral presentations of scholarship to include PechaKucha image-driven presentations, interactive porch presentations in the student neighborhood, visual art displays, and performances. And performing arts faculty are now serving on a task force to think about how the arts contribute to the institution's celebration of undergraduate scholarship. This is welcome dialogue when performing arts faculty are all too familiar with our creative scholarship going unrecognized, and facing the tenure process with trepidation as our work will be judged by peers in disciplines that only validate traditional research. Given that creative activity as research is fraught territory among even performing arts faculty, no wonder our colleagues in other disciplines are confused about how they should value our work. When we devalue entire knowledge bases in our own fields, in self-serving attempts to secure our own tenure, or protect our course offerings in acts of territorialism, then we are making civil war among the very troops that need to rally together to appropriately face this national crisis in front of us. The arts are under assault, devalued, and misunderstood in the turn toward vocational and career-ready consumerist models of education.

Missed opportunities for undergrads to present their performing arts experiences as research are unfortunately a common occurrence in many performing arts programs nationally. Within the performing arts fields, the Kennedy Center American College Theatre Festival is a place where undergrads present their research, but it is not framed in this way and instead is understood as competition-based. Students participate in hopes of receiving awards, not to get critical feedback about their creative activity as research. The American College Dance Association engages undergrads in adjudications of choreographed works, and again the focus is on competition rather than research. The College Music Society is mainly for music faculty, and even though there are student chapters, music undergrads are not often encouraged to present their research at conferences. These few examples of performing arts conferences demonstrate a common thread within our disciplines of missed opportunities to frame our students' creative output as research, and there are more. Therefore, both within and outside our closed disciplines, our undergraduates' creative activity as research is under-supported, and on a national level we can see from the most current NCUR conferences that the performing arts are underrepresented.

Overall, the national research profile of the performing arts is inconsistent, underrepresented, or unacknowledged. There are some colleges and universities where the performing arts as research has become a part of the academic culture of the institution, or where awards or grants are given to undergraduates to encourage a culture shift to normalize creative activity as research (see Vanderbilt, Michigan State, Drexel, Northwestern, Ohio State, and Virginia Commonwealth for some examples). And the new peer-reviewed journal of Performance as Research, *PARtake*, indicates a promising shift in the scholarship of Performance as Research (PAR), wherein the editors promote the term "scholartist" in hopes that it will take hold as a positionality of scholars/artists as they frame their creative activity as scholarship.[11] *PARtake*, and similar efforts, will influence "scholartists" to incorporate undergraduate research in the performing arts as part of their regular practice, and this trickle-down effect will begin to change performing arts curricula, and undergraduate experiences.

A silver lining of the recent turn to vocational training may be the space the upset opens for considering and valuing other modes of scholarship and educational models beyond traditional research approaches. Certainly the interest in experiential learning serves the performing arts. Similarly, when traditional education approaches, like the college essay, are being called into question as the most viable means to educate our students in required coursework, other means of presenting knowledge are being considered as more practical and meaningful to students' acquiring of knowledge.[12] This is a fertile climate to plant the seeds of creative activity as research, to advocate for the value of the arts as a part of a liberal arts education, and to provide students with research opportunities that appeal to those wary of the ivory tower focus on traditional written scholarship.

The much written-about millennial student has been found, namely in the Stanford Study of Writing, to engage in writing more than generations of students before them, only in significantly more performative forms that play with the representation of identity on multiple media platforms.[13] The Conference on College Composition and Communication has called for writing (read undergraduate research) to embrace non-traditional approaches, including artistic approaches.[14] To consider performance as research is to understand the contingency of knowledge, and to question objectivity. Undergraduates are inclined to consider published works as infallible, but can readily understand knowledge as positional and partial when it is embodied in their own creative activity.

The act of devising original work in theatre, dance, or music employs all the steps of more traditionally understood laboratory research and intellectual inquiry, but perhaps with fewer preconceptions, as Beth Watkins describes about the value of devising:

> Typically, academic researchers define the question they seek to answer, or the problem they wish to address, early in their investigation. For practice-based researchers, however, this is rarely the case. ... The traditional researcher tries to narrow and contain an argument. In practice-based research, reflexivity makes problem-formation necessarily messy and difficult.[15]

Another benefit of original works as undergraduate research is the dovetailing with an entrepreneurial perspective that can empower students to create and disseminate their creative output with the dynamics of the economies of artistic practice at the forefront of their experience. Now is the time to promote the performing arts as training ground for performing arts majors and non-majors to gain the skill-sets needed for creative industries and cultivate cultural literacy by engaging in performance as research.

The case studies in this chapter explore both the theory and practice of undergraduate research. Kathy L. Privatt describes how engaging students in a dramaturgy project of their own choice has been a fruitful model of individual research. Malaika Sarco-Thomas illustrates the benefits of integrating theory and practice in a dance project that gives undergraduates the framework in which to pursue their own research project.

Call to action:

- Administrators must advocate for tenure and promotion guidelines that fairly recognize the creative activity of faculty as research, and performing arts faculty must ensure that representation on tenure and promotion committees includes performing arts faculty whenever possible.
- Performing arts faculty need to get on the same page (forgive the logo-centric privileging) about what constitutes creative scholarship and advocate for one another by lifting up the creative activity of our colleagues and our students as viable research.
- Performing arts faculty must see to it that creative activity by performing arts students is showcased at events touting the research profile of their institution.
- Performing arts faculty need to bring more intentional presentation by undergraduates of creative activity as research to their discipline's professional conferences and organizations.
- Performing arts faculty and students must utilize the performing arts to solve problems in our local communities. Engaging students in devising original performances that necessitate their integration of knowledge across disciplines and utilize their liberal arts training in dynamic ways ensures that others will be able to recognize the value of creative activity as research and service to the community.
- Performing arts faculty need to encourage students to present interdisciplinary performing arts research at non-performing arts conferences (the NCUR and others). This will mean a culture shift: if your

students are only accustomed to interpretation and have never undertaken the challenge of creating interdisciplinary original work (adaptation, devising, choreographing, composing), there will be a period of pushback as students may fail to recognize that being content creators is a legitimate pursuit in obtaining a performing arts degree (regardless of Bachelor of Arts vs. Bachelor of Fine Arts majors). Expect pushback, not just from performing arts majors, but also from faculty who don't want the pressure of bringing new audiences to their work, who are wary of "agendas," and may be hostile to the idea that the performing arts needs to be legitimized by interdisciplinary inquiry to be valued (to name a few of the common resistances to evolving curricula and pedagogy in the performing arts).

- Performing arts faculty need to work with librarians, information technology departments, media and communication departments (academic and institutional), CUR, and learning/teaching centers to democratize methods of dissemination, so that creative activity in the performing arts can be appropriately archived (where not prohibited by copyright, another benefit of devising original works) and shared. This also includes acquiring resources particularly valuable to the performing arts, like high-quality performance films and subscriptions to media services. If our libraries (both the stacks and electronic resources) dissuade performing arts students from acknowledging their research as legitimate, the cycle continues. A common problem: performing arts students cannot easily search for plays and music, or locate a play collection in one place.[16]

- Performing arts faculty should not choose their production seasons in a vacuum. Pay attention to university mission, campus initiatives, invited speakers, symposia, or conferences, and consider ways your season offerings could collaborate with other units to create complementary programming (common intellectual experiences) and co-sponsorships. We have the opportunity to connect dots in an energizing and embodied way that students and colleagues can find illuminating and refreshing. Show your community how creative activity is research by demonstrating your valuable contributions to a larger campus initiative.

RESEARCH: DIGESTING CREATIVE FOOD

Kathy L. Privatt
Lawrence University
Appleton, WI, USA

In *Five High-Impact Practices: Research On Learning Outcomes, Completion, and Quality* by Brownell and Swaner, undergraduate research is characterized as a pedagogy that is becoming more widespread across institution types, but was spurred by and originated in the sciences.[17] While this sequence makes logical sense to me, particularly since research is the public face of the sciences, I would argue that research is the center of the creative heart of theatre as it is taught at colleges and universities. Whether it leads to a creative choice or impels one in reaction, research starts the work that results in our public face: the performance. At the small liberal arts college where I teach, research as dramaturgy is the major project in our theatre literature and history class sequence, and supports our departmental mission to engage students as theatre-makers.

The Dramaturgy Project assigned to all students in Theatre Traditions I and II at Lawrence University (LU) fulfills the definition/parameters put forth for high-impact undergraduate research: discovery-based, original creative activity that contributes new knowledge to the discipline.[18] The assignment involves choosing a play, researching that work, developing a suggested approach to studying or producing that play, and presenting that approach to the class. In more detail, the assignment is structured as follows: Each student chooses a play, musical, or opera not read for class, but written within the time period covered by the class. Once their choice is approved, they research two major categories of information: The Play in History and The Play as Text. Researching The Play in History includes investigating the playwright's biography for elements that might affect their writing, looking for common style elements and themes in other plays by the same author, locating or developing a production history (including revivals) of the chosen play, locating reviews and critical responses to the play, and considering theatrical developments contemporary with the writing of the play (and assuming shared class knowledge). The Play as Text includes researching Stanislavsky's given circumstances with an expanded understanding of that concept to include aspects such as economic forces, and political and religious thought within the play; the world around the play when it was written to consider its cultural background; and then analyzing the text for meaning and ideas contained or referenced, both in the play's own time as well as now, and grounding that analysis in textual evidence. The next step of the project is developing an approach to the play. Students are instructed to synthesize their research as creative "food," and propose what we should pay attention to in the chosen play, whether for study or for a production. Their default perspective is as a theatre generalist, but students may choose to frame their approach as a particular theatre artist (e.g., costume designer). As they write their approach, they are instructed to articulate the influential sources that fed that approach, even if the sources influenced by pushing the student in the opposite direction. The final product of the Dramaturgy Project is multi-part. Each student produces a notebook of all the materials they gathered and produced, including notes they took, research dead-ends they encountered, and their approach statement with the influential sources identified. Each student posts a synopsis of their chosen script (either original or appropriately cited) and a bibliography of their sources on Moodle (an online learning platform), making it available to all members of the class. Each student also creates two collages to explore or explicate the world of the play (researched as Given Circumstances) and the world at the time the play was written (researched as Cultural Background). The student presents those two collages to their classmates to guide them through their creative analysis as support for their proposed approach to the play. The class documents what they understood to be the approach offered, as well as key ideas or images. Those comments, as well as a grading rubric I use that covers both the notebook and the presentation, are given to the student as feedback in addition to a letter grade.

I have been using this basic assignment, with ongoing modifications, since 2005.[19] I substituted this Dramaturgy Project for a more traditional research paper option as a better match for the goals of the department mission statement that stresses the creation of theatre-makers, as this project requires the type of research necessary for all theatre artists as well as the resulting visual choices and oral communication of that research. When considering the learning objectives I had identified for this assignment, I noted the congruence between my observations, George Kuh's assessment of high-impact practices, and the general outcomes already measured in previous studies of Undergraduate Research assembled by Brownell and Swaner. Kuh includes the inherent interactions between a student, their peers, and faculty; first-hand knowledge of faculty strategies for "the inevitable challenges that crop up in the course of an investigation";[20] and the potential for a work that "can also be a springboard for connecting learning to the world beyond the campus."[21] Applicable outcomes that have been measured in previous studies of Undergraduate Research as high-impact practice include increased persistence, and improvement in written and oral communication skills, problem-solving, and critical thinking.[22] While my observations haven't risen to the level of a study, the data I've tracked does suggest similar results. The Brownell and Swaner study also noted the lack (at the time of writing the report) of discipline-specific outcomes measured.[23] In addition, I have embedded a theatre-specific outcome in this assignment that is best articulated by Nancy Kindelan, in her book *Artistic Literacy*. In a discussion of signature pedagogies, Kindelan describes the "unique, nonverbal language of theatre," coming from in-depth script analysis "within the frame of its historical context or by going beyond the traditional modes of inquiry" that facilitates seeing "how complexity and ambiguity contribute to cultural dispositions and social values." That language is composed of the "artful physical and visual images that evoke additional thought about the play's meaning and emotional content."[24] This Dramaturgy Assignment combines a research-based approach to script analysis with a final product of images thoughtfully chosen to reflect what the student chooses to express through and with that play. Again, my observations are just that at this point, but reveal a close match to this signature pedagogy that Kindelan translates into skills employers desire in the workplace[25] as well as the ability to make actionable connections to the world that Kuh puts forth as the ultimate goal of education.[26] In what follows, I use my learning outcomes as the framework to consider those measured in previous studies, and then consider an additional learning outcome that further supports the value of individual research.

Outcome 1—synthesize research to choose visual images to represent ideas—provides evidence of critical thinking, problem-solving, and oral presentation skills.[27] This outcome arose from the LU Department of Theatre Arts learning objectives to (a) integrate research to support creative choices and (b) synthesize cultural history. In the most recent iteration of the Theatre Traditions class, I found 1 student's set of collages that included images for all but two of the ideas presented, offering a clear opportunity for me to confirm the critical thinking that led to the representation of all the other ideas and to guide the student to a complete set of images to strengthen the presentation. I also found 6 presentations (out of 21 total) that spent a significant amount of time on a topic, but either didn't have an image paired to an idea or didn't tie the topic to the approach. The feedback to the students then guided them to use the assignment requirement like a two-way street: If the idea is important to the approach, find and use an image in one of the required collages. If the idea isn't important to the student's approach, leave it out of the presentation. Thus, the assignment requirements help students tackle the problem of the "favorite idea" that is superfluous to the central point of their communication. Perhaps surprisingly, this aspect of the assignment also teaches the necessity of persistence. After receiving their feedback, two of those six students approached me and "confessed" to failing to spend the time needed to fully complete the assignment. Overall, the project offers me clear information about where students are on the synthesize-information-through-critical-thinking-and-problem-solving scale versus the check-requirements-off-the-list approach that implies an absence of co-creation of new knowledge and more reliance on re-presentation of others' work.[28]

Outcome 2—synthesize research into a creative approach to the play, musical, or opera—also addresses the departmental learning objective of integrating research to support creative choices and identifies a discipline-specific outcome worth pursuing in a more formal study. This aspect of the assignment is the most recent modification, and was inspired by Nancy Kindelan's book, *Artistic Literacy*. As mentioned above, Kindelan describes theatre's unique linguistic goal to "transfer a play's historical, social and psychological ideas into the unique, nonverbal language of theatre—artful physical and visual images that evoke additional thought about the play's meaning and emotional content," and I realized that the Dramaturgy Project was stopping short of requiring this final stage of thinking, but was designed in a way that positioned students, even those without previous theatre experience, to effectively create an approach.[29] I had noticed some students choosing to add that focus to their presentations, and expanded that to an expectation of all students. In ways appropriate to a sophomore-level class, the requirement asks students to engage their ability to bridge scholarly research to creative choices. Out of 21 students in the most recent class, only 2 didn't include an approach statement in their presentation and notebook. This particular class was composed more heavily of theatre majors and minors than usual, with only two not in those categories, and they self-reported significant theatre experiences in their background. However, the successful percentage supports this requirement as an achievable objective. I find this result particularly gratifying, since several students have used the Dramaturgy Project as their first analysis of a play that they go on to propose for production as a Senior Experience.[30] Obviously, at that level, the synthesis of research into creative approaches is key for the overall department goal of creating theatre-makers.

Outcome 3—communicate main ideas orally and comprehend them aurally—fits neatly within improved communication skills,[31] and supports the departmental objective of integrating research into creative choices in a very pragmatic way. All students, when not presenting, are given feedback forms that ask them to record the approach as they heard it, as well as any key ideas or images. Students consistently identified those few who didn't include an approach in their presentation. Some recorded question marks in the space for Approach, and others recorded one of the key ideas with question marks in that space. I also observed that approaches that were short phrases, even sound bites, were reported most consistently, but I'm not planning to guide students toward that structure at this point as it is sometimes harder to let ideas evolve if a phrase chosen early ceases to fit. Students also frequently included some sort of self-identifier on the response form, despite the lack of a request for their names. I left the forms anonymous to encourage clear observations rather than "nice comments," but perhaps this isn't needed since other department courses don't use anonymous feedback. At this point, given the appropriate, observation-driven comments offered, anonymity is inconsequential to my concerns.

Outcome 4—engage in an analysis process that considers a variety of sources to draw conclusions—supports the benefits noticed from the increased interactions with faculty and peers as part of the individual research process, including knowledge of faculty research methods and ongoing self-reflection.[32] This outcome also aligns with the departmental objective to interrogate a text. The very structure of the assignment expands the contact with me, Library teaching staff, and the student's colleagues. In the second week of the term, the class meets with a Reference Librarian to explore resources to address parts of the Dramaturgy Project assignment using a play that all have read. The Reference Librarian uses that assignment to divide the students into groups and assign specific resources for them to investigate. The groups bring their findings back to the whole class to share, and that information then shapes further discussions of the play at the next class session. I approve each student's play choice prior to the meeting, and they are encouraged to schedule individual research appointments with the Reference Librarian as they work on their projects. The Digital Collections Librarian visits the class later in the term to walk them through finding images to match with the ideas they want to share. That session is also preceded by a jointly read play and class time spent creating a list of idea-linked images they're interested in pursuing that I forward to the librarian prior to the class session. Because the list is generated by the whole class, students see the potential rewards of more open-ended searches that can reveal or expose unconsidered directions in the text. The librarian uses that list to take the students through useful image sources, and then offers to do searches based on their individual projects also. At a halfway point in the due-date timeline, each student has an individual meeting with me to report on their findings so far and discuss any roadblocks. I also sometimes offer additional resources to consider or another line of inquiry for exploration, particularly if they've missed a standard source. At present, I simply use the assignment sheet as a guide to the discussion, but find a number of students who haven't made progress yet at that point. While having each student walk through the assignment as a check-off list at that meeting might increase compliance with the planned timeline, this might sabotage the self-directed agency embedded in this individual research project. After each presentation, students can ask questions or comment on what they heard. While not required, this is an additional avenue of communication, and is sometimes taken up informally as students leave the classroom, even in the absence of questions during class. Finally, students are given the rubric I use for grading when they receive the initial assignment, I reference it at each individual meeting, and then students receive their grade with the comments on that rubric. Interactions are both required and encouraged as an inherent part of this assignment, and students reflect on their research work at multiple points through the class, as well as after presenting it to the class.

An additional outcome Brownell and Swaner identified from summer research opportunities examined professional development skills as including understanding of one's self and capabilities.[33] This outcome also seems a likely gain from the Dramaturgy Assignment, based on my observations. The final step of the research process is developing an approach to the chosen play, musical, or opera. This step requires students to individually digest their research, and present it to their peers, and sometimes even to a peer who has chosen the same play. By design, and by allowing more than one student to choose any given play, the project acknowledges the personal in the scholarly/creative process, and the resulting projects vary in approach, confirming the individual approach to synthesis. Sometimes the approach is content- or idea-related, such as revenge as cyclical and endless in an English Renaissance play or pushing the boundaries of etiquette to explore hypocrisy in a Comedy of Manners. Other approaches are more related to structure or style, such as focusing on the Commedia dell'Arte aspects of a script because the social and political ideas don't translate well or viewing an Elizabethan play as a RomCom structure. Occasionally, the approach takes a highly personal turn, such as a focus on the fairies in the script by a student deeply interested in Celtic culture.[34] All of these approaches reveal something of the artist in the art, even at this early stage in a creative venture, and perhaps even more significantly, support the creative nature of individual research, even outside the arts.

Ironically, the potential for an additional learning objective with wide reach, beyond the world of the theatre, occurred to me as I worked on my own dramaturgical research for a production of *Gint*, by Romulus Linney. Linney sets Ibsen's *Peer Gynt* in Appalachia, so I was immersing myself in the region and found a book titled *Appalachia in the Classroom: Teaching the Region*, edited by Burriss and Gantt. In the Introduction, Burriss writes about the "value of place-based education" as it develops "cultural awareness and sensitivity," and lists categories of influences and circumstances that define a region.[35] I stopped reading, and just sat for a moment. That list was a close match for the categories of inquiry I use for the expanded Given Circumstances, as well as Cultural Background. The Dramaturgy Project requires searching for and investigating sources of information on the influences and circumstances within the world of the play as well as the world that surrounded the playwright at the time of writing. The students are acquiring skills to learn about places and cultures different from their own, and sometimes, dependent on the play chosen, their own. Granted, one of those worlds is fictionalized (to varying degrees), but I would hypothesize that the "fiction" holds additional learning "magic." Playwrights have frequently chosen another time or location to set a story that is actually critiquing the here and now (e.g., think *The Crucible* by Arthur Miller). Conventional wisdom says the setting creates a distance that lets us encounter challenging ideas in a less threatening way. Perhaps a play, by virtue of its status as fiction, can help us see past our bias-induced blind spots and societal politeness to really consider the information revealed about a place or a culture, and critically examine the source of that information. If I view this dramaturgy research assignment as place-based education more commonly pursued in other academic departments, will that reveal additional tools and resources for students to develop "cultural awareness and sensitivity?" And how will I know if they do? That will be the focus of my next iteration of this individual research project.

I openly admit that the Dramaturgy Project is one of my favorite assignments. The student projects are endlessly interesting for the very reasons cited above: they have chosen a play and invested in it (sometimes one I've never read); they have taken an individualized trip down the research path I've outlined and produced results influenced by their perceptions and understandings; they have translated that information and analysis into visual images arranged to support their approach to the work; they have shared those creative ideas with all of us in the room as colleagues and responded to each other as colleagues as well. The projects are always unique in some ways, built on theatre traditions in some ways, offer some new knowledge of that particular play, musical, or opera in some ways, and sometimes even result in a production. A theatre-maker needs research to feed their creative heart, and I would hypothesize that this Dramaturgy Project is effectively promoting the skills and approaches necessary for that incorporation. With further investigation, I may also hypothesize that acquiring individual research skills appropriate for theatre-makers changes the way students connect to their world.

QUESTIONING THROUGH DOING: SHAPING PRAXIS THROUGH THE INDIVIDUAL DANCE PROJECT

Malaika Sarco-Thomas
University of Malta
Msida, Malta

Introduction

How might flow theory explain dancers' experience of technique class? Can auditory learning stimulate a deeper understanding of tap dance? How does "play" build group cohesion in improvisation? These and other questions can spark undergraduate dance research.[36]

Artistic research at the undergraduate level creates an opportunity for students to exercise a range of skills as scholars, facilitators, and performers. This case study will look at the Individual Dance Project (IDP) as integral to the Bachelor (Honors) in Dance Studies course offered by the University of Malta's School of Performing Arts as an example of high-impact teaching where students are guided and challenged to build unique projects which investigate a phenomenon in both theory and practice. Inspired by the current of practice-led performance research that began to gather force in the United Kingdom in the 1990s, IDP emphasizes skills in reflective practice and facilitation, preparing students for critical thinking and creative action in work and postgraduate study. This chapter gives examples of student projects that imaginatively drew on individual curiosities to show how systematic discovery can strengthen self-awareness via praxis: artistic practice as research.

Dance Studies in higher education has taken upon itself the task of closing a perceived gap between thinking and doing in performance.[37] Proponent of Practice as Research (PaR), Robin Nelson, points out that the uneasy relationship between the university and the performing arts conservatoire has been expressed in the dichotomy of "university = academic, research criteria, theory; conservatoire = practitioner, aesthetic criteria, practice,"[38] which in recent years is challenged through the mergers of a number of conservatoires with academic institutions. Reference can be made to Dwight Conquergood's observation that for practice to be valued properly, performance disciplines have a duty to resist "the deeply entrenched division of labor, apartheid of knowledges, that plays out inside the academy as the difference between thinking and doing, interpreting and making, conceptualization and creativity."[39] As a step toward integration of theory and practice, abstraction and embodiment, doing studio-based dance research is an opportunity for movers to articulate their own experiences of dancing, and to value this in dialogue with scholars and artists in the field.

Background

The University of Malta's IDP sits at the start of the final year of a three-year Bachelor Dance Studies course. Its two parts: IDP Essay and IDP Presentation, balance one another (each represents five European Credit Transfer System [ECTS][40] credits) in line with the interweaving of practice and theory at the core of the course's ethos. Students choose a problem in dance that interests them, and which can be investigated both in theory (tested by the essay) and in practice (tested by a lecture demonstration on the outcomes of a series of workshops the student facilitates, and a viva or oral exam). The study unit prepares dancers for research at postgraduate level, particularly within the climate of dance practice as research as it has developed recently in Europe and the United Kingdom. Inspired by the interventions of the Practice as Research in Performance (PARIP) group based at Bristol University in the 1990s, which sought to usefully blur the distinction between professional and scholarly practice,[41] conducting research through practice has gained footing within higher education institutions. Today PaR is a key mode of valuing performing arts' contributions to academia, and the practice-based MA and PhD are rapidly growing arts-specific forms of postgraduate study.[42]

Literature produced by PARIP identifies a number of qualifiers for performance research, which are translated into IDP: (1) posing a clear and pertinent research question, (2) identifying a systematic mode for investigating this question through reading and through doing, or physical practice, (3) analyzing the collection of data in order to shed light on the original question.[43] In her reflections on methodologies for PaR, Melissa Trimingham[44] acknowledges the unpredictability and characteristic messiness of the creative process, noting that in this field, methodologies of performance research will vary, but a systematic mode of enquiry should be revisited regularly in order to shed light on the topic. She acknowledges that an historical enquiry can offer a useful context for a practice-based research topic, as can a mixture of a hermeneutic method (the self-reflective spiral) and logical, post-positivist modes of thinking (identifying clear aims and objectives to tackle a specific problem). To this end, Donald Schön's reflective practice, Graham Gibb's reflective cycle, and Kurt Lewin's Action Research methods can offer useful processes through which to investigate practice. A literature review pertaining to the phenomena and to the chosen theoretical framework should always be used to give context to the enquiry. Finally, analysis via mixed methods, or a grounded theory approach, can aid in the comprehension of data by identifying key "terms," "categories," or "codes" by which to draw conclusions and connections back to the original research question.

Delivery

Rather than "taught," IDP is guided through a series of four lectures on research methods in the arts: (1) Doing Dance Research: Questions and Methodologies; (2) Reflective Practice and Action Research for Dance; (3) Ethics in Dance Research; and (4) Analyzing and Presenting Dance

Research Data. Action Research and reflective practice encourage students to take an active role in reconsidering the effectiveness of their methods of delivery from one workshop to the next, and a spiral mode of discovery through planning, acting, observing, reflecting, revising the plan, acting, observing and reflecting again, and so on,[45] is used to understand processes of research through practice (see Fig. 7.1).

Students are introduced to qualitative and quantitative data-collection instruments such as questionnaires, focus group discussions, semi-structured interviews, participant observation, drawing, photography, and video. These lectures segue into weekly tutorials for individual students. At the end of their second year, students submit a proposal for a topic that can be investigated both in theory and in practice; this is often something which has been touched on in the first two years of study but crucially relates to the student's own interests. A tutor then advises each individual in the gathering of research materials for the essay, and the designing of 3–6 workshops for 2–10 participants. An ethics statement is also completed in order to prepare for the recruitment of participants. Many students choose to work with other Dance Studies or Performing Arts students, while others may test a specific subject group, such as non-dancers, professional dancers, young people, Belly dancers, or Hip Hop dancers. It is important to note that we see IDP as sitting separately from the Dissertation, which is necessarily a very different topic and focus. However, the methods exercised in IDP may be applied to the larger scale dissertation project if desired. Studio space and time is made available for students to plan and conduct their workshops.

Importantly, IDP builds on dance science research skills formed in year one and two through projects such as the Individual Fitness Plan (IFP) in the Healthier Performer study unit, wherein a dancer identifies an area (e.g., upper body strength, mental attitudes toward training) they wish to develop and then design and undertake a bespoke practice schedule to target this. The IFP is designed with tutorial support, where scholarly articles inform the content, frequency, and application of chosen exercises, and before and after photos (or equivalent means of testing one's degree of fitness in the chosen area) are analyzed to show evidence of change.

Examples

At year three, the IDP offers a greater scope for creativity and investigation of individual concerns. Defining one's research question is the central

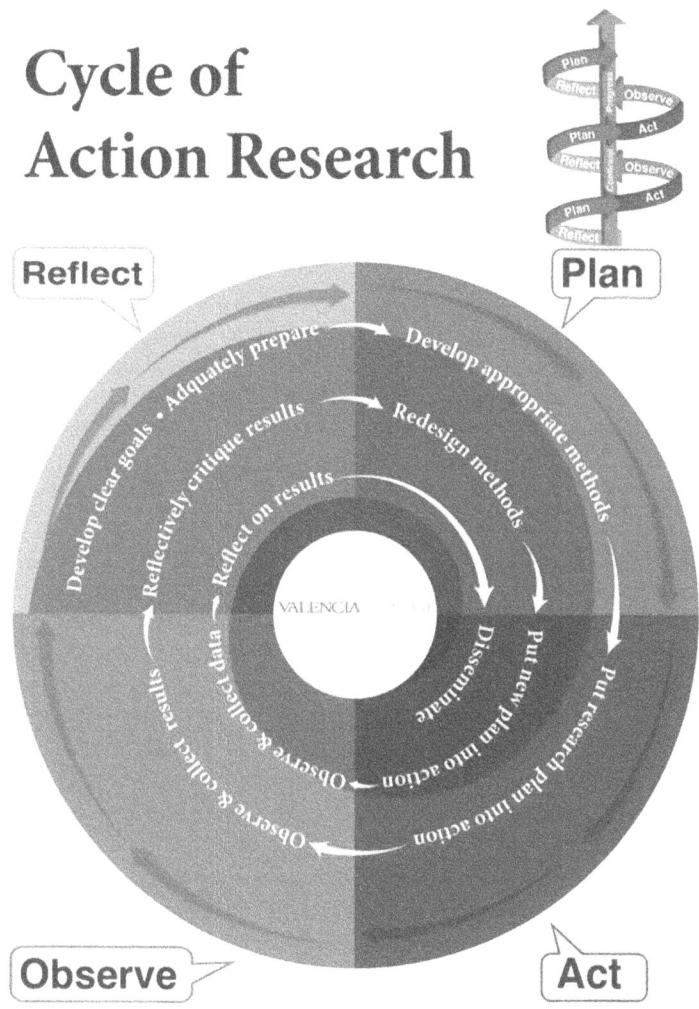

Fig. 7.1 Cycle of action research. Image: Valencia College

challenge of IDP, and articulating this at proposal stage is fundamental to the project's success. Students may either seek to identify a theory that can be tested in practical experimentation, or to take an aspect of personal experience and set up a means of examining this. An example of the theory-into-practice approach might be working with Rudolf Laban's effort theory, which describes movement as a combination of dynamics rooted in "states" and "drives," and investigating this with regard to processes of composing narrative solo dances. Shanon Deguara used Niel Fleming's visual, aural, read/write, kinesthetic (VARK) learning theories[46] to identify effective practices in tap dance pedagogy with regard to incorporating auditory methods in teaching a set British Theatre Dance Association (BTDA) syllabus, and furthermore compared these with the divergent discovery style identified by Elizabeth Gibbons in *Teaching Dance: The Spectrum of Styles*. The essay paved the way for her investigation of how student-centered learning can be encouraged via auditory methods in tap. Mihaly Csikszentmihalyi's theory of flow may be used to understand dancers' experiences of engagement throughout a learning process, as in Rochelle Gatt's project. This approach of investigating a theory through practice is indicated in the white areas of the chart below.

Another route is to identify a phenomenon of practice and develop a more holistic understanding of this through multi-modal research. Examples of this kind of project include: questioning the relationship between cross-disciplinary arts practices such as drawing and dance-making, investigating the therapeutic effects of Authentic Movement for dancers, and researching connections between rhythm, musicality and emotion for disabled people. This approach of practice-into-multi-modal-research is identified in the gray areas of the chart.

Selected IDP essay and presentation topics are below. In some cases the title/question remains the same throughout the project, and in some cases the essay and presentation have a slightly different focus, when the application of theory to the practice has led into a somewhat new area for discussion (see Figs. 7.2 and 7.3).

Assessment

IDP is assessed in terms of students' ability to choose an appropriate topic, relate theory with practice, design and carry out a multi-pronged research project, locate their research within artistic and scholarly discourse, problem-solve, reflect upon the findings and limitations of the project,

Essay	Presentation	Student
Pick-up, Shuffle Wing Toe-tap. An examination of the possibility of using multiple learning and teaching styles during a tap dance class for teenagers. Apart from visuals, how can auditory learning be incorporated into dance cognition?		Shanon Deguara, 2015
Fragmentation of Expression and the Expression of Fragmentation: Juxtaposing Bausch and de Keersmaeker's Choreographic Methods		Anna Armato, 2017
Raving Mad: social, somatic and psychological experiences of dance in contemporary clubbing with special reference to neo-tribalism as a framework for shared understanding of ritual		Shlomit Weidenfeld, 2016
Embodied drawing: How can flow in improvisational practice influence a practitioner's mindset and a fluidity of creative expression in dancing and drawing?	Finding flow in dance improvisation and drawing: applying principles of automatic drawing to develop creativity and expression across art forms	Eszter Joo, 2017
"The feeling of joy": Facilitating experiences of flow in dance technique classes	"The feeling of joy" : Facilitating experiences of flow in classes of Contact Improvisation, Gaga and Contemporary Technique	Rochelle Gatt, 2015
Feeling Vibrations: the Music and the Dance	Emotional Impacts of Music, Rhythm and Vibrations on Dancers' Experiences of Improvisation	Rachel Calleja, 2015
How can creative dance positively affect study/work-related stress and be a tool for self-expression?	Analyzing the positive effects of creative movement and Authentic Movement in relation to stress and self image through the case study of "Dance for Ease"	Blanka Fekete, 2017
Therapeutic dance for people with dementia symptoms and Alzheimer's disease, and those with Parkinson's disease: physical and psychological benefits	Dance facilitation approaches for the elderly: a case study comparing work with adults with dementia, and adults with Parkinson's Disease	Natalie Muschamp, 2017
Facilitating Play: How can movement and improvisation override creative inhibition?	Using Play within Group Improvisation to Encourage Empowerment and Creativity	Marie Keiser-Nielsen, 2017
Facilitating Improvisation: Towards Empowerment and Creativity in Performance: Exploring Belly Dance and Contact Improvisation within a Cultural Context	Facilitating Empowerment and Creativity in Performance: Bringing Contact Improvisation Skills to Belly Dance Training	Yasmin Falzon, 2017

Fig. 7.2 Selected IDP topics, University of Malta, 2015–2017

Fig. 7.3 "Contact improvisation skills for bellydance" IDP workshop. Photo by Yasmin Falzon

and communicate their findings through an 3500-word essay, a 15-minute lecture demonstration, and a 15-minute viva. Students should be encouraged to take risks, and to question their findings in relation to initial hypotheses and theoretical frameworks in order to "arrive at thoughtful, well-supported conclusions."[47] Because the essay is handed in several weeks prior to the workshop series, it should provide a sound foundation for practical research, including an historical, terminological, and theoretical context for the study to be conducted. Based on their written research, students design workshops and data-collection methods appropriate to the scope of the topic.

The most satisfying IDPs integrate practice and theory in unexpected yet rigorous ways, and offer clear applications for students' future practice in teaching, choreography, or group facilitation. Rachel Calleja's project on rhythm, for example, has informed her subsequent work as dance coordinator for Opening Doors, a performing group for adults with learning disabilities in Malta, whereby the theories investigated have brought about inroads into movement creation that taps into emotion and shared experience within the group. Marie Keiser-Nielsen brought her working knowledge as a theatre director to be tested during a series of improvisation-based sessions with secondary school children in Malta, in order to see how "play" as a theory and teaching approach develops group cohesion, creativity, and empowerment in a devising process. Eszter Joo investigated

Fig. 7.4 "Embodied drawing" IDP workshop. Photo by Eszter Joo

her passion for illustration and improvisation by seeing how an automatic drawing process impacted dancers' readiness to make creative leaps within improvisational tasks. Her project pushed her to find definitions of creativity across art forms and look for these characteristics within cross-disciplinary examples of studio work (see Fig. 7.4).

Ways In

At the undergraduate level, the IDP is not attempting to develop new theories from scratch, but students are encouraged to test the validity of established theories to areas of their interest, or to seek a new perspective on an experienced phenomenon by linking it with an existing theoretical framework. These two approaches can be considered first as theory-into-practice, and second as practice-into-theory. The shape of the study unit, in which the essay is produced first, offers a kind of hybrid of the two approaches. Theory informs the development of the workshops, and reflection informs the analysis of the workshop findings, to the degree that the successful project will expand upon or articulate the original theory in new ways as a result of the dance experience.

Toward the first method, Penelope Hanstein outlines a number of useful ways that theories can inform, and be formed by, dance research in the chapter "Models and Metaphors: Theories and the Creation of New Knowledge" in *Researching Dance: Evolving Modes of Enquiry*. Toward the second method, a dancer can work with a tacit, embodied artistic knowledge, experience, intuition, or a hunch—for example, the sense of finding cohesive sense of musicality or "groove" within dance improvisation practice—to identify elements that define and characterize such an event, and in order to articulate such a phenomena in light of existing theory. Toward the second mode of research where theory is used to make sense of practice, IDP can be a process of articulating the "expert intuitive processes"[48] a dancer already possesses, while also developing their artistic, organizational, facilitatory, and analytical skills.

Skills

Aesthetic and analytic skills both featured in Anna Armato's 2017 project "Fragmentation of Expression and the Expression of Fragmentation," which applied contrasting approaches from Pina Bausch's, and Anne Teresa De Keersmaeker's choreographic strategies, as identified through Nietzschean aesthetic principles, in order to see how composition can convey Apollonian and Dionysian qualities of individual dancers within a group. The systematic nature of the workshop series, which generated material from performers' emotional memories and then worked with repetition, isolation, and juxtaposition of contrasting dynamic moments among the group's movement, demonstrated the application of two methods of modifying and directing movement material. Its outcome was a four-minute group choreography, framed by a lecture. The next layer of questioning within the project asked how such methods might highlight the opposing forces of order and emotion within an aesthetic product, and a further direction for research was identified in how such systematic approaches to isolating and reconstructing qualities such as "frenzied," "ecstatic," "buoyant," and "dejected" with different body parts can enable a dancer to understand the subtle physical initiations of emotion-based movement.

Owning such processes develops the skills of the dance student as researcher, facilitator, reflective practitioner, and communicator. The problems set by the project brief to "question, research, discuss, and test a problem or phenomenon of interest to you in your experience of dance"[49] encourage valuing the dancer's visceral experience as inherently worthy of research. At the same time, students exercise their ability to identify, apply, and analyze modes of thinking and working through dance. This is in line with the planning, doing, observing, and analyzing stages of reflective practice and Action Research, whereby new insights are articulated at each level.

Praxis

As Nelson points out, the value of a performance praxis as research is always in terms of the "insights" offered in relation to criteria by which it is judged, whether that be public audiences who witness its presentation or the scholars who assess its relevance to the field.[50] Because IDP students articulate their own aims for their project, they exercise a degree of control over how it is seen, understood, and evaluated. To this end, performance-making is understood as a key mode of knowing in IDP.

Melrose's testament to performance-making as an "expert intuitive" mode of knowing problematizes the perceived worthiness of written versus performance outcomes within academia. Recent years have seen an expanded use of the term praxis in the performing arts in higher education as a way of identifying knowledge generated by practice imbricated with theory. Robin Nelson expands on this through his multi-mode model for PaR epistemology in arts praxis. Drawing on Gilbert Ryle's influential terminology to discuss dance, Nelson identifies artistic knowledge as "know-how" or the insider's embodied knowledge of dance-making; "know-what" or critical reflection on the artistic tools of composition, methods, terms, and processes which "work"; and finally "know-that," defined as an outsider's knowledge of how something can be theorized, discussed, or framed[51] (see Fig. 7.5).

Praxis is evidenced in projects that develop a workable method for facilitating a dance process, in a way that such methods can be named and considered in terms of the aesthetic and experiential effects they provoke. Marie Keiser-Nielsen expanded her "know-how" as a theatre facilitator by investigating "pedagogies of creativity" as routes for developing group collaboration as a form of "know-that," and finally gathering "know-what" in terms of a series of exercises that worked to develop camaraderie, risk-taking, and enthusiasm among her young participants. As a result of the IDP, her practical knowledge of group improvisation deepened through reflecting on applications of creative pedagogy.

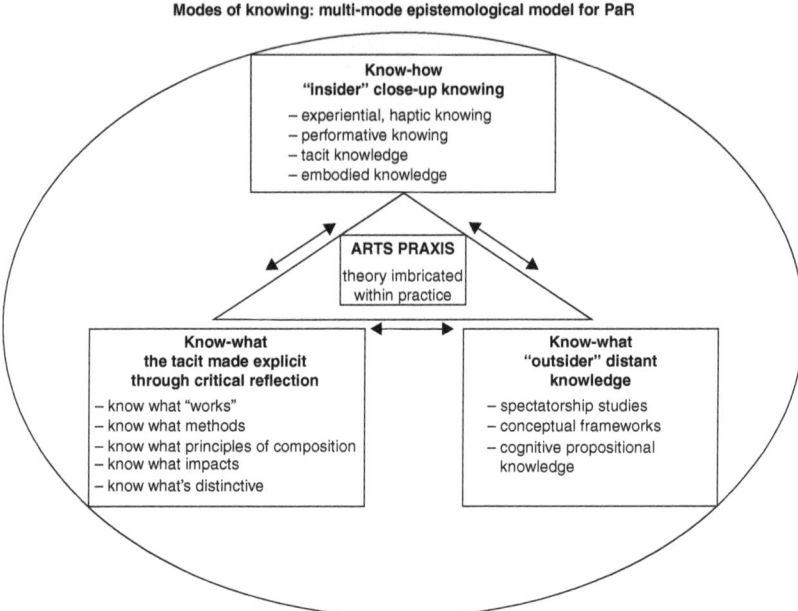

Fig. 7.5 Robin Nelson's PaR modes of knowing[52]

Conclusion

By using practice-as-research methodologies, IDP empowers student dancers to systematically study their experience of moving, and share reflections in a lecture demonstration that draws on their abilities in performance, composition, and analysis. The project exemplifies a high-impact educational practice by challenging artists to take ownership of their praxis by showing what dance can do, how it happens, and why this is important. By questioning, testing, and communicating discoveries about movement in various formats, not least of which is through performance, IDP sharpens creative capacities for critical reflection through action.

Notes

1. Carl Diehl, *Americans and German Scholarship, 1770–1870*, 147–148.
2. Joyce Kinkead, "What's in a Name? A Brief History of Undergraduate Research," 22.

3. Kinkead, "What's in a Name?," 23.
4. See the book introduction, Chapter 1, for more information about STEAM, the movement to insert the Arts into STEM education.
5. NCUR's 2017 Conference Program.
6. See NCUR's published proceedings available online at ncur.org.
7. See ncur.org.
8. NCUR's 2017 Conference Program, 8.
9. See Randy Bass' "Disrupting Ourselves" for a discussion on post-course curriculum that opens up space for creative activity as research.
10. See Malaika Sarco-Thomas' case study in this chapter for an example of undergraduate research that embraces performance as research, and her endnote listing numerous PhD programs outside the United States in performance as research.
11. William W. Lewis and Niki Tulk, "Why Performance as Research?"
12. Rebecca Schuman, "The End of the College Essay: An Essay."
13. Jenn Fishman, Andrea Lunsford, Beth McGregor, and Mark Otuteye, "Performing Writing, Performing Literacy."
14. See the "Position Statements on Writing" on the National Council of Teachers of English website for more about a broadening approach to writing in the classroom.
15. Beth Watkins, "Working from Scratch: The Pedagogic Value of Undergraduate Devising," 171.
16. See Jennifer Mayer, "Serving the Needs of Performing Arts Students," for a librarian's perspective on how to improve user experience for performing arts students.
17. Jayne Elise Brownell and Lynn E. Swaner, *Five High-Impact Practices*, 31. This is a follow-up to George Kuh's *High-Impact Educational Practices: What They Are, Who Has Access to Them, and Why They Matter*.
18. Boyer Commission on Educating Undergraduates in the Research University. *Reinventing Undergraduate Education: A Blueprint for America's Research Universities.*, quoted in Brownell and Swaner, *Five High-Impact Practices*, 32–33.
19. Special thanks to Beth Watkins for the original idea to use a dramaturgy project rather than a research paper, and Denise Massman for introducing me to collages as integral to undergraduate design coursework.
20. George D. Kuh and Carol Geary Schneider, *High-Impact Educational Practices: What They Are, Who Has Access to Them, and Why They Matter*, 14.
21. Kuh and Schneider, 17.
22. Brownell and Swaner, *Five High-Impact Practices*, 32–33.
23. Brownell and Swaner, *Five High-Impact Practices*, 32.
24. Nancy Kindelan, *Artistic Literacy*, 137.

25. See Kindelan, Chapter 9: Artistic Literacy and the Twenty-First-Century Workforce p. 135–143.
26. Kuh and Scheider, *High-Impact Educational Practices*, 13.
27. Brownell and Swaner, *Five High-Impact Practices*, 32–33.
28. Boyer Commission on Educating Undergraduates in the Research University. *Reinventing Undergraduate Education: A Blueprint for America's Research Universities.*, quoted in Brownell and Swaner, *Five High-Impact Practices*, 32–33.
29. Kindelan, *Artistic Literacy*, 137.
30. A Senior Experience is required of each student at LU. In the Theatre Arts Department, the student proposes a project that will showcase their strengths in an area they plan to pursue with further study or employment. Students frequently propose producing a play, and in those cases, this Dramaturgy Project is frequently the first work they do on the play, as well as the first time they publicly solicit interest from their colleagues.
31. Brownell and Swaner, *Five High-Impact Practices*, 33.
32. Brownell and Swaner, *Five High-Impact Practices*, 33, 56–57. Kuh, *High-Impact Educational Practices*, 14.
33. Brownell and Swaner, *Five High-Impact Practices*, 33–34.
34. These examples are all generalized approaches noted from the last two iterations of the class.
35. Theresa L. Burriss and Patricia M. Gantt, eds., *Appalachia in the Classroom: Teaching the Region*, xiii–xiv.
36. With thanks to Professor Jo Butterworth for her comments on a draft of this essay, and to the graduates who gave permission for their IDP research topics to be shared.
37. Courses which balance theory and practice, such as the University of Malta's Bachelor (Hons) in Dance Studies, are one example of this, but the need to value both experiential and contextual studies has been central to Dance Studies' disciplinary identity. In *Dance as Education* Peter Brinson notes that "the fundamental principle of dance scholarship is a partnership between verbal and nonverbal knowledge requiring a balance between theory and practice and a broad interdisciplinary approach," 90–91. Since authoring the first curriculum for dance in higher education at the University of Wisconsin in 1926, Margaret H'Doubler's philosophy "that dance must be taught conceptually and that the individual learns best through structured experience" (*A History of Dance in American Higher Education*, 100) has been instrumental in fostering balanced theoretical and practical approaches toward researching dance. Recently in *Thinking Through Dance: The Philosophy of Dance and Performance Practices*, Bunker et al. observe,

"Modern and contemporary dance tend toward self-reflexivity and have a self-conscious relationship to their own history, arguably embedding a research—even a philosophical—imperative within the dance practice itself," 5.
38. Robin Nelson, "On the Methodology of Practice as Research," 16.
39. Dwight Conquergood in Richard Schechner. *Performance Studies: An Introduction*, 18.
40. ECTS credits indicate values assigned to study units as per the European Credit Transfer System, instigated by the Bologna process to enable parity for courses across Europe, and transferability for international and Erasmus students.
41. Angela Piccini and Baz Kershaw, "Practice as research in performance: from epistemology to evaluation," 87.
42. Institutions offering PaR PhDs in performance include University of Central Lancashire; University of Lincoln, De Montfort University; University of Exeter; Canterbury, University of Kent; Goldsmiths, University of London; Trinity Laban; Plymouth University; Cheshire, Manchester Metropolitan University; Royal Holloway University; Stockholm University of the Arts; University of Surrey-Guildford.
43. For further reflection on PARIP in higher education see Jo Butterworth and Sita Popat, *The Art and Science of Nurturing Dance-Makers: Papers from the Greenhouse Effect Conference*.
44. Melissa Trimingham, "A Methodology for Practice as Research," 54–60.
45. Stephen Kemmis, Robin McTaggart, and Rhonda Nixon, *The Action Research Planner: Doing Critical Participatory Action Research*, 89.
46. Niel D. Fleming and Colleen Mills, "Not Another Inventory, Rather a Catalyst for Reflection," 137–155.
47. Learning outcomes from the IDP study unit, part of the University of Malta's Bachelor (Hons) in Dance Studies course which was written by Jo Butterworth in 2009 and validated in spring 2010.
48. Susan Melrose "…just intuitive" and "Expert-intuitive processing and the logics of production: struggles in (the wording of) creative decision-making in 'dance'."
49. Malaika Sarco-Thomas, "IDP Essay & IDP Presentation Launch document."
50. Nelson, "On the Methodology of Practice as Research," 22.
51. Anna Pakes addresses the implications of these forms of knowing explicitly for choreography and dance in "Knowing through Dance-making: Choreography, Practical Knowledge and Practice-as-Research."
52. Nelson, "On the Methodology of Practice as Research," 19.

Bibliography

Bass, Randy. 2012. Disrupting Ourselves: The Problem of Learning in Higher Education. *Educause Review* 47 (2): 23–33.

Brinson, Peter. 1991. *Dance as Education: Towards a National Dance Culture*. London: Falmer Press.

Brownell, Jayne Elise, and Lynn E. Swaner. 2010. *Five High-Impact Practices: Research on Learning Outcomes, Completion and Quality*. Washington, DC: Association of American Colleges and Universities.

Bunker, Jenny, Anna Pakes, and Bonnie Rowell, eds. 2013. *Thinking Through Dance: The Philosophy of Dance Performance and Practices*. Binsted: Dance Books.

Burriss, Theresa L., and Patricia M. Gantt, eds. 2013. *Appalachia in the Classroom: Teaching the Region*. Athens: Ohio University Press.

Butterworth, Jo. 2010. Individual Dance Project: Essay and Presentation. Study Unit Description, Bachelor (Hons) Dance Studies Handbook, University of Malta.

Butterworth, Jo, and Sita Popat, eds. 1999. *The Art and Science of Nurturing Dance-Makers: Papers from the Greenhouse Effect Conference*. Wakefield: Centre for Dance and Theatre Studies at Bretton Hall.

Diehl, Carl. 1978. *Americans and German Scholarship, 1770–1870*. No. 115. New Haven: Yale University Press.

Fishman, Jenn, Andrea Lunsford, Beth McGregor, and Mark Otuteye. 2005. Performing Writing, Performing Literacy. *College Composition and Communication* 57: 224–252.

Fleming, Niel D., and Colleen Mills. 1992. Not Another Inventory, Rather a Catalyst for Reflection. *To Improve the Academy* 11: 137–155.

Gibbons, Elizabeth. 2007. *Teaching Dance: The Spectrum of Styles*. Bloomington, IN: AuthorHouse.

Hagood, Thomas K. 2000. *A History of Dance in American Higher Education*. Lewiston, NY: Edwin Mellen Press.

Hanstein, Penelope. 1999. Models and Metaphors: Theory Making and the Creation of New Knowledge. In *Researching Dance: Evolving Modes of Enquiry*, ed. Penelope Hanstein and Sondra Fraleigh, 62–88. University of Pittsburgh Press, Dance Books.

Kemmis, Stephen, Robin McTaggart, and Rhonda Nixon. 2014. *The Action Research Planner: Doing Critical Participatory Action Research*. Singapore: Springer.

Kindelan, Nancy Anne. 2012. *Artistic Literacy: Theatre Studies and a Contemporary Liberal Education*. New York: Palgrave Macmillan.

Kinkead, Joyce. 2012. What's in a Name? A Brief History of Undergraduate Research. *CUR Quarterly* 33 (1): 20–29.

Kuh, George D., and Carol Geary Schneider. 2008. *High-Impact Educational Practices: What They Are, Who Has Access to Them, and Why They Matter.* Washington, DC: Association of American Colleges and Universities.

Lewis, William W., and Niki Tulk. 2016. Editorial: Why Performance as Research? *PARtake: The Journal of Performance as Research* 1 (1): 1.

Mayer, Jennifer. 2015. Serving the Needs of Performing Arts Students: A Case Study. *Portal: Libraries and the Academy* 15 (3): 409–431.

Melrose, Susan. …Just Intuitive. http://www.sfmelrose.org.uk/justintuitive/. Last Modified April 2005.

———. 2009. Expert-Intuitive Processing and the Logics of Production: Struggles In (the Wording of) Creative Decision-Making in 'Dance'. In *Contemporary Choreography: A Critical Reader*, ed. Jo Butterworth and Liesbeth Wildschut, 23–37. New York: Routledge.

National Conference on Undergraduate Research. NCUR.org. http://www.cur.org/conferences_and_events/student_events/ncur/. Accessed 30 June 2017.

———. NCUR Conference Program. NCUR.org. http://www.memphis.edu/ugresearch/links/ncur_conference.pdf. Accessed 30 June 2017.

National Council of Teachers of English. NCTE Position Statements on Writing. http://www.ncte.org/positions/writing. Accessed 30 June 2017.

Nelson, Robin. 2014. On the Methodology of Practice as Research. *Choros International Dance Journal* 3 (Spring): 12–25.

Pakes, Anna. 2009. Knowing Through Dance-Making: Choreography, Practical Knowledge and Practice-as-Research. In *Contemporary Choreography: A Critical Reader*, ed. Jo Butterworth and Liesbeth Wildschut, 10–22. London and New York: Routledge.

Piccini, Angela, and Baz Kershaw. 2004. Practice as Research in Performance: From Epistemology to Evaluation. *Digital Creativity* 15 (2): 86–92.

Sarco-Thomas, Malaika. 2016. IDP Essay & IDP Presentation Launch Document. Department of Dance Studies, School of Performing Arts, University of Malta.

Schechner, Richard. 2002. *Performance Studies: An Introduction.* London: Routledge.

Schuman, Rebecca. The End of the College Essay: An Essay. http://www.slate.com/articles/life/education/2013/12/college_papers_students_hate_writing_them_professors_hate_grading_them_let.html. Accessed 30 June 2017.

Trimingham, Melissa. 2003. A Methodology for Practice as Research. *Studies in Theatre and Performance* 22 (1): 54–60.

Valencia College. 2017. The Cycle of Action Research. https://valenciacollege.edu/faculty/development/tla/actionResearch/elements.cfm. Accessed 20 July 2017.

Watkins, Beth. 2016. Working from Scratch: The Pedagogic Value of Undergraduate Devising. *Theatre Topics* 26 (2): 169–180.

CHAPTER 8

Diversity and Global Learning

George Kuh acknowledges that the high-impact practice (HIP) of diversity and global learning often emphasizes that students interrogate "difficult differences" via coursework and experiential learning such as study abroad.[1] Additionally, "alternative spring breaks" and other service experiences can be beneficial toward realizing the goals of this HIP. Jiali Luo and David Jamieson-Drake detail the many benefits associated with student engagement in diverse learning environments in "A Retrospective Assessment of the Educational Benefits of Interaction Across Racial Boundaries." These benefits include enhanced learning and social life, academic and social self-confidence, growth in cultural awareness, open discussion of race-related issues, greater civic interest, interracial friendships, interpersonal and leadership abilities, problem-solving and critical thinking skills, higher retention and graduation rates, and greater college satisfaction.[2] Importantly, Luo and Jamieson-Drake's study found that "students who engaged in substantial interracial interaction were considerably more likely than students who had no or little interracial interaction to question their beliefs about other races or ethnicities." These students were also able to challenge their own belief systems about sexual orientation, politics, and religion, as well as the value systems and beliefs of the larger society.[3]

Notable for those of us in the performing arts is Luo and Jamieson-Drake's finding that these same students who reported substantial interracial interaction also "reported higher levels of development in two additional areas: (a) appreciating the arts and (b) identifying moral and ethical issues." They also engaged in the following extracurricular activities during their college career: intramural sports, performing arts or music, and visiting speakers.[4]

The data collected by Luo and Jamieson-Drake are not surprising to those of us in the performing arts in the academy. Indeed, many faculty and students produce their creative scholarship with the intent that audiences have a self-reflexive response and grapple with the issues of diversity that the performing arts elicit. The performing arts are a flashpoint for how we understand, engage, and articulate diversity. Because the performing arts rely on the fact of bodies occupying the same space, this embodiedness becomes the irrepressible vehicle for representing our diverse identities, cultural values, and communities.

The major institutions of the performing arts in the non-academic sphere frequently become battlegrounds for culture wars, where contestations over identity and representation are commonplace.[5] One only has to reflect on the reactions to Vice President Mike Pence's attendance at the musical *Hamilton* to know that representation and diversity in the performing arts is a political and loaded cultural site.[6] Venues that are driven by the need to sell tickets and please their subscribers often choose "safe" shows, performing artists and companies, rather than take risks on shows or performing artists who are pushing boundaries and challenging the status quo. The result of conflict over cultural representation and community identities is often a diversity mission statement in which the institution posts ambitious goals on its website to address diversity blind spots, with insufficient follow-through.

In higher education, academic freedom and less pressure to create financial revenue should mean that we are insulated from the quagmire of unfulfilled diversity missions and promises. However, there are many ways that the academic performing arts can reproduce the same exclusionary practices seen in the professional sphere, despite this relative freedom.[7] There have been positive strides happening at the intersection of diversity and the performing arts, but the academy is slow to change.

The most recent Strategic National Arts Alumni Project (SNAAP) data from performing arts graduates indicates that over 75% of our majors are engaging with students that are different from them. In answer to the question about how frequently performing arts majors "had serious conversations with students who are different from you in terms of their ethnicity, religious beliefs, political opinions, or personal values," 41.4%

answered "often," 34.8% answered "sometimes," 17.8% answered "rarely," while 6% answered "never."[8] It is unfortunate to see that 23.8% of performing arts graduates surveyed answered that they "rarely" or "never" engaged in serious conversations with students who are different from them. We are not delivering on the high-impact learning practice of diversity if we are not challenging our students by engaging in dialogue across difference in our classrooms. The performing arts has to be self-reflexive about diversity, because when it is not, that naiveté and insensitivity often comes back to bite via disgruntled audiences, critical reviews, and tarnished reputations. The performing arts puts bodies on display, and a lack of attention to issues of diversity in season selection, casting, performances, and audience is painfully visible.

Dance may be the most obvious performing art that harbors an expectation of the "ideal body," and certainly the professional dance world has a long way to go before eradicating this harmful bias toward an idealized thin, tall, and white dancer. In academic dance, there has been much attention given to the necessity of welcoming all bodies into the curriculum and diversifying dance beyond only Western forms. But similar to academic music programs, dance departments face significant challenges in recruiting diverse students and incorporating meaningful diversity learning objectives into the curriculum. Academic music and dance programs have more work to do (theatre does not require "classical training" for entry) in reconsidering audition processes and curriculum to meet these challenges. Many performing arts programs in theatre, dance, and music in academia tend to relegate diversity to a handful of courses on "world music," or "world theatre," or particular genres of non-Western dance, rather than seriously overhaul curriculums to include a diverse perspective of the performing arts in a comprehensive way in all coursework.

Taking only one "diversity" qualifying course during an academic career would do little to reframe hegemonic thinking in any discipline, and can feel like a token offering. Luo and Jamieson-Drake's study warns that

> Undergraduate students are developmentally highly sensitive to hypocrisy, particularly in authority figures. To the extent that an institution's commitment to engaging diversity appears episodic to them, students will reject even well-meaning efforts to change as superficial, or worse, they will join in them initially and then be disillusioned as they discover their efforts are being undermined or ignored by other elements of an institution's message or polity.[9]

How do we send the appropriate message of diversity and inclusion to our performing arts students? How do curricula in the performing arts deliver on an institution's mission around diversity? Are we living up to the diversity splashed on our promotional brochures? Each discipline has had a different road to travel in its progress on diversity and inclusion, though there are common threads among the trajectory of academic music, dance, and theatre.

The Society for Ethnomusicology and the International Society for Music Education were both founded in 1953 and marked a turning point in music education, when there was an acknowledgment of the importance of studying world music. However, music education's inclusion of world music curriculum has been more focused on the curricular diversity of the music itself, rather than the student population it serves.[10] Overall, music education in colleges and universities has been slow to change, in spite of calls for a reimagining of curriculum. While music journals have been publishing articles lamenting the lack of diversity in music education for decades, like C. Victor Fung's "Rationales for Teaching World Musics", published in 1995, many music programs in higher education have done little to change a paradigm in music education that privileges European and Western music traditions. Fung identified the commonly held notion that the privileging of Western music is indeed a problem in music education: "The belief that Western art music is more natural, complex, expressive, and meaningful than other musics has come to be seen as both an intellectual and a moral problem."[11] Since 1995, there has certainly been some progress in music education, as documented by Bennett Reimer in his 2012 article, "Another Perspective: Struggling Toward Wholeness in Music Education":

> The burgeoning competencies we are developing in areas such as the teaching of composition, of improvisation, of a broad range of concern with issues of social justice, of expertise in adapting ourselves to the latest music-making and music-disseminating technologies, and of accepting a world of diverse musical genres and practices as having genuine value and quality—all are signs of life-sustaining, relevancy-enhancing opportunities for wholeness that we need to support with urgency.[12]

While Reimer acknowledges the important strides toward diversifying music education, he also urges a reconsideration of the most fundamental obstacle to true diversification of music curricula: the emphasis on performance. Reimer pushes for music education to be as robust as music is experienced in everyday life in "Reconceiving the Standards and the School Music Program":

> Rather than constraining all students to being musically the same, as we tend to do now, a good general education in music will have the opposite effect—to encourage as much diversity of involvements as there are musical opportunities. An effective, reality-based general music curriculum will explore each role for its particular challenges, satisfactions, and ways to think and do. And it will demonstrate how each of the other roles enriches the one being studied. To make this possible, we must devise a sequential program that unifies general music as a school subject while encouraging the diverse approaches our very diverse society requires.[13]

Reimer is far from alone in calling for different approaches to music education. Allen Clements also argues that the privileging of performance as the ultimate measure of success in music programs is a barrier to diversifying the music student body in "Minority Students and Faculty in Higher Music Education":

> No established college or university music program in the United States wishes to abandon the rich heritage of European classical music. In fact, for many current college music faculty members, it is precisely this music that first motivated them to pursue a career in music. At the same time, it behooves these schools of music to recognize the fact that there are many musicians (both practicing and potential) who have no interest in becoming orchestral performers, conductors, opera singers, or college music professors. It is to these musicians that alternative curricula and outreach programs are likely to appeal.[14]

Clements acknowledges that music schools that have initiated early recruitment efforts like outreach programs in middle and high schools have close interaction with high school music faculty, maintain a diverse faculty to create a welcoming environment, and offer an alternative curriculum to Western music, and have had notable success in diversifying their student body. General music programs and music therapy programs are best poised to make radical changes to curriculum, and indeed these are the programs that have already begun to adapt to the challenges of training the next generation of music students. Ethnomusicology, music therapy, music education, and performance faculty committed to inclusion are contributing necessary course development in diversity and powerful cultural immersion experiences in music programs worldwide.[15] However, diversifying the music performance major's curriculum to reflect the breadth of career options postgraduation, as well as diversifying the music student population, is a work in progress.

Similarly, dance programs in higher education are facing the same challenges that music performance programs are struggling with: access and socioeconomic factors that limit the kinds of students in the position to apply and audition for these programs. Doug Risner and Susan Stinson describe some of these challenges in "Moving Social Justice: Challenges, Fears and Possibilities in Dance Education":

> the limitations of current multicultural efforts in postsecondary dance often ignore socioeconomic diversity and minimize differently abled populations. The ability to enter dance programs usually privileges previous training, normally extensive study in ballet and modern dance. In this respect, auditions serve as a socioeconomic barrier, filtering out students whose backgrounds have not allowed access to formal dance training. From the outset, these sorting mechanisms build homogenous programs as they simultaneously reduce diversity.[16]

In the face of this homogeneity, where the majority of dance students are white and female, many dance programs in academia have been attentive to inclusivity by welcoming all bodies, including students with disabilities, into the dance studio. While this is a significant difference from most professional dance companies (with notable exceptions[17]), Jill Green cautions that dance faculty may be unaware of the power they wield over dancers' bodies in "Socially Constructed Bodies in American Dance Classrooms":

> Dance educators often attempt to "free" up students or open them up so that their bodies may be used as "expressive" instruments. ... Yet, dance teachers do not always attempt to be self-reflexive regarding the ways the student dance body may be mechanized or habituated into an ideal form that represents the teacher's learned belief system and presumed ideas about what the body should be and do. It is not common to find dance educators reflecting on how power enables them to mold student bodies and standardize bodily behavior in class.[18]

Green's discussion of how dancers' bodies are the "docile bodies" of Foucault's theory of self-regulation in power regimes asserts that "[i]f

Foucault studied dance education as culture he might say that students' bodies in the dance class are constantly under surveillance."[19] Nevertheless, dance faculty have the opportunity to be clear in their pedagogy about inclusive practices. Susan Petersen and Karen Kaufmann describe pedagogical tactics to employ in the dance studio to model inclusivity in "Adaptation Techniques for Modeling Diversity in the Dance Class":

> The teacher's directions should encourage students' thoughts, feelings, and ideas to freely manifest themselves in movement. Most important in this form of exploration is the encouragement to see all movement responses as "right" and valuable. ... For example, a teacher might initiate directions with an open-ended question such as, "Can you find your own way to...?" or "How many ways can you...?" These statements convey the value of individuality to students. Successful classes support and challenge students to discover their uniqueness.[20]

Here again, we see a call to honor each student's individuality, rather than attempt a one-size-fits-all curriculum and insisting that all students learn the same things. This pedagogical approach is necessary to be inclusive of all bodies, including students with disabilities. Meeting the needs of music and theatre students with disabilities is also happening on many campuses, and similar articles can be found encouraging music and theatre faculty to practice inclusive pedagogy.[21]

Many performing arts departments struggle to recruit first-generation college students and students from working class and poor families.[22] These sought-after students are often discouraged from majoring in the performing arts by their parents and will often feel obligated to pursue a "practical" degree instead that their families believe will provide financial security. In academic theatre, there are fewer of the socioeconomic barriers to access that music and dance struggle with, and therefore theatre stages and classrooms on campuses are in general more diverse than other performing arts units. There is not the expectation of formal theatre training for the undergraduate theatre student, and access to bachelor of arts theatre programs in particular is relatively within reach of diverse students. Bachelor of fine arts programs can be fiercely competitive in academic theatre, but this is not specific to underrepresented students. However, greater access does not guarantee that inclusion is a priority in any theatre program. Curricular revision, while less burdened by an expectation of exclusive study of the Western canon than music or dance, can still privilege Western theatre forms while treating "world" theatre as an add-on elective.

Academic theatre has been plagued by misguided casting and superficial engagement of diversity issues in productions, and these missteps sometimes make national news headlines. These stories remind us that some theatre faculty are not prepared to deal with diversity issues sensitively, or have not themselves been schooled in the politics of representation and critical race, gender, or queer theory. Of course, the same could be said of faculty in music and dance as well, but their performances do not usually spotlight representation and diversity issues in such explicit ways as to garner the attention (if unwanted) of national media outlets.

Because theatre is staging the work of playwrights that have indicated casting considerations, scripts that carry the weight of problematic historical contexts, and new works that confront diversity issues head on, academic theatre often takes center stage in the campus culture wars of the politics of diversity. To the extent that these wars are waged productively to increase the capacity of local community to dialogue about diversity issues, they are well fought and theatre program faculty and students are often the brave ground zero.[23]

There are a growing number of performing arts faculty devoted to a performing arts practice for civic engagement and social justice, and they are having a tremendous impact on realizing diversity educational goals at their home institutions through various means: producing diverse production seasons and new works festivals, providing interdisciplinary engagement via performance panels, and bringing applied theatre, music, and dance work to on and off campus community partners.[24]

Theatre, dance, and music tell stories, and when the performing arts stage stories that would otherwise go unheard in the mainstream media and culture, it becomes a site for the democratic practice of dialogue and empathy. As Florence Samson describes in "Drama in Aesthetic Education: An Invitation to Imagine the World as if It Could Be Otherwise," the performing arts have the ability to transport audience members to worlds they had never imagined. Samson invited Ping Chong Company to perform *Secret History: Journeys Abroad, Journeys Within*[25] for her education students as part of the Lincoln Center Institute Teacher Education Collaborative. She describes their collective experience of empathy for the refugee stories shared in the performance:

For many of us, engagement with Chong's drama was as close as we could come to the authenticity of being a refugee, of being an outsider. Chong's approach to drama would not allow us to remain indifferent to the inhumane plight of the refugee. How could an audience engage with this particular drama or work of art and remain unaffected, unaware of the need for change? As a member of the audience, I had been moved and educated at a deep and intense level.[26]

Samson and her students' experience of transformative learning occurs frequently in the performing arts. For our students engaging with the performing arts as performers or audience members, the potential for self-reflection and increased cultural competence is an obvious correlation. It is our responsibility to ensure that we take the necessary steps to evolve pedagogy and curriculum in pace with the diversity of our cultural realities. Whether elicited by a piece of music, dance, theatre, or a combination of those, the performing arts can strike at the emotional and intellectual core of the human condition and form an empathic bridge connecting our difference.

The case studies in this chapter consider various forms of bridge building enabled by innovative pedagogy and impactful experiential learning. Julius Bailey has students explore philosophical approaches to diversity through hip hop music, building bridges between popular culture and critical race philosophies. Michelle Hayford and Katie O'Leary work with college students to facilitate a summer theatre camp for youth with autism spectrum disorder (ASD). The mutual exchange that occurs during the summer camp exemplifies the imperative of diverse learning communities that expose students to life experiences, identities, and worldviews divergent from their own.

Call to action:

- Administrators need to provide professional development opportunities for performing arts (and all) faculty in the areas of diversity, inclusion, implicit bias, intergroup dialogue and other pedagogies that would serve your student body.
- Administrators need to collaborate with their performing arts departments on curricular and co-curricular initiatives to work toward realizing their institution's diversity and inclusion goals in innovative and impactful ways.
- Performing arts faculty need to ensure that search committees and hiring practices recruit diverse faculty, and advocate for institutional

policies and strategies to retain them (including re-examining the role of student evaluations in tenure and promotion policies as they have been demonstrated to tell us more about student bias toward the gender, race, and discipline of their faculty than the quality of teaching[27]).

- Performing arts faculty must implement recruitment and retention strategies for diverse students.
- Performing arts faculty must engage students in diverse local communities (reference chapter 9 on the HIP of community engaged learning and service learning).
- Performing arts faculty need to revise curriculum for meaningful inclusion of diversity learning objectives, beyond superficial add-on electives. Build self-reflection and intercultural competence into diversity learning objectives throughout the curriculum.
- Performing arts faculty must eradicate any hypocrisy between the institutional or departmental diversity mission statement and the curricular and programmatic offerings of their program.
- Performing arts faculty need to produce diverse performances and work by underrepresented playwrights, composers, and choreographers.
- Performing arts faculty need to collaborate with campus colleagues in other disciplines to offer panels contextualizing a presented work, with a focus on a meaningful issue of diversity on your campus.
- Performing arts faculty should reconsider their audition procedures. If students audition to gain access to your program, consider the implications to the diversity of your student body.

The "Real" Versus the "Represented" Self: First-Year Students Seek Identity Through Kanye West

Julius D. Bailey
Wittenberg University
Springfield, OH, USA

Utilizing hip hop pedagogy at the undergraduate level presents a host of challenges. Chief among these is the easy-A misconception. Undoubtedly, some students attempt to take a less than rigorous approach to class materials because they are familiar with so much of the course content. However, students of hip hop soon learn that their knowledge of the culture is far more superficial than they imagine. This superficial understanding is not the result of any unwillingness to immerse themselves in the art form, but, rather, a lack of familiarity with philosophical inquiry.

With its existentialist elements viewed through the lens of the black predicament and its emphasis on subjectivity and identity formation, Kanye West's 2008 song "Pinocchio Story" is a pedagogical vehicle perfectly suited to travel these ill-lit and narrow avenues of philosophical inquiry. On the one hand, West is the conscious rapper who speaks for and as the marginalized other; on the other hand, he is undeniably self-centered—an egomaniac of the first order. This tension is nowhere clearer than in "Pinocchio Story."

West is the artist in search of his genuine, untainted self—the black artist par excellence who resists the trappings of celebrity stardom (materialistic faux identity). West's search for identity destabilizes "the self" in a process of disavowal, leading toward a highly liberatory emergence of the black artist as subject. This responds to the growing levels of alienation, isolation, and marginality that attend upon black stardom. Kanye West in particular and the genre in general explore and attempt to overcome this existential angst, yet the pedagogical value of this exploration is often overlooked.

To promote engagement with difficult concepts, I encourage my first-year students to explore the following questions over the course of three sessions. First, how does the music of Kanye West contribute to his search for an authentic self? Second, how does Kanye West both represent and disturb our notions of the African American artist? Third, how does Kanye West represent and resist the post-colonial condition? Since the tangible remnants of colonial conditions and conditioning continue to shape the identities, languages, and cultures of the formerly colonized and enslaved, the answers to these questions lean heavily upon a post-colonial framework, which we explore over the course of three classroom sessions.

The goal is not just to introduce difficult philosophical concepts, but also to explore how the college experience in our Liberal Arts-centered institution demands upon them. Most explicitly, to forge these common intellectual experiences (most of whom have never looked at hip hop and philosophy together) and to foster discussions that emphasize diversity and inclusiveness—we draw on the often-diverse nature of the hip hop centered classroom. For black students, the hip hop focus offers them an opportunity to explore a culture they readily identify with; for non-black students, it means a chance to explore a culture and the perspectives that inform it that are very different from those to which they are accustomed.

Day One—Kanye West: The Man or the Image?

The goal of the first session was to facilitate students to think critically about and engage with West's positioning as post-colonial subject, but also to interrogate their own individual identities as well. Naturally, this begins with the questions: Who is Kanye West? Who do we know him to be? And perhaps most importantly, who does he think he is?

On the cusp of the new millennium, Kanye West began to emerge as a hip hop icon (an emergence that accelerated rapidly with each new game-changing release). The son of a university professor and a photojournalist, Kanye displayed an early affinity and passion for the arts. He was writing and producing music and selling it to aspiring Chicago hip hop artists when he was still only in junior high.[28] After high school, he studied English at Chicago State University, but he dropped out when he was still early in his studies to devote himself to his musical career full time. His decidedly middle-class upbringing and liberal education colored his early work (and continue to do so).

His first six albums reached platinum status, and five of them debuted at Number 1. He's won an astounding 21 Grammy Awards, and scores of critics have placed him in the hip hop pantheon.

Kanye's achievements—as formidable and frequently discussed as they might be—only account for a relatively small portion of his star power. The consummate self-promoter, West has worked tirelessly to shape his public persona. He pushes his epistemology of race, self, and legacy to the very front of his brand: he is the conscious rapper, the justified egoist, the genius who will not be denied. He sees himself at the apex of musical history, part of (perhaps the culmination of) the spectrum of black artists who struggled to be heard and to BE in America—a country that continues to struggle to give black artists their due. Highly visible and bullhorn brash, Kanye antithesizes black America's historical invisibility.

West realizes that notwithstanding his economic privileged background, he cannot escape his blackness. Rampant masculinity and expressive egotism in "My Beautiful Dark Twisted Fantasy" (2010), "Watch the Throne" (2011), and "New Slaves" (2013) are performances that West knows will inflame his opponents (non-assimilative) while enlisting his supporters (assimilative). Nick Krebs argues that by "Sticking to the rules of the Neoliberal system—his raps as [capitalist] labor"—West seizes power of the product and "produces an exclusive manifesto of pride aimed at disturbing the dominant narrative" and Neoliberal political fantasy.[29] These elements of the self are familiar themes for West, including black oppression and material success. Kanye West lays bare the process of his identity-making:

> Yeah, I just think about when Jay-Z would be like, "I do this for my culture, I do this for the hood." I'm doing it for that. I'm doing it for where I came from. ... But I had to come to the realization, it wasn't just the search for something different, but something better, a better solution. I never forget that... It feels like I'm on the right path.[30]

West draws attention to his origins, "*where I came from*," laying claim to something without pinning it down. Instead, he defines himself as something other—someone who does that which is "different" from the norm, something "better." During a *Nightline* interview in 2007, West said, "I just don't fit into, like, the cookie cutter, you know ... who you're supposed to be as a rapper or who you're supposed to be as a black man or who you're supposed to be as an entertainer, who you're supposed to be as a celebrity, you know I don't, I don't just follow those rules."[31] His invocation of Jay-Z, of "my culture" and "the hood," shows that West connects to a legacy of black music and its traditions while simultaneously resisting and interrogating those traditions. This goes as much for what black artists believe and say of themselves as it does for what the wider culture expects of blackness or have perceived it to be. Teaching in my small Midwestern University, where the majority population came from high schools that were exclusively (or near) white, this is often the point of disruption in the course and where good teaching can begin.

When discussing this facet of West's persona in the classroom, it becomes possible to introduce Frantz Fanon into the discussion—whose penetrating insight into the destructive manifestations of colonialism can help establish a foreground for our post-colonial reading of "Pinocchio's Story." Drawing on his own experiences as a black colonized subject, Fanon explored the consciousness of the colonized and the colonizer, doing so as a way to answer his deep yearning for both political and psychic survival. To read Fanon's *Black Skin, White Masks* is to hear the tension and struggle between his many (sometimes ambivalent, often antagonistic) authorial voices[32]—a presence that is just as deeply felt in Kanye's lyrics. In his article "Remembering Fanon: Self, Psyche and the Colonial Condition," Homi Bhabha argues that

> The analysis of colonial de-personalization alienates not only the Enlightenment idea of "Man," but challenges the transparency of social reality, as a pre-given image of human knowledge. ... For the very nature of humanity becomes estranged in the colonial condition.[33]

Identity is, therefore, seen as an emergent, framed as an "enigmatic questioning": What does the Black Man want? Ostensibly students "find themselves" within these discussions and seek to minimalize race and highlight place/space as a way of forging some commonality with the colonized subject.

To push these enquiries and engagements with philosophical enquiries yet deeper, I introduce students to post-structuralism and Marshall McLuhan's ideas related to media and self, particularly as these ideas relate to authenticity. In "Pinocchio Story," Kanye repeatedly claims that he wants to be a "real boy." The meaning of this is clear enough in the context of the Pinocchio story, but less so when it is not a puppet but, rather, a hip hop superstar. What does Kanye mean, and how can this meaning be explored with the aid of philosophical perspectives?

For McLuhan, media determines not only intellectual life but also emotional and even physical being in the world. It sets the conditions of possibility. For McLuhan, how we answer the question "Who am I?" is at least in part a reflection of our media preferences. If man recreates himself by extending himself through his use of media, then the particular result is contingent on (and at least partly determined by) the particular modes of extension involved. Through a range of media (as a producer, rapper, fashion designer, social media icon, etc.), Kanye creates and is created. His heavily constructed persona is at once shaped by and a shaper of the media through which he extends himself. The degree to which he is shaped is what leads Kanye to question his authenticity, saying that he is "just a façade on TV." Simultaneously, his undeniable role as shaper leads him to lay claim to the boast (which he places in the mouth of the many), "Kanye, he keeps it real, boy."

His reference to his own (falsely) represented televised image marks a splitting of the post-colonial subject, who is both seen (as a representation of the black artist) and unseen as a constrained human subject—one who is trapped in "hell" and "prison" (golden chains and all).

Day Two—"Pinocchio Story": A Post-Colonial Reading

For students unfamiliar with hip hop or partial to other musical genres, it can often be difficult to engage deeply with hip hop's content. There are barriers between the uninitiated listener and the artist, the message, and the philosophy at its core. This barrier is, in effect, identical to the one that separates the colonizer from the colonized, between the self and the other.

By exploring hip hop's lyrical content (often for the first time), students are encouraged to forge a connection—perhaps positive, perhaps negative—with the artist, the genre, and the philosophy.

This philosophy is one of resistance, but this is too often, too readily confused with resistance against power in its many forms—political, social, military, economic, and so on. But Kanye's resistance moved both outward and inward. In "Pinocchio Story," he laments the lost authentic self—the wages of success—and he longs for a simpler, truer (but, for him, foreclosed) existence. Franz Fanon says, "It is through the effort to recapture the self and to scrutinize the self, it is through the lasting tension of their freedom that men will be able to create the ideal conditions of existence for a human world."[34] Is this not, I ask the students, what Kanye is doing in "Pinocchio Story," and, if so, how might this necessitate a re-evaluation of Kanye as an artist and a philosopher (if, indeed, it might do this at all).

Much of the discussion that often follows focuses on the exact nature of Kanye's "sacrifice," on his agency in his rise to pre-eminence, and his foreknowledge of the attendant issues of superstardom. West simultaneously seeks his audience's adoration and pity, but some students grant him neither. Though Kanye evidently envies his audience their presumably easier path to authenticity, this strikes a false note for some. Is Kanye's quest for authenticity, they ask, yet more inauthentic posturing? How, after all, can we take seriously laments about a lack of guidance from someone who positions himself at the vanguard—as the greatest of all time? The rhyme of "sell" and "hell" suggests a powerful defiance of capitalist machinery, but Kanye's brand (which orbits the man himself) has luxury and conspicuous consumption at its core.

In the midst of these conversations surrounding Kanye's apparent hypocrisies and inconsistencies, it becomes possible to reintroduce theories about the post-colonial subject—a subject divided, a subject at war with itself. Deep within the heart and mind of the subject a battle rages between the colonizer and the colonized, the self and the other, the subject and the object. Identity-making happens as we drive our stakes in the ground on this battlefield. The stakes couldn't be higher: in the balance are authenticity and intellectual freedom. The artist *par excellence* undeniably has the latter (at least in as much as they shape more than they are shaped), but the former is more elusive, and for the deep-thinking artist—even Kanye's sternest critics must grant him this title—bridging the gulf between the authentic life and the "flashing lights" demands increasingly stringent self-analysis and (frequently) abnegation.

A tangible urgency laces so much of "Pinocchio's Story" that students often—while conceding the possibility that his search for authenticity might be inauthentic—are willing to take Kanye's claims at face value. We are all familiar with the search for "real love," with the disappointments that attend upon consumerism, with the attempt to locate and inhabit more authentic modes of being, so students are inclined to empathize with Kanye's predicament. They are particularly drawn to the impossibility of Kanye's vision—his desire to return to a lost innocence, to the loving arms of his recently deceased mother (the "only one" whose "real love" was beyond question). To hear this in Kanye's lyrics is to humanize the would-be superhuman. It demands a re-evaluation of Kanye and his heavily constructed identity.

It is in the ambivalent interstices of this identity that Kanye's post-colonial condition and subjectivity rise to the surface. He longs to be that which he is not—and cannot be. Egoist though he is, he is uneasy in his own skin. His is an antagonistic and "agonistic" identity-making.[35] Perhaps most interesting (and a fecund source of classroom discussion) is the way he, as a post-colonial subject, vacillates between subject positions. He alternates between puppet and puppet-master, boy and man, wise man and novice. The reasons for these movements are rooted in his post-colonial subjectivity—in his blackness, which shapes his relationship with both the outside world and his internal self. This post-colonial condition comes to be enunciated from what Bhabha refers to as a "hybrid space," where the "very question of identification only emerges *in-between* disavowal and designation."[36] At the very least, West performs this struggle. Likely, he lives it as well.

The aim of this post-colonial reading is to expose students to new ways of understanding the precarious conditions of their own and others' subjectivities. West creates a disjunctive subject, one who seeks to be whole, who regrets, who can recognize his own superficiality. He straddles these ambivalent subject positions with a shifting and hybrid identification: the celebrity who feels invisible, even when all eyes are on him; the wooden thing dreaming of being a real boy.

Day Three: Forging the Personal Connection

The final session is also the most inspiring and fruitful one, at least from a pedagogical perspective. After introducing a number of sophisticated lines of philosophical inquiry, it is possible to unlock deeper (often personal) levels of meaning. The classroom is primed to discuss topics relating to diversity and inclusiveness and the mental conditions that attend upon marginality. While I need to facilitate much of the conversation during the first two sessions, during the last session, students need very little prodding. They are bursting with ideas, comments, and questions, not just for me, but for each other as well. The conversations that result are enriched in terms of perspectives and vocabulary—the latter often displaying a deep understanding of complex concepts: subjectivity, identity formation, and the post-colonial condition among them. By and large, students view Kanye through a more charitable lens, seeing him as a conflicted postcolonial subject who is inextricably linked to the history of the African American—to the tragic history of the colonized, enslaved, and circumscribed black minds and bodies in this country.[37]

Perhaps the most productive pedagogical outcomes involve the students' newly developed insights into their own positioning as post-colonial subjects. Black male students identify with West's fraught position; female students identify with his otherness, his foreclosed marginalization; white students identify with his struggle for authenticity and the tension between the real and the represented. Thanks to our earlier discussion of McLuhan, the role that the mass media plays in each of these frequently enters the discussions, and this opens up yet more avenues of philosophical enquiry that lead through Adorno and Horkeimer and countless others.

Ultimately, what students most appreciate about "Pinocchio Story" is West's attempt to destabilize his media-imposed identity, which gives the putative superhuman a face creased with human cares and concerns (even if the mask only falls away for a moment). Students openly admire and identify with West's search for an alternative identity, one that better reflects his own perception of himself as a loving and creating subject.

At the end of the final session, I broaden the conversation to include the genre as a whole. Students come to realize that the seductions of hip hop are not categorically different from those of other art forms, though the social vectors of blackness and masculinity have had a particular effect in narrowing the range of affective associations available to rappers. It is in this seduction that we can see how hip hop audiences and artists alike can easily fall into the trap of the glorified (and lucrative) celebrity image. At the same time, an artist and his or her art do not necessarily have to be one and the same—indeed, they often are not. The artist undoubtedly identifies (either strongly or completely) with what they produce and present. The philosophical task is interrogating both image and artist and locating, as much as it is possible to do so, where they diverge and converge. It lies in seeing oneself (the real and the represented self) in what is being represented for us and who is doing the representing. It is generally the case that when the students go to serve their ten hours of community service, which is a requirement in my course, they tend to work with middle-school and high school students on this dichotomous question of "the real" versus "the represented" self, particularly in the age of social media.

Whether inside or outside of hip hop celebrity, personal identity and the postmodern search for recognition and authenticity are exhausting. With new vocabulary and concepts, though, it becomes easier to articulate the roots of the postmodern disease. It becomes possible to sympathize and empathize with the marginalized, opening the door to new perspectives on life at the center of African American and celebrity culture and to life in America's wide margins and capacious gutters. The result is a more broad-minded classroom—one with inclusion at its core.

MAKING BRIGHTER CONNECTIONS

Michelle Hayford
University of Dayton
Dayton, OH, USA

Katie O'Leary
Brighter Connections Theatre
Columbus, OH, USA

The Centers for Disease Control and Prevention describes Autism Spectrum Disorder (ASD) as "a developmental disability that can cause significant social, communication, and behavioral challenges" in 1 out of every 68 children. Additionally, the "learning, thinking, and problem-solving abilities of people with ASD can range from gifted to severely challenged."[38] The cause of ASD is unknown and cannot be detected until the age of two years old, at the earliest. Families are often challenged to find extracurricular activities that are welcoming for their children with ASD. Necessary therapies are expensive and budgets are often strapped, but the need for a creative outlet for children with ASD to socialize and learn new skills is in higher demand than ever, as noted by Kim et al. in their article

"Neurodiversity on the Stage: The Effects of Inclusive Theatre on Youth with Autism":

> Creative interventions for individuals with ASD, like those that involve theatre, provide an important opportunity for youth and their families to receive innovative and affordable support services that serve to cultivate a sense of belonging which in turn promotes self-esteem, empathy, and more trusting relations with others.[39]

Brighter Connections Theatre (BCT) is a summer theatre camp for youth with differing needs, namely children with autism, co-facilitated with the University of Dayton (UD) Theatre, Dance, and Performance Technology (TDP) program. The foundation of the BCT model is built upon the same strategies and accommodations typically made for students in the classroom, applied in a youth theatre program, therefore positively impacting a child's social, communication, and behavior skills, and meeting a local need for families. Because this kind of opportunity for families is rare, questions that arise from parents new to BCT who are anxious about their child's participation include "Will my child fit in? Will s/he be supported in rehearsals? What if s/he can't keep up?" We reassure parents that BCT is a welcoming environment for their child, and our goal is that they thrive in theatre camp. With up to 16 children in the youth and young adult programs, the ability to meet needs at different levels is paramount. Between the UD students, faculty, and BCT community volunteers, we can realize a ratio of 16 children to 13 camp facilitators in order to provide the one-on-one attention that many of the cast members require.

Facilitators for the BCT camp are Katie O'Leary (co-author, founder, and director of BCT), several community member volunteers not affiliated with UD, as well as UD students and theatre faculty, including Michelle Hayford (co-author, director of UD's TDP program, and co-director of BCT summer camp). Katie has been facilitating BCT summer camp for youth with ASD for five summers. Her career as an Intervention Specialist in a public middle school, as well as a regular improv actor and theatre enthusiast, has enabled her to successfully train the UD and community collaborators to co-facilitate the BCT programming each summer. Michelle's expertise in applied theatre and creating original theatre, in collaboration with community partners to address social needs, allows her to bring an appreciation for the value of this applied theatre endeavor to the UD student participants.

The Dean's office of the College of Arts and Sciences at UD awards student fellowships in the form of a stipend that enables students to stay in Dayton over the summer to conduct research with faculty mentors.[40] For the last two summers, students have been able to serve as College of Arts and Sciences (CAS) student fellows and co-facilitate the BCT summer theatre camp in collaboration with the UD TDP program.[41] This experience provides mutual rewards for both the UD students and the youth with ASD. For the UD students, there is the opportunity to engage with life experiences and worldviews that differ from their own, thereby meeting the goal set forth in the Association of American Colleges and Universities (AAC&U's) HIP of diversity. For the cast members with ASD and other disabilities, the opportunity to socialize and create friendships with college-age students is welcomed, and the genuine relationships that result are rewarding for all involved.

The camp is six weeks long for youth ages 8–14, and five weeks for young adults ages 15–18 and both are held at UD in TDP facilities, including a classroom and the Black Box Theatre. The makeup of the 2017 youth cast included a total of 11 children. There were six boys and five girls. Eight had been identified with ASD, two had other diagnoses, and one had no diagnosis. Three students had limited language skills, including a nonverbal child with reading and writing skills several grade levels below average, and a child with Attention Deficit Hyperactivity Disorder (ADHD) and minimal coping skills. Other diagnoses in place of, or in addition to ASD, included psychosis, obsessive compulsive disorder, and attention deficit disorder. In a previous summer, we had a cast member with Asperger's who read college level texts at the age of eight. All five of our young adult cast members had ASD. Each of our cast members comes to us with distinctly different needs. Five UD students, two UD faculty, and six community volunteers worked jointly to provide quality theatre camp programs for these two age groups. For the youth cast members, two specific goals were identified for each child after a discussion with parents before the start of the program. These goals are set up similarly to an individual education plan (IEP), and are measurable, attainable, specific, and time-oriented objectives. Student fellows, volunteers, and directors took notes on progress toward these goals during and after each rehearsal in assessment binders. Examples include:

- Cast member will initiate and hold a conversation for at least two turns with a peer or volunteer by asking questions or making remarks about the other person one time per rehearsal.

- Cast member will participate in group activities with no more than one reminder per activity in two out of three observations.

This case study will consider our summer BCT camp experience of 2017, and describe the benefits to undergraduates of the HIP of engagement with diversity when working with youth and young adults with ASD and other diagnoses. We will also assess the multiple rewards of the camp experience for the cast members, while acknowledging the limitations of traditional IEP assessment for inclusive artistic practice.

"Can I Be Mary?"

Each rehearsal includes a couple of warm-ups, one or two games, a role-play session, and either the development or practice of original skits for the final performance at the culmination of the six-week program. During warm-ups and games, the first objective is to gauge how the group is feeling. Camp facilitators can perceive who is in a good mood, or having a bad day, lack of focus, and stress and frustration levels within the first five minutes. Sometimes, the detailed schedule is altered within the warm-up in order to meet the clear need for a different approach, such as a game that emphasizes concentration. The second objective of the warm-up and games is to engage each cast member. Many cast members are accustomed to being by themselves and with their own thoughts, and would stay on the periphery of the room if not encouraged by the beginning group activities.

The purpose of role-play in our rehearsals is to enable the cast members to practice life skills, as Autism Theatre Network leaders Andrew Nelson and Parasuram Ramamoorthi emphasize, "[y]oung people with ASD often … lack the ability to plan and prepare for novel settings and events." Therefore, "rehearsed response or role-play techniques can be used to help prepare for social situations."[42] Using guidelines from Nelson's *Foundation Role Plays for Autism*, we establish a purpose and procedure from the first rehearsal.[43] There is a semi-circle seating arrangement that is specifically used for role-play sessions, as well as two taped boxes showing students where to stand when playing the scene. Students are handed index cards to read the script. Following a routine is important for any child with different learning needs, as they associate the setup with the activity itself, therefore becoming more comfortable with the practice, and allowing them to become an active participant. We focused on the following life skills in our role-plays: ways to start a conversation, how to sustain a conversation, how to handle frustration, and how to let someone know you're upset.

Following role-play is dedicated time to developing or rehearsing original scripts. The UD students and BCT volunteers participate in every stage of rehearsal: warming up, playing games, role-play, and facilitating the development and rehearsal of skits. BCT is a peer model, where the UD students and BCT volunteers are also incorporated into the final show as actors. This peer model approach has the cast members with ASD and other diagnoses performing alongside neurotypical same age peers, UD students, and volunteers. Kim et al. describe the efficacy of the peer model in their description of The Miracle Project's (TMP) theatre with youth with ASD:

> Instead of teaching youth with ASD to follow conventional behavioral expectations, TMP encourages neurotypical individuals to join the world, and thus follow the lead, of youth with ASD, all in the context of theatrical play, performance, and experimentation. This process allows neurotypical individuals to identify with, and often celebrate, the experiences of youth with ASD on their own terms, and to engage others with openness, compassion, and empathy. Additionally, youth with ASD are able to develop relationships with neurotypical peers, which has been widely documented as having positive effects on the socialization and communication skills of those with ASD.[44]

The above description of the peer model process illustrates how BCT functions. UD students and community volunteers co-create with the cast members with ASD and other diagnoses, to bring the cast members' original stories to the stage. During the process of facilitating many writing workshops in the early weeks of camp, the UD students and volunteers work individually with cast members to find out what interests them, and build trust and relationships forged by a collective creative process.

Penelope[45] is 14 years old and returned for her second summer at BCT. Penelope is shy and tends to wear a hoodie to hide her face. In her first summer with BCT, she often preferred to watch the activities and was not interested in participating in games and role-plays. This summer, Penelope connected with one particular UD student, and their friendship gave her the confidence to fully participate and make progress on her personal goals. One of Penelope's goals was to initiate a conversation with a peer or volunteer once per rehearsal. She achieved this once in week one, three times in week two, three times in week three, and then six times in week four. Most of these conversations were initiated with Penelope's new friend and UD student, Betsy. This new friendship translated into more confidence and even encouraged Penelope to ask for a substantial role during one rehearsal, when she voiced her desire to be a more interesting character being played by a UD student by asking "Can I be Mary?," to which Mary said, "Of course, you'll be great at this part!"

Penelope was feeling down before one of the performances and didn't want to take off her hoodie to put on the cast tee shirt everyone wore for performances. Betsy was able to talk to her for ten minutes about other things and lift her mood, so that when a director asked Penelope again to put on her show shirt she quickly complied. Relationships like Penelope and Betsy's are invaluable, and every summer special friendships between cast members and students and community volunteers are the most rewarding part of BCT.

"Theatre Is Stupid!"

Ben was the first BCT cast member in five years who refused to perform. He demonstrated that for all cast members, the process is as valuable as the presentation of the "product," or the show that we put on for the audience at the end of the camp experience. Ben was one of five cast members with ASD in our inaugural year of the young adult camp for 15–18-year olds. He displayed some typical autistic behaviors, such as difficulty with communication, social interaction, and imagination. Namely, his limitations in using his imagination particularly challenged him in his daily experience of BCT camp. While he had a sophisticated sense of humor, he also was very literal and found theatre and acting to be silly and contrived. He repeatedly told us that "Theatre is stupid!" or "Acting is stupid!" When challenged to play improv games or read a scene, he would get frustrated, agitated, and humiliated, insisting that "No one would ever do this!" or "I would never say this!" Ultimately, he enjoyed the camp for the limited successes he had in socializing with one friend that he already knew coming into camp, but never was able to overcome his belief that "Theatre is stupid!" and had nothing to teach him. On the day of the young adult showcase for family and friends, he refused to come into the room to perform, and instead he sat in the hallway with his dad, while his mom watched the scene that he had helped write be performed without him.

While we could see Ben's non-participation in the showcase as a failure, Sara Jane Bailes reminds us that "failure works."[46] For Bailes, "a failed objective establishes an aperture, an opening onto several (and often many) other ways of doing that counter the authority of a singular or 'correct' outcome."[47] For Ben, the other ways of doing that were more fruitful for him in the end were providing stagehand assistance and technical support for the run of the youth shows in week six. He found his stride when placing props for a scene or running sound cues in the booth. In his case, the singular outcome of performing in a show was not a value to him, but working as part of the backstage team was satisfying. While running sound cues with a UD student operating the board, Ben thrived on the specific task, able to appreciate the computer software and technology that made it all possible.

Ben's exposure to supporting the world of imagination by assisting the storytelling on stage increased his capacity to see what imagination looked like in practice. This is the special purview of theatre: to create worlds, and to imagine what the world might be, as well as show us with focused attention what it means to be of the world. For Ben, his "failure" to perform led him to find a different way to cultivate his imaginative faculties by providing technical theatre support to the show while also increasing his ability to work as part of a team. The UD students that assisted Ben in the technical booth encouraged his enthusiasm for sound design and learned to have sensitivity toward youth with ASD who have specific learning preferences.

"Can We Move On?"

> Making mistakes is not easy, and making mistakes in front of others is even harder, but since this class is a democratic, collective community of theatre practitioners, all members become more and more trusting of their voices, their language skills, the levels of embodied practices, and what they can offer to the whole group.[48]

Similar to the theatre class described above by Kelly Brunetto in "Performing the Art of Language Learning," BCT is a safe place for making mistakes and figuring out how to be a part of a team. Many children with ASD tend to be loners who have difficulty in making friends, and therefore they tend to become rigid in doing things their way, impatient with others, and frustrated by the compromise and collaboration that is required in theatre.

Jessie is 13 years old, and was eager to make friends in her first summer with BCT. She took to acting quite naturally, as she easily interpreted characters off the page and had a great stage presence. However, she was not readily amenable to working as a part of a team, in that she insisted that her way was the *right way* and did not care to take direction or input from anyone else when rehearsing. She had little patience for other cast members and the process of trial and error required in the theatre. While rehearsing blocking, or stage movement, she would frequently ask in frustration, "Can we move on?" Early in the process, she did not appreciate the need to give other cast members time to work on their parts and blocking, and wanted to jump to the parts that involved her and be done with it.

When we made the transition from the theatre classroom to the Black Box Theatre for rehearsals, Jessie was particularly upset. The move to the theatre made the whole thing too real for her and she had stage fright during our first rehearsal in the space. At the start of her first scene, she looked down in fear and said "I can't do this." It was evident that Jessie not only didn't have patience for others, but that she also was hard on herself and was afraid of making mistakes and humiliating herself. The directors reassured her that rehearsals were the place to make the mistakes and that everyone would mess up and that was part of the process.

During a rehearsal, one of the UD students forgot a line, which in turn caused great confusion for the rest of the scene. Jessie saw that even college students mess up. The UD students who made mistakes in rehearsals were able to model the ability to have confidence, even when taking responsibility for an error and being embarrassed. The UD students were able to normalize making mistakes in front of others for the cast members with ASD. Jessie slowly got comfortable with the new pressure of being in the theatre and realized that in fact everyone was making mistakes and it was okay. Jessie was able to be more accepting of herself and others by acknowledging that mistakes and trial and error are a part of the creative process. This acceptance enabled her to develop more patience for herself and other cast members as the weekend of final performances approached, and she even took responsibility and apologized to the directors for her impatience at a previous rehearsal. During the shows, Jessie become a leader among her peers, helping other cast members to get through scenes and quietly cueing them when it was their turn to speak.

"Boss Hog!"

One of our favorite games and warm-up activities for the young adult camp was a Dukes of Hazard theatre game. We stood in a circle for the game and in turn each cast member would say one of the following commands, prompting the rest of the circle to repeat the command and the associated choreography:

- "Daisy Dukes," accompanied by miming thumbs in belt loops and twirling toes on the floor
- "Get them Duke boys," followed by everyone running to find a different place to stand in the circle
- "Boss Hog," accompanied by miming the pulling of suspenders and lunging forward

Everyone enjoyed this game because it created laughter, brought us together, and lifted the mood in the room. In particular, Tyler loved this game. Tyler is 16 and was with BCT for his first summer. He often needs to be prompted to engage in conversation, and does not typically initiate dialogue with others. Theatre is a great tool for creating space for multiple communication modalities. Through the semiotics of performance, namely the body and its relationship to space, as well as gesture, movement, and choreography, cast members who are uncomfortable with speaking can find other ways of communicating. Theatre games that use the entire body, including a verbal command, can encourage cast members with ASD to participate fully and take comfort in the multitude of cues for effective communication.

Tyler loved to yell "Boss Hog!" when it came his turn in the circle, and he took pleasure from the rest of us repeating the command with him as we did the movement gesture to accompany it. Saying "Boss Hog!" and completing the choreography made Tyler laugh loudly, and in response we all laughed together. The multiple languages of theatre, where a repeated movement sequence and silly verbal command communicate volumes among the ensemble performing it, create trust and community among all the players and is one of the reasons why BCT is successful. Tyler experienced effective communication every time he gave us the "Boss Hog!" cue, and the successful performance that called on his voice, body, and emotions built his confidence and his sense of belonging. Theatre games create trust and camaraderie among the ensemble. For the UD students, playing games with the cast members with ASD created a common vocabulary not based solely on language, and opened up alternative and nonverbal modes of connection unique to theatre semiotics.

"Hold Hands."

In their book "Inclusive Arts Practice and Research: A critical Manifesto," Alice Fox and Hannah Macpherson suggest that in practicing inclusive arts, facilitators need to be responsive to diverse forms of communication: "This might involve sitting quietly with a person, speaking very little but choosing particular materials that help the person speak or feel through an artwork."[49] For Julia and Clarissa, two sisters with ASD who were mostly nonverbal, sitting with them while they drew pictures or simply looking out the windows with them were the ways of communicating that they preferred.

Amber is 14 years old and is almost completely nonverbal. She has ASD, a sensory processing disorder, and compulsions. Her parents forewarned us that she particularly liked to hold people's hands. We quickly learned that once she had a hold, it was extremely difficult to redirect her. One of Amber's goals was to understand others' need for personal space, and to ask to hold hands instead of just grabbing another's hand. In her first week of camp, Amber would only listen to redirection when it came to personal space in 4 out of 14 observations. By holding hands with others, Amber is able to stimulate her senses. Sensory processing disorder is common in children with autism, and in Amber's case, holding hands with another would become her sole focus. To enable Amber to get more out of her camp experience, we asked her parents to bring in different sensory items from home that Amber valued, let her stroke a clothing item on a volunteer or the tops of fingernails when she asked first, and rewarded her with positive reinforcements (often a snack) when she went for a certain amount of time respecting others' personal space. We succeeded in getting her to ask to hold hands instead of grabbing hands unexpectedly. She frequently approached UD students and other BCT volunteers with her request by saying "Hold hands." Depending on what else was happening in the room, her request could be accepted and we would hold her hand, or we would attempt to redirect her attention to participate in the activity.

For the UD students, working with Amber increased their sensitivity to other ways of being in the world. Getting to know Amber and seeing the world through her need for sensory stimulation while honoring their own needs for personal space was a challenging and rewarding negotiation. By week three, the frequency of hand grabbing immediately decreased as she began to tune into her parts in the scripts. One of Amber's goals was following stage directions while rehearsing. This included saying lines on time and performing her blocking with her partner in the scenes. Every night during one of the skits, she had three lines to read at separate times over the microphone in the booth, while everyone on stage collectively stopped to listen for her voice. In rehearsals, Amber needed several reminders on any given night to say her line. However, during all three performances Amber said her line immediately and clearly into the microphone. Performing her blocking was a bit more challenging, as she walked onto stage twice in the middle of scenes that she was not acting in, as well as laid down during one of her scenes on stage after saying "Tired." But, the fantastic thing about BCT is that all her behavior is accepted, and we just rolled with it. It makes for an unpredictable show! Amber's overall growth from the beginning of the program until the end impressed us. She made strides in respecting others' need for personal space, in communicating her desires, and in responsive verbal communication.

"This Is Not Going to Be Easy."

Connor is a 15-year-old cast member with ASD, who has participated in BCT for the last five summers. He has grown tremendously in his communication skills and social interactions during his time with BCT. Connor routinely says, "This is not going to be easy," while in the midst of fully participating in a game, role-play, or scene. Even while we were taking cast pictures and losing patience with arranging everyone to fit within the frame of the picture, Connor said, "This is not going to be easy." And he is always right.

Theatre is not easy. It is challenging for anyone, because it's a playground where we practice being human, and being human is hard. Theatre teaches us resilience when we fail through all our trial and error, it challenges our rigidity, it forces us to compromise and play well with others, it requires us to be empathic, and use our entire selves to communicate. The same skills necessary for theatre are the very skills that most youth with ASD need to cultivate. Many studies have been published that recognize the therapeutic value of theatre for people with ASD, including increased empathy, self-esteem, comfort with others, and trust.[50] Theatre has also been shown to improve social responsiveness, acknowledgment of the perspective of others, participation, and cooperation for participants with ASD.[51] Theatre practice with a peer model approach, like BCT, has been shown to lessen anxiety during social interaction for those with ASD, increasing their social competence.[52]

It is the personal triumphs of cultivating more patience, resilience, understanding, empathy, and a sense of belonging that are hard to capture through traditional assessment means. Our assessment collection has historically been modeled on the IEP, as this is a framework that both Katie and our BCT parents find comfortable and familiar. However, Michelle has posited and Katie has agreed, that moving forward we need to have alternative ways of gathering assessment data so that we can account for the skill sets gained that the parents could not have anticipated when they had their initial conversation about goals before camp began. Fox and Macpherson remind us that "[u]nlike some forms of research, which advocate designing research at the outset and then 'applying' that research design to a group, when working with people with learning disabilities in arts settings it is essential to be flexible and open to change."[53] Indeed, in addition to the quantitative data and qualitative surveys we collect,

> We can add to a list of possible findings properties such as gestures, habits, images and sounds. In this way, arts-based research calls into question what might traditionally be conceived as a research finding or output, where presenting arts-based research findings doesn't mean turning people into clichéd one-dimensional narratives.[54]

The positive benefits of engaging with theatre do not come easily. Our BCT cast members are challenged, and there are inevitable frustrations and tears as a result of facing some of the obstacles that theatre challenges them to overcome. For the UD students, faculty, and community volunteers, our capacity for empathy, understanding, and compassion is increased, and our collective worldview broadened. Together, we all experience moments of discovery and celebration that accompany personal triumphs, and the satisfaction of being a part of a theatre community that stands by you when things are hard.

NOTES

1. George D. Kuh and Carol Geary Schneider, *High-Impact Educational Practices: What They Are, Who Has Access to Them, and Why They Matter.*
2. Jiali Luo and David Jamieson-Drake, *A Retrospective Assessment of the Educational Benefits of Interaction Across Racial Boundaries*, 67–69. These pages summarize numerous studies on diversity in higher education.
3. Luo and Jamieson-Drake, *A Retrospective Assessment*, 75.
4. Luo and Jamieson-Drake, *A Retrospective Assessment*, 78.

5. Read about the protest of productions of *Angels in America* in Texas and North Carolina in Patrick Healy, "*Angels in America*" Earns Place in Pantheon. Most recently, the Public Theatre in New York had protests of a Trump-inspired *Julius Caesar*, see Konerman, *Protesters Interrupt Trump-Inspired "Julius Caesar."*
6. See the recent debate about bias in theatre criticism and the democratization of culture in the following articles: Gwendolyn Alker, "A Collective Call Against Critical Bias"; P. Carl, "Becoming a White Man in the Theatre"; and Chris Jones, "Like it or Not, We are in the Midst of a Second Arts Revolution."
7. See Jennifer Schuessler, "Cancellation of College Production of "Jesus in India" Over Casting of White Actors Prompts Debate," for an example of casting controversies.
8. SNAAP survey data.
9. Luo and Jamieson-Drake, *A Retrospective Assessment*, 83.
10. Patricia Shehan Campbell, "Music Education in a Time of Cultural Transformation."
11. C. Victor Fung, "Rationales for Teaching World Musics: C. Victor Fung Discusses the Importance of Introducing Students to Multicultural Music by Including it in School Curricula," 36.
12. Bennett Reimer, "Another Perspective: Struggling Toward Wholeness in Music Education," 27.
13. Bennett Reimer, "Reconceiving the Standards and the School Music Program," 35.
14. Allen Clements, "Minority Students and Faculty in Higher Music Education," 55.
15. See Donna T. Emmanuel, "An Immersion Field Experience: An Undergraduate Music Education Course in Intercultural Competence," for an example of a cultural immersion experience for music students and S. Kim and Annette Whitehead-Pleaux, "Music Therapy and Cultural Diversity" to see how music therapy as a field has approached inclusion.
16. Doug Risner and Susan W. Stinson, "Moving Social Justice: Challenges, Fears and Possibilities in Dance Education," 7–8.
17. See Axis Dance Company in Oakland, BalaSole Dance Company in New York City, ILL NANA/DiverseCity Dance Company of Toronto for examples of diverse professional dance companies.
18. Jill Green, "Socially Constructed Bodies in American Dance Classrooms," 156.
19. Green, "Socially Constructed Bodies," 159.
20. Susan C. Petersen and Karen A. Kaufmann, "Adaptation Techniques for Modeling Diversity in the Dance Class," 17.
21. For example, see Alice-Ann Darrow, "Dealing with Diversity: The Inclusion of Students with Disabilities in Music" and Sally Bailey, "Exemplary Theatre Practices: Creating Barrier-Free Theatre."

22. See Ernest T. Pascarella, Christopher T. Pierson, Gregory C. Wolniak, and Patrick T. Terenzini, "First-Generation College Students: Additional Evidence on College Experiences and Outcomes," for a broad view on first-generation college students' experience, including the fact that on the whole they engage less in fine arts curriculum when compared to other students.
23. See Reid Davis, Peter Harrigan, Marietta Hedges, Maya Roth, Monica Stufft, and Christine Young, "To Thrive: Social Justice Theatre on Six Catholic Campuses" for examples of such battles on Catholic campuses.
24. For an introduction to applied theatre, see Monica Prendergast and Juliana Saxton, *Applied Theatre: International Case Studies and Challenges for Practice*. For an example of an international play festival see Joan E. Robbins, "Forging Cultural Dialogue with an Undergraduate International Play Festival."
25. Ping Chong and L. Modirzadeh, *Secret History: Journeys Abroad, Journeys Within*.
26. Florence Samson, "Drama in Aesthetic Education: An Invitation to Imagine the World as if it Could Be Otherwise," 76–77.
27. See Anish Bavishi, Juan M. Madera, and Michelle R. Hebl, "The Effect of Professor Ethnicity and Gender on Student Evaluations: Judged Before Met," for one of many recent studies about student bias in teacher evaluations.
28. Donda West and Karen Hunter, *Raising Kanye: Life Lessons from the Mother of a Hip-Hop Superstar*.
29. Nicholas D. Krebs, "Confidently (Non)cognizant of Neoliberalism: Kanye West and the Interruption of Taylor Swift," in Julius Bailey, *Cultural Impact*, 196.
30. Peter Macia, thefader.com, "Fader 58: Kanye West Cover Story and Interview," http://www.thefader.com/2008/11/25/fader-58-kanye-west-cover-story-and-interview/, (accessed August 24, 2017).
31. Eric Johnson, abcnews.go.com, "Kanye West: Hip-Hop's 'Creative Genius'," http://abcnews.go.com/Nightline/story?id=3640219&page=1 (accessed August 24, 2017).
32. Hiddleston, Jane, "The Perplexed Persona of Frantz Fanon's Peau Noire, masques blancs," 3.
33. Homi K. Bhabha, "Remembering Fanon: Self, Psyche and the Colonial Condition," in Patrick Williams and Laura Chrisman, eds., *Colonial Discourse and Post-Colonial Theory: A Reader*, 114.
34. Homi K. Bhabha in Franz Fanon and Richard Philcox. Black Skin White Masks, xxiv.
35. Homi K. Bhabha, *The Location of Culture*.
36. Homi K. Bhabha, *The Location of Culture*, 72.
37. This point will be better explained in the final presentations/findings that the students discussed. Kanye's post-colonial subject is wrestling with his "New Slave" status, namely an appropriation of white male hegemony through the domestication of the mind. The students queried how can Kanye, through his music, force the (black) listener to see what capitalism

does to us, but he, in turn, is himself a non-European subject turned into a European construct for exploitative purposes? Some argued that one way is to reduce him to animal, yet retain the ability to sympathize with him (Bergsonian tradition). Also it was surmised that colonization also involves the usurpation of cultural traditions in order to force the emergence of a pseudo-homogeneous culture. You do this by pretending to incorporate him into your superstructure and infrastructure. Sha'Dawn Battle suggested in an interview "Give Kanye access to the fashion industry, but only in a way that you may exploit him and reinvest the capitalist gain into the (white) male economy—one that he does not have access to. You'll have to think about how this happens. Also, he must be a reformed subject. In what ways has Kanye proven to have internalized the need for his reformation, and how has he reified it? Next, the colonial governing structure operates through the grotesque and obscene—or through a system of venality. How does bribery and venality manifest in the music industry, and not necessarily as enacted from the top down? (i.e. ... think neocolonial power ... the African regime ... the colonized subject is now the new colonizer ..., but how does he maintain, stabilize and disseminate his power through venality?)."

38. See cdc.gov.
39. Ah-Jeong Kim, Sarah Stembridge, Christopher Lawrence, Vincent Torres, Nancy Miodrag, Joong-Won Lee, and David Boynes, "Neurodiversity on the Stage: The Effects of Inclusive Theatre on Youth with Autism," 29.
40. Many thanks to our administrators and friends at the University of Dayton for making this partnership possible: Jason Pierce, Dean of the College of Arts and Sciences, Don Pair, Associate Dean for Interdisciplinary Research and Experiential Initiatives, Phyllis Bergiel, Coordinator for Academic Initiatives, Eric Spina, President of University of Dayton, Karen Spina, Board Member of Brighter Connections Theatre, and Matt Evans, Technical Director of Theatre, Dance, and Performance Technology. And special thanks to Donna Beran, former Costumer and Lecturer for Theatre, Dance, and Performance Technology, for bringing the authors together and supporting the initial partnership.
41. UD CAS Student Fellows for Summer 2017s Brighter Connections Theatre summer camp were Elizabeth Mazza, Beth Fuchs, Mary Stoughton, and Andrew Martin. Additionally, Jordan Hightower received internship credit.
42. Parasuram Ramamoorthi and Andrew Nelson, "Drama Education for Individuals on the Autism Spectrum," 2.
43. Andrew Nelson, *Foundation Role Plays for Autism*.
44. Ah-Jeong Kim et al., "Neurodiversity on the Stage," 29–30.

45. Names of youth and young adult cast members were changed to protect their anonymity.
46. Sara Jane Bailes, *Performance Theatre and the Poetics of Failure*.
47. Bailes, *Performance Theatre*, 2.
48. Kelly Kingsbury Brunetto, *Performing the Art of Language Learning: Deepening the Language Learning Experience through Theatre and Drama*.
49. Alice Fox and Hannah Macpherson, *Inclusive Arts Practice and Research: A Critical Manifesto*, 86.
50. Ah-Jeong Kim et al., "Neurodiversity on the Stage: The Effects of Inclusive Theatre on Youth with Autism."
51. Suzanne Reading, James Reading, Robert J. Padgett, Samantha Reading, and Pete Pryor, "The Use of Theatre to Develop Social and Communication Behaviors for Students with Autism."
52. Blythe A Corbett., Scott D. Blain, Sara Ioannou, and Maddie Balser, "Changes in Anxiety Following a Randomized Control Trial of a Theatre-Based Intervention for Youth with Autism Spectrum Disorder."
53. Fox and Macpherson, *Inclusive Arts Practice and Research*, 143.
54. Fox and Macpherson, *Inclusive Arts Practice and Research*, 144.

Bibliography

Alker, Gwendolyn, et al., A Collective Call Against Critical Bias. *Howlround*. http://howlround.com/a-collective-call-against-critical-bias. Accessed 25 July 2017.

Ashcroft, Bill, Gareth Griffiths, and Helen Tiffin. 1989. *The Empire Writes Back: Theory and Practice in Post Colonial Literatures*. London and New York: Routledge.

Axis Dance Company. http://www.axisdance.org/. Accessed 25 July 2017.

Bailes, Sara Jane. 2011. *Performance Theatre and the Poetics of Failure*. New York: Routledge.

Bailey, Julius, ed. 2014. *The Cultural Impact of Kanye West*. New York: Palgrave Macmillan.

Bailey, Sally. Exemplary Theatre Practices: Creating Barrier-Free Theatre. *2013 VSA Intersections: Arts and Special Education*: 25.

BalaSole Dance Company. http://www.balasoledance.org/. Accessed 25 July 2017.

Bavishi, Anish, Juan M. Madera, and Michelle R. Hebl. 2010. The Effect of Professor Ethnicity and Gender on Student Evaluations: Judged Before Met. *Journal of Diversity in Higher Education* 3 (4): 245.

Bhabha, Homi K. 1994. *The Location of Culture*. London and New York: Routledge Classics.

———. 2004. Writing Rights and Responsibilities. (U. O. T.V. Interview), October 10.

———. 2015. Remembering Fanon: Self, Psyche and the Colonial Condition. In *Colonial Discourse and Post-Colonial Theory: A Reader*, ed. Patrick Williams and Laura Chrisman. New York: Routledge.

Brunetto, Kelly Kingsbury. 2015. *Performing the Art of Language Learning: Deepening the Learning Experience Through Theatre and Drama*. Blue Mounds, WI: Deep University Press.

Campbell, Patricia Shehan. 2002. Music Education in a Time of Cultural Transformation. *Music Educators Journal* 89 (1): 27–32.

Carl, P. Becoming a White Man in the Theatre. *Howlround*. http://howlround.com/becoming-a-white-man-in-the-theatre. Accessed 25 July 2017.

Centers for Disease Control and Prevention. Facts About ASD. CDC.gov. https://www.cdc.gov/ncbddd/autism/facts.html. Accessed 18 July 2017.

Chong, Ping, and L. Modirzadeh. 2004. Secret History: Journeys Abroad, Journeys Within.

Clements, Allen. 2009. Minority Students and Faculty in Higher Music Education. *Music Educators Journal* 95 (3): 53–56.

Corbett, Blythe A., Scott D. Blain, Sara Ioannou, and Maddie Balser. 2017. Changes in Anxiety Following a Randomized Control Trial of a Theatre-Based Intervention for Youth with Autism Spectrum Disorder. *Autism* 21 (3): 333–343.

Darrow, Alice-Ann. 2003. Dealing with Diversity: The Inclusion of Students with Disabilities in Music. *Research Studies in Music Education* 21 (1): 45–57.

Davies, Carole Boyce. 1994. *Black Women, Writing and Identity*. London: Routledge.

Davis, Reid, Peter Harrigan, Marietta Hedges, Maya Roth, Monica Stufft, and Christine Young. 2015. To Thrive: Social Justice Theatre on Six Catholic Campuses. *Theatre Topics* 25 (3): 277–284.

Derrida, Jacques. 1995. *The Gift of Death*. Chicago: University of Chicago.

Emmanuel, Donna T. 2003. An Immersion Field Experience: An Undergraduate Music Education Course in Intercultural Competence. *Journal of Music Teacher Education* 13 (1): 33–41.

Fanon, Frantz. 1963. *The Wretched of the Earth*. New York: Grove Press.

———. 1968. *The Wretched of The Earth*. New York: Grove Press.

Fanon, Frantz, and Richard Philcox. 2008. *Black Skin, White Masks*. New York: Grove Press.

Fox, Alice, and Hannah Macpherson. 2015. *Inclusive Arts Practice and Research: A Critical Manifesto*. New York: Routledge.

Fung, C. Victor. 1995. Rationales for Teaching World Musics: C. Victor Fung Discusses the Importance of Introducing Students to Multicultural Music by Including it in School Curricula. *Music Educators Journal* 82 (1): 36–40.

Gilroy, Paul. 1995. *The Black Atlantic*. Cambridge: Harvard University Press.

Green, Jill. 2001. Socially Constructed Bodies in American Dance Classrooms. *Research in Dance Education* 2 (2): 155–173.

Healy, Patrick. 'Angels in America' Earns Place in Pantheon. http://www.nytimes.com/2010/10/25/theatre/25angels.html. Accessed 25 July 2017.

Hiddleston, Jane. 2008. The Perplexed Persona of Frantz Fanon's Peau Noire, masques blancs. *Postcolonial Text* 4: 3.

ILL NANA/DiverseCity Dance Company. https://illnanadcdc.com/. Accessed 25 July 2017.

Jones, Chris. Like It or Not, We Are In the Midst of a Second Arts Revolution. http://www.chicagotribune.com/entertainment/theatre/ct-culture-critics-jones-ae-0702-20170701-column.html. Accessed 25 July 2017.

Kim, S., and Annette Whitehead-Pleaux. 2015. Music Therapy and Cultural Diversity. *Music Therapy Handbook*: 51–63.

Kim, Ah-Jeong, Sarah Stembridge, Christopher Lawrence, Vincent Torres, Nancy Miodrag, Joong-Won Lee, and David Boynes. 2015. Neurodiversity on the Stage: The Effects of Inclusive Theatre on Youth with Autism. *International Journal of Education and Social Science* 2 (9): 27–39.

Kofman, Kirby Dick, and Amy Ziering Kofman. 2002. Directors. *Derrida* [Motion Picture].

Konerman, Jennifer. Protesters Interrupt Trump-Inspired 'Julius Caesar'. http://www.hollywoodreporter.com/news/protesters-interrupt-trump-inspired-julius-caesar-theatre-production-1014455. Accessed 25 July 2017.

Kuh, George D., and Carol Geary Schneider. 2008. *High-Impact Educational Practices: What They Are, Who Has Access to Them, and Why They Matter*. Washington, DC: Association of American Colleges and Universities.

Luo, Jiali, and David Jamieson-Drake. 2009. A Retrospective Assessment of the Educational Benefits of Interaction Across Racial Boundaries. *Journal of College Student Development* 50 (1): 67–86.

McLuhan, Marshall. 1994. *Understanding Media: The Extensions of Man*. Cambridge: Massachusetts Institute of Technology.

Nelson, Andrew. 2010. *Foundation Role Plays for Autism: Role-Plays for Working with Individuals with Autism Spectrum Disorders, Parents, Peers, Teachers and Other Professionals*. Philadelphia, PA: Jessica Kingsley Publishers.

Pascarella, Ernest T., Christopher T. Pierson, Gregory C. Wolniak, and Patrick T. Terenzini. 2004. First-Generation College Students: Additional Evidence on College Experiences and Outcomes. *The Journal of Higher Education* 75 (3): 249–284.

Petersen, Susan C., and Karen A. Kaufmann. 2002. Adaptation Techniques for Modeling Diversity in the Dance Class. *Journal of Physical Education, Recreation & Dance* 73 (7): 16–19.

Prendergast, Monica, and Juliana Saxton, eds. 2009. *Applied Theatre: International Case Studies and Challenges for Practice*. Chicago: Intellect Books.

Ramamoorthi, Parasuram, and Andrew Nelson. 2011. Drama Education for Individuals on the Autism Spectrum. *Key Concepts in Theatre/Drama Education*: 177.

Reading, Suzanne, James Reading, Robert J. Padgett, Samantha Reading, and Pete Pryor. 2015. The Use of Theatre to Develop Social and Communication Behaviors for Students with Autism. *Journal of Speech Pathology & Therapy* 1 (1).

Reimer, Bennett. 2004. Reconceiving the Standards and the School Music Program. *Music Educators Journal* 91 (1): 33–37.

———. 2012. Another Perspective: Struggling Toward Wholeness in Music Education. *Music Educators Journal* 99 (2): 25–29.

Risner, Doug, and Susan W. Stinson. 2010. Moving Social Justice: Challenges, Fears and Possibilities in Dance Education. *International Journal of Education & the Arts* 11 (6): n6.

Robbins, Joan E. 2010. Forging Cultural Dialogue with an Undergraduate International Play Festival. *Theatre Topics* 20 (1): 65–76.

Said, Edward. 1979. *Orientalism*. New York: Vintage.

Samson, Florence. 2005. Drama in Aesthetic Education: An Invitation to Imagine the World as if It Could Be Otherwise. *The Journal of Aesthetic Education* 39 (4): 70–81.

Sanderson, George. 1984. *Marshall McLuhan: The Man and His Message*. Colorado: Fulcrum Inc.

Schuessler, Jennifer. Cancellation of College Production of 'Jesus in India' Over Casting of White Actors Prompts Debate. https://artsbeat.blogs.nytimes.com/2015/11/16/cancellation-of-college-production-of-jesus-in-india-over-casting-of-white-actors-prompts-debate/. Accessed 25 July 2017.

Strategic National Arts Alumni Project. Snaap.indiana.edu. http://snaap.indiana.edu/pdf/2016/SNAAP15_16_Recent_Grads_Aggregate_Report.pdf. Accessed 24 July 2017.

Thorogood, T. 2008. Kanye West Opens Up His Heart. London, November 12.

West, Donda, and Karen Hunter. 2007. *Raising Kanye: Life Lessons from the Mother of a Hip-Hop Superstar*. New York: Simon and Schuster.

CHAPTER 9

Service Learning and Community-Based Learning

Since at least the founding of Campus Compact in 1985, when the university presidents of Brown, Georgetown, and Stanford decided to formalize their commitment to local communities and the democratic project, community-engaged learning has been a major player in the higher education landscape.[1] Colleges and universities have to benefit their surrounding area if they are to thrive and be welcome contributors to the local community. It is, of course, in the college or university's best interest to have mutually beneficial relationships with local community stakeholders as this can bring more visibility to an institution as well as positively impact the institutional image. With over 1000 colleges and universities now participating in Campus Compact, it is clear that the pedagogical practice of community-based learning, and service learning, is embedded in higher education. The quality of these experiences varies dramatically according to each institution's capacity to support this high-stakes learning. While some universities have institutes or centers focused on community engagement with full staff support, other less resourced colleges and universities may rely on individual faculty members alone to make their reputation in the local community via the development of service or community-based learning in coursework.

Because of the ubiquity of service learning and community-engaged learning now required of students as they matriculate, colleges and universities are starting to understand the necessity of properly resourcing and assessing these endeavors. Initiatives aimed at faculty development that

© The Author(s) 2018
M. Hayford, S. Kattwinkel (eds.), *Performing Arts as High-Impact Practice*, The Arts in Higher Education,
https://doi.org/10.1007/978-3-319-72944-2_9

seek to ensure consistent ethical practice of community-based work are common on many campuses. The tracking and assessment of community-engaged learning are occurring on many campuses, especially those seeking or maintaining the coveted Carnegie Community Engagement Classification, initiated in 2006. Currently, 361 colleges and universities have earned the Carnegie Community Engagement Classification, having provided evidence of robust infrastructure, faculty development, and assessment practices to support the community-engaged and service learning happening on their campuses.[2]

When community-based learning and service learning are incorporated into the culture of an institution and faculty feel supported in providing their students the opportunities for mutual exchange, the benefits are well documented. Faculty report that their pedagogy improves, and that students make connections between curriculum and community issues when engaged in community-based learning.[3] Of course, there are also hurdles faced by many administrators who would like to invest in more infrastructural resources to support community-based learning, but are faced with difficult budget scarcities. In those cases, community-based learning still transpires on campuses and the burden falls on faculty members to provide this enrichment with little to no financial support by way of course release or stipend, nor infrastructure support in the way of transportation and staff assistance. But the most common problem for faculty who engage in community-based learning is the lack of recognition of this kind of scholarship for their promotion and tenure portfolios. While Ernest Boyer called for a broader definition of scholarship to include community engagement in his 1990 book *Scholarship Reconsidered*, too few institutions have meaningfully changed tenure and promotion polices to evaluate non-traditional research.[4] The "publish or perish" paradigm is very much alive and well, even when universities have included community engagement as part of their mission or identity. It is rare that an institution goes beyond the feel-good verbiage of community engagement splashed on their websites and promotional materials to revise what is at the heart of the university's long-term commitment to its faculty: its criteria for tenure and promotion.[5] Until tenure and promotion criteria become flexible enough to credit the time-consuming practices of community-based research, faculty who engage in community for their pedagogy and scholarship do so at their own peril as the tenure clock ticks, and for their own unrewarded personal and pedagogical commitments to social justice and service. This is an exploited group of faculty, and we all need to do what we can to properly advocate for recourses and recognition for ourselves and our colleagues who perform research and teach in partnership with community.

Amy Driscoll reviewed the data submitted by colleges and universities applying for the Carnegie Community Engagement Classification in her "Analysis of the Carnegie Classification of Community Engagement," and found that the impact of community-engaged learning on faculty is indeed overlooked in assessment practices, as are the following:

- Assessing community perceptions of institutional engagement;
- Assessing the impact of community engagement on faculty, community, and institution;
- Initiating and maintaining mutuality and reciprocity in partnerships with community and specifically in terms of ongoing feedback mechanisms.[6]

Indeed, a special issue of the journal *Feminist Teacher* is dedicated to community-engaged learning as feminist praxis and the co-editors Lee Nickoson and Kristine Blair caution:

> All too often, concepts such as "service-learning," "connecting the undergraduate experience," or "the scholarship of engagement" can become academic and cultural buzzwords. These concepts are deployed less to work with and for communities and more to simulate the appearance of institutional presence in local contexts to foster the perception of accountability to economic and political stakeholders who question the limited use value of higher education in the larger culture.[7]

So, what does it mean then for an institution to engage in community-engaged and service learning in an ethical manner? How do colleges and universities get it right? There are many resources one can find from Campus Compact that can guide assessment practices, and seeking out faculty colleagues at campuses that have earned the Carnegie Community Engagement Classification for peer mentoring and guidance is a great place to start. However, undertaking community-engaged research, teaching, and learning is not a one-size-fits-all arrangement. In fact, a greater sensitivity to the specific needs of any one community partner is called for in Daniel Banks' "The Question of Cultural Diplomacy: Acting Ethically." Banks describes the work he does with Theatre Without Borders (TWB) in partnership with community:

> An ongoing conversation in TWB is the move away from the notion of fixed "best practices," toward recommending a more fluid application of what works in each individual situation—often now referred to as "better practices." We hope to shift the thinking that there is a discrete or stable approach to the work of cultural exchange and diplomacy. Each situation is different, laden with its own complexities and paradoxes, and requires a methodology that can be adapted to its uniqueness.[8]

It is the uniqueness of any one community-engaged learning partner that makes consistent assessment hard to accomplish. However, we must continue to solicit feedback about community-engaged learning with our local partners to ensure reciprocity and mutual benefit. As Elizabeth Tryon and Randy Stoecker have detailed in *The Unheard Voices: Community Organizations and Service-Learning*, a common problem reported by community partners is communication. The short-term service and engagement sometimes dictated by the academic calendar exacerbates this communication problem, and also explains inadequate relationship building. Other areas for improvement noted by Tryon and Stoecker are the management and evaluation of students and their cultural competency with community partner clientele.[9]

The Center for Performance and Civic Practice (CPCP) is a wonderful resource for performing arts programs, faculty, and the communities that they serve.[10] CPCP engages in, and facilitates, innovative and efficacious partnerships between arts programs, artists, and community partners to address social justice concerns in communities nationwide. Michael Rohd, founder of Sojourn Theatre and Institute Professor at Arizona State University's Herberger Institute for Design and the Arts, is CPCP's Executive Director. Rohd, with assistance from Shannon Scrofano, CPCP's Director of Design, facilitated a workshop for the Association for Theatre in Higher Education's Leadership Institute in the summer of 2017, in which he shared CPCP's incisive language for understanding the diverse needs of community partners when engaging artists in partnerships:

Community Partner Needs:

Advocacy—help increase visibility and propel mission/message;
Dialogue—bring diverse groups into meaningful exchange with each other;
Story-Sharing—gather and share narratives from a particular population or around a particular topic;
Civic Application—engage the public and decision-makers together in acts of problem-solving and crafting vision;
Cross-Sector Innovation—leverage skills and experience from different fields or disciplines to create and manifest new knowledge;
Capacity Building—develop needed skills within the existing human resources of an organization to accomplish goals through current or new strategies.[11]

Rohd also shared that artists need to be very clear about determining how a partnership with a community organization will take shape by using precise language to describe and understand shared expectations about the parameters of the collaboration. CPCP offers clarifying language to describe the variety of arts and community organization partnerships that is useful in understanding and describing the scope of a shared project. To this end, CPCP has articulated three discrete forms of art-making that transpire in a spectrum understanding of these partnerships:

Articulating a **spectrum** of art-making in relation to process and intentions:

Studio Practice: Artists make their own work and engage with neighbors and residents as audience.
Social Practice: Artists work with neighbors and residents on an artist-led vision in ways that may include an intention of social impact beyond a traditional audience experience.
Civic Practice: Artists co-design project with neighbors and residents; the spoken intention is to serve a public partner's self-defined needs.[12]

Incorporating community-engaged learning or service learning in performing arts curriculum happens in numerous ways unique to each community that partners with an institution of higher learning to provide a site for mutual exchange with college students. The performing arts student can frequently be found in K–12 classrooms, via applied theatre, dance, or music lessons for youth, or bringing performing arts experiences to local service agencies, health and wellness centers, or hospitals. Wherever we bring our students, we must prepare them for an ethical encounter with the community partner. As Banks reminds us:

> [P]rojects of cultural diplomacy work best when all parties—agency, facilitators, and participants—are in regular, early dialogue and time is dedicated to discussing all aspects of a program, including, especially, philosophy and methodology. Initiating this type of communication may prove challenging, as many agencies plan multiple projects simultaneously and do not yet recognize the need for a deep level of contact beyond logistics. However, we have discovered that an explicit discussion of values is crucial. The politics of these relationships are complex and often difficult to perceive.[13]

The practical tool of cultural mapping is proposed to help students approach community partners ethically in Graeme Evans and Jo Foord's "Cultural Mapping and Sustainable Communities: Planning for the Arts Revisited."[14] Mapping a community's assets and resources enables students to understand the wealth and values of a community partner in context and prevent the community "outreach" model that assumes lack and would position community engagement as charity work. Cultural mapping also provides students the opportunity to learn about local communities and engage with the values of local citizens as they take inventory. Fenn et al. discuss the value of cultural mapping for their students in "Training Community-Engaged Culture Workers at a Public University": "Such direct involvement helps illuminate points of convergence and divergence around values, activities, and perceptions that residents understand as constituting 'community.'"[15] Cultural mapping has students negotiate what community means in practice, and encourages them to reflect on citizenship, their future role in communities, and diversity. Fenn et al. encourage students to engage in critical fieldwork with community partners:

> This application of theory to practice requires the painstaking work of being curious and asking questions, doing research, listening intently, and being aware of one's own cultural biases. As such, encouraging students to

practice fieldwork skills such as observation, interviewing, building trust, and data analysis for the purpose of communicating with a broad public is essential.[16]

Engaging in community-based learning and service learning in the performing arts can have a profound impact on students and local communities when faculty have been supported to provide ethically sound exchanges. The key to promoting ethical practices in community-engaged learning and service learning is self-reflection. Students need to be able to interrogate their own biases before entering the field, and any course including community engagement must allow the time and space for this necessary reflection. Banks describes this kind of engagement as cultural diplomacy:

> Cultural diplomacy, at its most human and aware, would be self-reflective: constantly striving for better ways to interact; consciously working to deconstruct multiple levels of hierarchy in a room; and seeking the space of pure presence where participants paradoxically celebrate the implicit humanity that connects all people, while learning about significant differences.[17]

The following case studies describe two different approaches to community engagement: co-curricular community-based learning that invites community members to campus to engage in dialogue around performance and community engagement embedded in curriculum that brings students into the community. Michelle Hayford and Brandon Kliewer consider how a performance that invited veterans to campus connected public narrative and empathy to civic leadership practices. Trudi Wright explains how her students deliver oral presentations in a series of community engagement lectures at a local church with an active arts ministry.

Call to action:

- Administrators should advocate for a meaningful inclusion of community-engaged learning and service learning pedagogy and research in merit, tenure, and promotion processes and policies.
- Administrators need to encourage ethical community-based learning practices by providing high-impact resources: creation of a center or

office with staff dedicated to community-engaged learning, flexibility of student schedules, transportation, accessible and welcoming space on campus for community members.
- Administrators must provide performing arts faculty and staff professional development opportunities in ethical community-engaged and service learning practices: faculty training, community visits, tours, and immersions.
- Performing arts faculty should embed community-based learning in their curriculum. The most recent SNAAP survey data revealed that 22.5% of graduates in the performing arts "never" served their community while enrolled in their institution, while 27% answered "rarely," 32.2% answered "sometimes," and 18.4% answered "often." Compared to their visual arts peers, performing arts majors engage in their communities less during their college years.[18] We can do better, and we need to provide more students with the high-impact practice of community-based and service learning in the performing arts.[19]
- Performing arts faculty should coordinate with campus colleagues already involved with community partners; don't poison the well or reinvent the wheel because you hadn't reached out to colleagues already engaged with a potential partner.
- Performing arts faculty must build self-reflection into courses that incorporate community-engaged and service learning. Time and space must be provided for critical dialogue around cultural biases and improving cultural competence in order for students to ethically engage in community-based learning or service learning projects. Faculty need to model self-reflexivity and pursue training in ethical community-based learning pedagogies, as well as critical examination of personal biases and blind spots regarding intercultural competencies.
- Performing arts faculty should strive for sustainability with community partners. Find ways to continue future work (enabling previous student work to be handed off to future students) so that a feedback loop can be established and trust can build, leading to reciprocal exchange and mutual benefit for students and campus partners.
- Performing arts faculty should collaborate with community partners to offer programming affiliated with your production season. Tap the off-campus expertise in your backyard.[20]

Performative Organizing: "Spark-ing" Civic Leadership and Inclusive Modes of Public Narrative

Michelle Hayford
University of Dayton
Dayton, OH, USA

Brandon W. Kliewer
Kansas State University
Manhattan, KS, USA

Recognizing the intersection between performance studies, applied theatre, leadership development, and democratic theory, our project produced a staged reading of a play as a site of democracy that acknowledged specific challenges women veterans face when returning from war. Our community-engaged scholarship was specifically interested in creating a leadership development opportunity that connected public narrative to common community values of empathy. Our campus–community partnership supported a community-based reading of Caridad Svich's play *Spark* and a post-performance panel and civic dialogue that was focused on civic leadership development. Our partnership created a community engagement space that was interested in demonstrating, modeling, and practicing leadership that connected public narrative to common community values of *empathy* and *mutual understanding*.[21]

The specific circumstance of women veterans returning to civilian life from war served as the context of leadership development. The play's protagonist is a woman veteran returning from war to a bleak civilian economy and a society ill-equipped to handle post-traumatic stress (PTS). The performative space created by applied theatre empowered veterans and members of our university and local communities to dialogue about issues associated with women returning from war. The democratic site of the theatre supported an intimate encounter between veteran and civilian citizens to consider a series of questions usually unacknowledged—"how should I treat a veteran in class?," "how do veterans define mental health?," "what did you experience as a woman soldier in the Middle East?" Feminist methods of democratic engagement and the performative element of the partnership produced a *liminal space*, a betwixt and between collapse of actor/spectator that encouraged participants to reconsider dimensions of inclusion.[22] Not only did this space allow our community to engage an important issue, the space was structured to highlight many lost practices of democratic engagement and civic leadership.

When we collaborated on this project, the authors of this case study were colleagues at Florida Gulf Coast University (FGCU), which values civic engagement as a core guiding principle, and central to the mission of the institution. Each of us places democratic engagement at the heart of our teaching, research, and service scholarship. Michelle was an assistant professor and director of the theatre program at FGCU. She creates original works and applied theatre projects in partnerships with communities and non-profits. Brandon was an assistant professor of civic engagement and campus director of the FGCU American Democracy Project. His teaching, research, and service scholarship is focused on revitalizing the habits and institutional spaces of democratic life and civic leadership. We feel that it is important to share dimensions of our professional subjectivity with readers as they consider and evaluate the performative and dialogue spaces that were created in relation to principles of community-engaged scholarship.

Although the voice in this scholarly paper is primarily our own, members of the various communities contributed to development, execution, and analysis of this community inquiry. We created many spaces to include multiple conceptions of community voice. Community members from Veteran Services of Fort Myers and the American Red Cross played an instrumental role in co-creating the structure of the campus–community event. Fort Myers/Lee County, FGCU, and national-level community members shaped the topic that served as the basis of the performance and dialogue, the structure of the performance, the framework for the dialogue, and the themes discussed in this scholarly paper. Drawing on Akwugo Emejulu's analysis of feminist community development, D. Soyini Madison's conception of a performance of possibilities, and Iris Marion Young's modes of inclusive political communication, we assessed the value of our community-based staging of Caridad Svich's *Spark* as a performative form of feminist civic engagement and practice of public narrative and civic leadership. We will demonstrate the potential of applied theatre to link values of empathy to public narrative and forms of community engagement. Our campus–community partnership not only demonstrates a strategy to mobilize a broad-based movement that supports women veterans but also provides community framework for public narrative and civic leadership development.

Applied theatre, as a site and a practice, is one of the few cultural spaces that includes marginalized voices, valuing *dialogical performance*.[23] Applied theatre serves as an *interstice*, understood by Karl Marx as profit-less space and theorized by Nicolas Bourriaud as non-imposed *inter-human commerce*.[24] Applied theatre relies on dialogue and negotiation not stifled by a democratic process where "appeals to a *common good* are likely to perpetuate

... privilege."²⁵ Applied theatre serves as a physical gathering space and a community-building experience that allows both actors and spectators to take back participatory democracy through intentional acts of civic leadership. D. Soyini Madison theorizes such a democratic space as a "performance of possibilities," in which "the possible suggests a movement culminating in creation and change. It is the active, creative work that weaves the life of the mind with being mindful of life, of merging the text with the world, of critically traversing the margin and the center, and of opening more and different paths for enlivening relations and spaces."²⁶ Our *Spark* event lived up to Madison's conception, allowing for possibilities unimagined by the participants as they entered the theatre that night: vulnerable sharing, surprising revelations, and changed outlooks and behaviors.

Exercising the ability to empathize is a key habit of civic leadership and public narrative. Empathy allows individuals to accept political contestation from a range of perspectives. If the democratic process, and subsequent dialogue, is to achieve compromise, individuals need to be able to empathize with competing factions and contested concepts.

D. Soyini Madison names this leadership development position, as "the interrogative field," which "is the point at which the performance of possibilities aims to create or contribute to a discursive space where unjust systems and processes are identified and interrogated. It is where what has been expressed through the illumination of voice and the encounter with subjectivity motivates individuals to some level of informed and strategic action."²⁷ The staged reading of *Spark* propelled the participants into this interrogative field together, collectively yearning for actions we discovered during the post-performance dialogue that were available to all.

Description of Spark *Planning Process and Performance*

The *Spark* event was made possible by playwright Caridad Svich and NoPassport theatre alliance's embrace of theatre for social change. Svich put out a call for participants in an international staged reading scheme for *Spark*. Svich and NoPassport generously made her new play, *Spark*, available for performance royalty-free during the month of November in 2012 to venues that would endeavor to honor local veterans and draw attention to the special circumstances of women veterans. *Spark*'s story of a woman veteran's uneasy transition to civilian life was the perfect entry into a post-performance civic dialogue with local veterans, and Svich encouraged this kind of community collaboration as a part of the international scheme. In the end, 42 staged readings of *Spark* occurred in four countries, and numerous directors blogged about the successful dialogues in their communities as a result of the performances on NoPassport's website.[28]

At FGCU, a talented student director handled the crafting of the performance with student actors, while the co-authors structured a post-performance civic dialogue. We made contacts with local veterans' service agencies and partnered with the Students Who Served student organization to create a diverse panel of local veterans. Members of the university community and Fort Myers/Lee County, Florida, community attended the event.

Michelle and Brandon developed several drafts of questions that would create the basic structure of the dialogue. The questions were shared with the community members before the event. We met with the student cast and student director during one of the rehearsals to discuss the panel questions and the research that informed them to provide a greater context and appreciation for their performances. As a result, the dialogue framework was truly the collaborative product of multiple communities within FGCU and Fort Myers/Lee County, Florida.

A senior theatre major directed his peers[29] for the staged reading, holding several rehearsals in order to *block* (create stage movement for) particular scenes, adding depth to the typical convention for staged readings of actors reading from scripts on music stands and remaining seated on stage when not speaking. The staged reading was performed in our black box theatre on campus, with the house lights on. The playing space was not a proscenium stage, but rather the black painted floor the audience walks on to their seats. The lighting did not leave the audience in the dark, and everyone could potentially make eye contact. The lack of a raised stage and focused lighting allowed for an intimate and liminal space where the distinctions between playing space/audience and actor/spectator were blurred. The actors wore black. Minimal props were used. A row of chairs upstage and several music stands downstage were the only *set* utilized.

All this simplicity is not to suggest, however, that the performance itself was not complex or artistically realized, because it most certainly was. In fact, the student actors performed with more heart and integrity than usual given the nature of the performance. There was a feeling of wanting to *do right* by the veterans in the audience by authentically portraying the truth of the veteran's painful coming home story. The burden of realizing the power of representation was not lost on the cast, many of whom had studied the pitfalls of misrepresentation in their applied theatre courses. Before the show, nerves were running high as the cast prepared to merely dramatize what many veterans in the audience had actually survived.

We do not mean to minimize the power of live, embodied theatre, however, by detailing the student cast's concerns around the ethics of their performance. To be clear, while the performers did fret over doing the material and the veterans in audience *justice*, the veterans experienced the elation of seeing their lives and struggles, usually ignored in the public sphere, take center stage. Several veterans acknowledged their satisfaction with being rendered visible in such an intimate and communal way. This is applied theatre's unique calling card: embodied communion in safe democratic space to collectively grapple with a relevant social issue.

The powerful student performances created a direct link to the creation of a civic space where participants were compelled to experiment with inclusive forms of feminist democratic engagement in the post-performance panel and dialogue. Applied theatre, as an increasingly visible form of community activism and development, fits Bourriaud's description of art that has stepped into the space vacated by modern rationalism's avant-garde; "today's art is carrying on this fight, by coming up with perceptive, experimental, critical and participatory models."[30] Even though Bourriaud is theorizing *visual* art, we appropriate his analysis for applied theatre as the staged reading of *Spark* was contextualized by a *participatory model* of inclusion that foregrounded the post-performance dialogue as an integral aspect of the event. All in attendance understood that their willingness to participate in a democratic dialogue was crucial to the success of the event, as this intention was clear when soliciting veteran panelists, in the promotion of the event, and the announcements made before and after the performance. The structure of the performance created the critical subjectivity to consider and experiment with community engagement practice intended to disrupt the status quo and position participants toward informed and critically aware action.

There was a five-minute intermission immediately after *Spark* before the panel and dialogue began, and nearly every audience member returned to the theatre to participate. During the intermission, the theatre was arranged with chairs for the veteran panelists and cast members in the shape of a half-circle with either end meeting up with audience seating. The effect was an inclusive circle, inviting all to participate and maintain the liminal quality of reciprocity and collapse between actors/panelists and spectators/audience the performance had created.

As Bourriaud suggests for visual art, the performance had "shown us something" and transported us to an in-between-ness: "When an artist shows us something, he uses a transitive ethic which places his work between the 'look-at-me' and the 'look-at-that.'"[31] The *Spark* event was situated exactly in this transitive space of empathy and critical reflection. The performance, organization of the event, and substance of the dialogue were focused on illuminating essential techniques of feminist democratic engagement.

Post-Performance Democratic Engagement and Inclusion: Greeting, Acknowledgement, and Recognition

Young demonstrates that including public narrative as a legitimate mode of discussion will empower "relatively disenfranchised groups to assert themselves publicly; it also offers a means by which people whose experiences and beliefs differ, so much, that they do not share enough premises to engage in fruitful debate can nevertheless reach dialogical understanding."[32] Achieving a space of commonality, or even the capacity to understand the position of another from a perspective of empathy, is essential to democratic communication. Applied theatre creates a space of community engagement that supports practices which advance more equitable and inclusive ways of being necessary for democracy to flourish.

We observed participants asserting themselves publically in ways that would not be perceived as legitimate in spaces consumed by white-masculine-hetero and neoliberal hegemony. A woman veteran and FGCU student panelist shared her need to "assert [herself] publicly" during our post-performance panel:

> TW: To explain to someone what it was like where I had been [in Afghanistan] is just too difficult. I have made no friends in college ... I made no friends at [work]. I would literally go to school, go to work, go home and that is all I did and even now, I have to force myself to have interactions. That is why I come to things like this or I tell people in class that I have PTSD. I have done these things because it is the only way I don't go crazy in my own head. ... I have to confront these things.

We witnessed TW's relief at sharing her experience as a woman veteran during the post-performance panel and dialogue. Her need to express and *confront* her trauma with personal narrative in a public forum is a coping strategy that was particularly welcomed in the democratic space of the theatre. TW and the participants bore witness to a method of democratic communication that aligned with elements of community development. With her narrative, TW was able to realize a level of self-determination. The participants were able to observe and feel what it was like to recognize these forms of democratic communication in public space, as in the following dialogue between TW, and TT, a male student veteran:

TW: Today was another hard day. We had a KIA [killed in action]. One of my brothers on our bases in Afghanistan. So that is why I ... um, I apologize, it is just one of those ... [cries]. It is so hard to come back here. You feel out of place, you feel uncomfortable, you do not feel like you can relate. ... I have more life experience. I don't know what it was like to be 19 and be in college, I do not understand that. Where you [fellow civilian college students in audience] cannot understand what it was like to be in a foreign country hoping that you survive the next day. No matter how long I have been in college, or I have been out, I am still there. I will never get out of that. I look back, and days like this are really, really hard. I am always there.

TT: That is one thing we see on campus, actually on all college campuses, is you're going to see the veteran coming back and they are going to start reacting to things in ways you do not understand. They're going to be the student that sits in the back of the classroom with their back against the wall so they know what is around them. They are going to be the one that sits directly by the door so they can get out quickly because they feel enclosed and stressed out. ... So just keep in mind that the reaction to the way you act, someone could act adversely to it that has PTS—you could drop something and you do not understand why this person is starting to crouch down. They could be crouching down or they could be scared to death because of an experience they had. That is one reason I pushed for a resource center for student veterans over at Edison [College] and that is one of my pet projects here [at FGCU], is that they need someplace where they can go. Where they can release and relax, know that there is a place that is comfortable and they don't have to worry about all the noises and stresses of a college campus.

TW: I brought forward to my class one time that there was 31 deaths in a month. Not a single person in my class knew about any of them. Not one. 31 of our generation died in one month and no one knew about it.

The transcript above conveys the educational dimension of our democratic dialogue and the efficacy of personal narrative to enable civilian students, faculty, and all present, to become aware of their own ignorance, in a way that is transformative as opposed to confrontational. Not only was there a level of introspective enlightenment included in the event, but it provided participants a clear path to action. The dialogue, displays of recognition, and expressions of empathy gave students a path to action. Faculty, community members, university members, students, and administrators, that were not veterans, began to have a more robust understanding of their own privilege. Participants began to assume an empathic position for veterans because they had a better understanding of how invisibility impacts the lives of veterans. Understanding structures of privilege is essential to cultivating the type of empathy necessary for democratic life. The practical expression of empathy and perspective understanding portrayed in this dialogue personifies the democratic habits our communities need to revitalize.

Emejulu notes that a hallmark of feminist community development should be the expression of divergent points of view in which "complex claim-making and struggles for building solidarity between different people are not seen as a problem to be surmounted before the 'real politics' can start, but as the central purpose for a feminist community development that is interested in achieving social justice."[33] Minimizing elements of ideology that obscure the true topic of dialogue is essential to position modes of democratic communication to maintain inclusive spaces. A moment of *real politics* that minimized ideological influences to focus more precisely on the point of political contestation and discussion, occurred when Michelle and Brandon's read on mental health of the protagonist in the play *Spark* was extrapolated into unexamined assumptions. The woman veteran protagonist, "Lexie," has an epiphany while drunkenly talking to a specter alone in a cemetery. The co-authors framed a question about veterans' mental health around the assumption that veterans should not be relegated to hallucinatory isolation to have a personal break-through. However, CI, a professor who specializes in military and veteran research took issue with the premise of the question by insisting that we not dictate the larger community's role in the ways veterans heal:

> CI: I think we need to question the assumption that you need community—there are times when you need to withdraw, look into your own position and find an acceptable reason to be there. We need to be less demanding that they need to talk, come out and do things, and somehow fit our perception of what is right about how they are readjusting, and be more respectful of how they may need to do it. Provide a tent and let people go in and out of that tent.

This moment in which CI questioned the assumption in the question we posed was felt as a radical moment of productive *tension* theorized by Emejulu as "how individuals are both subjects within a community development discourse—possible creators of their own identities—and also subjected to a discourse—their identities and behaviors are structured and ordered by dominant ways of interpreting reality."[34] In this case, both the co-authors, particularly Michelle who served as moderator, and the panelists traded places as creating subjects and ordered subjects, as assumptions were made and refuted. This point in the dialogue reflects a transformative moment in which the structure of neoliberalism, which normally values certain forms of expertise and modes of communication, was disrupted.

Our post-performance panel and dialogue not only demonstrated the role personal narrative can have as it moves into the public realm, but provided an illustration of how to receive and recognize counter-normative modes of democratic communication. This moment represents the point when the position of their critique moves into the realm of action. The hope is that transformative spaces of democratic communication will give participants the knowledge and capacity to disrupt hegemony within and outside structures of theatre and dialogue events.

The performance created an atmosphere of experimentation and visually represented situations in which characters confronted serious public issues from positions of reciprocity and vulnerability. The performative dimension and dialogue modeled the types of empathetic behaviors that are consistent with feminist democratic engagement.

Augusto Boal provides a theoretical framework to distinguish between intransitive and transitive democratic performance.[35] According to Boal "conventional theatre is governed by an intransitive relationship, in that everything travels from stage to auditorium, everything is transported, transferred in that direction—emotion, ideas, morality…"[36] The goal of our civic work was to transform the spectator, from an idle observer to an empowered actor that is transitive, participatory, and interactive.

The structure of applied theatre practice can cultivate the habits and institutional spaces of democratic engagement that have been diluted by neoliberal ideology. Communities reconsider commitments to democratic engagement when brought face-to-face with fellow citizens in a theatre, allowing storytelling and personal narrative to take center stage in a vital democratic practice of empathy that leads to action.

Democratic education will play a key role in reminding communities that the power of community lies in the collective and coordinated action of many. The performative space of applied theatre, connected to democratic theory, has the potential to create more informed democratic action. In the case of *Spark*, feminist community engagement produced an empathic space where the usually marginalized experiences of veterans were placed at the center of our inquiry, resulting in compassion, understanding, self-reflection, and commitments to action. The theatre served as a site for the community to manifest ways of knowing and moving in the world that resulted in heightened sensitivity, awareness, and trust, *Spark*-ing greater understanding of our civic responsibility to one another.

PREPARING TO ENGAGE THE COMMUNITY WITH PUBLIC SPEAKING PERFORMANCE CLASSES

Trudi Wright
Regis University
Denver, CO, USA

Each year, the second-semester freshmen of Regis College (a small, Jesuit liberal arts program in Denver, Colorado) "engage in effective communication as a means to promote understanding through the cultivation of [their] public voice."[37] Because it is so important for us as a college community to promote critical thinking and intellectual discourse, the faculty also shares the following statement: "We [as scholars] develop our public voices when we actively listen to those around us and can articulate what we think in relation to them in a manner that takes into consideration how what each of us believes, values, and desires may impact everyone else."[38] These goals play out in my American Musical Theatre class, an oral communications-intensive course, which concludes with a series of community engagement lectures delivered by the students at Trinity United Methodist Church. My aim is to teach students how to establish and publicly voice their stance on concepts, theories, and ideas through the process of writing, practicing, and delivering public, oral presentations, while also creating a community of supportive learners.

Upon entering Regis College, students select into a First-Year Seminar, which features a writing-intensive course in the fall semester and a communications-focused class in the spring. The courses are linked by theme and the students work together as a cohort for the whole of their first year. These cohorts are made up of incoming students who have declared various majors, or have not yet declared a major at all (in other words, a class of non-music majors).[39] Because I am a musicologist, my communication-intensive course focuses on the history of the American musical, but also (and maybe more importantly) teaches the art of public speaking through three oral presentations where the stakes, the length, and the depth of the assignments increase throughout the semester. As stated above, these projects culminate in a community engagement experience where students publicly deliver pre-concert-style lectures at a local church, which sponsors a School for the Arts within their Music and Arts Ministry.[40] Along with providing opportunities for students to take low-stake risks in these oral "performances," the course encourages the study of human culture, intellectual, and practical skill development including written and oral communications and teamwork, personal and social responsibility through their civic engagement with the church, and integrative and applied learning, all essential learning outcomes of "successful" college students of the twenty-first century.[41]

The course begins with five weeks of critically studying musical theatre through show case-studies, with an emphasis on the idea of integration.[42] We explore a brief history of the musical, introduce musical terms and basic song analysis, and practice these skills by viewing, writing about, and discussing current and historic musical productions.[43] This introduction and the oral presentation assignments that follow, ask students to review and revisit the American musical, an art form that may be familiar to them, but with new information and through different scholarly lenses. They consider the content of the show and how it is delivered by the performers, and make metacognitive moves by thinking about how they receive the show and how the people of the historical period might have received it, as well. This understanding of the roles of performer and audience is then synthesized and demonstrated through their creation, performance, and reception of the oral presentations.

In order to prepare students for creation and delivery of a good public address, we discuss the components of a good speech (the script) and how that oral presentation can be delivered most successfully (the performance) to an audience. The students are then assigned their first oral presentation, a three-minute speech on Rogers and Hammerstein's *Oklahoma!*.[44] After watching and discussing the show, students complete readings (with significant bibliographies for further research opportunities) on this significant American musical and then write a three-minute speech focusing on one aspect of the show that made it successful/beloved in the United States. Speech topics may include a specific song, a performer, the composer or lyricist, its place in history, the choreographer or specific dance number, the costumes, the sets, the sales figures, or anything else the student finds compelling. The guidelines for the assignment are below:

Guidelines for Three-Minute Oklahoma! Oral Presentation[45]

- The speech must be 3–4 minutes long. Time yourself as you practice to ensure you stay within the time limit. You will "get the hook" if you are over your time.
- Hand in a full-sentence outline.
- Use three to five sources, each of which must be verbally cited in the speech at least once (you may use Leve, *American Musical Theatre* as one of them). A Chicago/Turabian works cited page should be attached to your outline.
- These sources cannot solely be websites:
  - You may cite only one, credible website
  - The remaining sources should be from scholarly sources, newspapers, and/or books.
- This speech should be persuasive. You need to prove your thesis with evidence.
- This speech will be delivered extemporaneously—not memorized or read from your outline, but spoken conversationally using only note cards.
- Make sure to organize your speech to follow a logical format that you can identify. Be sure to include a clear introduction, body and conclusion that fulfill the necessary criteria reviewed in class.
- You must only have 2–5 main points (which should be clearly previewed in your introduction) and they need to be connected by transition statements.
- You must give your speech on your scheduled day. If you are absent, you must be in contact with your professor about the possibility of delivering your work on an alternative day.

Important tips to remember:

- Start early in your preparations—there is no better time than the present!
- When doing an extemporaneous speech you must prepare more than with other styles. Here is the drill:
  - Research and write out your full speech. Transfer this manuscript into the full-sentence outline formula.

- Read your speech aloud 6–7 times trying different inflection, rate, emphasis, pause, and volume to determine how your speech sounds. (Record yourself and listen back. This is very easy with a smart phone.)
- Using your full-sentence outline and your practice session as a guide, transfer the speech onto note cards. These note cards should include:

  Keywords and phases
  Delivery cues "look up," "more volume," "slow down," and so on
  Include exact source citations and quotes on your note cards—
     things you want to say exactly and correctly.
  Things you tend to forget (transitions, figures, etc.)
  Figurative language and rhetorical devices you want to remember
     to use
  Card numbers—in case you drop them!
  Outline format to keep your organization in tact

- When the note cards are finished, practice with them 6–7 times. It is best to practice in front of someone to get some constructive criticism. Also, practice in front of a mirror to see your facial expressions and hand gestures, or record yourself!

• A good persuasive speech should be one that you feel passionate about. This assignment is about finding your public voice through your connection to the theatre arts. Being verbally persuasive and convincing will help you in many areas of your adult life.

These guidelines demonstrate the oral presentation assignment's reliance on the students' previous writing experience from their fall semester's writing-intensive course. The students must organize their speeches to make logical sense, support their points with current scholarly evidence, and work through the drafting process.

Along with the assignment's guidelines, I also introduce the rubric (found in Figs. 9.1 and 9.2), which covers the evaluation criteria for both the content and delivery of the oral presentation. This allows students the opportunity to discuss the evaluation categories before they begin researching and crafting their speeches. During this discussion, I demonstrate how the desired content of their presentations features writing concepts learned in their first-semester writing class. The students are expected to focus on the

Persuasive Presentation Peer Evaluation Form

Speaker's Name: _____ Date: _____
Evaluator's Name: _____

Please use the appropriate mark to evaluate each aspect of the speaker's oral presentation listed below.
"+" = Excellent; "✓" = Satisfactory; "–" = Needs Improvement

Content and Organization   **Comments**

_____ Effective attention getter

_____ Thesis statement was evident

_____ Preview statement was clear

_____ Main points and subpoints were clear, substantive

_____ Speaker presented compelling argument

_____ Speaker supported argument with evidence

_____ Speaker cited sources of evidence

_____ Presentation was organized well

_____ Review of major points included in conclusion

_____ Concluding statement - presentation ended smoothly

Delivery   **Comments**

_____ Speaker was confident and/or enthusiastic about topic

_____ Appropriate and effective eye contact

_____ Appropriate vocal variety (rate, pitch, volume)

_____ Appropriate and effective gestures and movement

_____ Appropriate and effective use of language

_____ Appropriate and effective articulation and pronunciation of words

_____ Absence of vocalized pauses or vocal fillers

_____ Visual aids were easily seen by audience

_____ Visual aids provided additional information and were effective

Fig. 9.1 Persuasive presentation peer evaluation form

formation of a strong thesis supported by scholarly evidence for each point they make. The writing, however, is only one portion of the assignment. As a class, we also discuss how the theses and evidence are given orally, a medium which allows the audience only one chance to take in their words, much like the way we experience live music or theatre. This creates a space for me to highlight the importance of the "performance" aspects of oral presentation.

In addition to continued practice of their writing skills, students learn the importance of practicing their oral presentations in order to experience

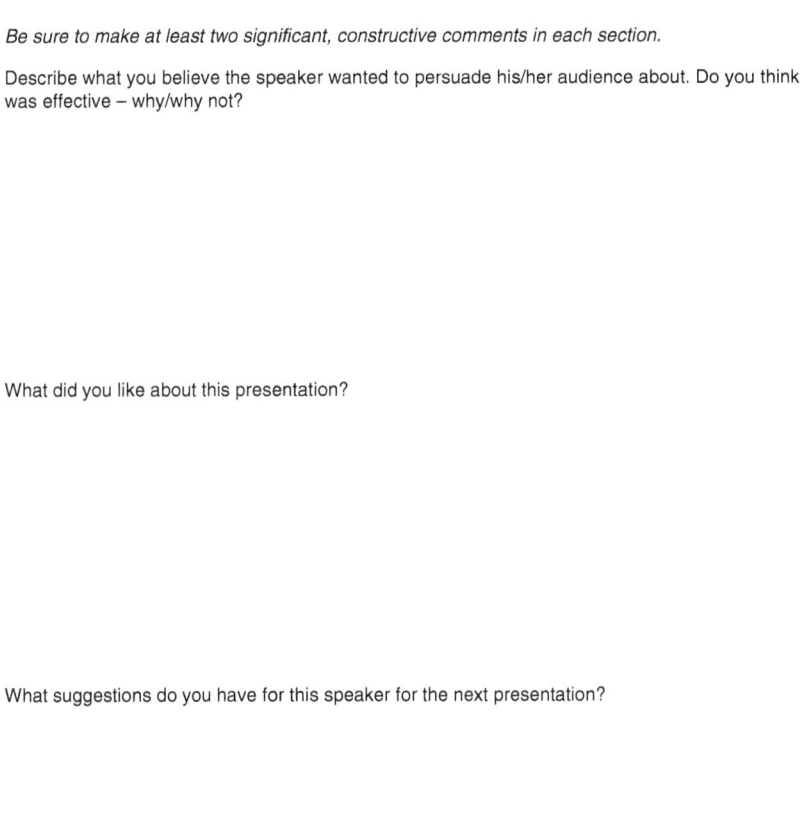

Be sure to make at least two significant, constructive comments in each section.

Describe what you believe the speaker wanted to persuade his/her audience about. Do you think it was effective – why/why not?

What did you like about this presentation?

What suggestions do you have for this speaker for the next presentation?

Source: Schaller, K. (2002). *Principles of Effective Public Speaking: Student Workbook.* Boston, MA: McGraw-Hill.

Fig. 9.2 Persuasive presentation peer evaluation form

a smooth performance. Instead of "practice makes perfect," our class motto is "practice makes prepared." My main objective is to teach students that the act of practicing their well-crafted argument is the surest way to "sell" their points. Even if they write the most convincing speech, if it is delivered too quickly, too quietly, with filler words, without passion, or with any number of other presentation issues, the content will be undermined or even lost due to an unrehearsed performance. It is my hope that the discipline of practicing for public speaking opportunities will follow them as they become active members of their professional and social communities.

Persuasive Presentation Peer Evaluation Form

When presentation day arrives, each student not only delivers his/her speech (taking our theories of successful public speaking and putting them into practice) but also acts as a member of our "public speaking performance class." Every student fills out the rubric they first used as a tool for preparation, but that now functions as a guide for peer assessment (see Figs. 9.1 and 9.2). Each class member is required to offer thoughtful, oral comments to at least one speaker during the class period. In order to set up a safe and productive environment, we orally comment first on something we like about the speech and then suggest a place where the speaker shows "an opportunity for growth." It is very important to use this specific phrase so students understand that the workshops' function is to encourage improvement, not to point out the mistakes and missteps of others. The commenter can focus their suggestions on content, mechanics, or delivery.

As one would guess, most of the students are nervous about delivering their work orally and, many times, uncomfortable with giving and receiving public comment. This performance class format, however, allows for immediate peer-to-peer feedback on their work, collective improvement on both content and delivery (they take in the feedback on all presentations, not just their own), and the development of trust and community within the classroom.

The oral commenting portion of the performance class is graded for very low stakes. The students receive full class participation credit for the day if they have given oral comments to at least one speaker (although many students give comments to multiple speakers), and if they have given thorough written comments for every presentation. After I have had a chance to review the feedback on these rubrics, and add my own, I return all the written comments to the speaker, along with their grade. It is my desire that the returned rubrics allow the speaker to reflect on their oral presentation experience through the concrete feedback from their oral and written comments, in order to improve their next speech.

The second oral presentation of the class centers on an historical show of their choice and increases in length to eight minutes. The premise of the assignment is to convince the room (who are acting as potential investors) that the show on which they are presenting should be revived on Broadway. This speech assignment, worth 10% of their grade, continues to employ student research, writing skills, speech rehearsal, and the performance class method of evaluation. I stress that I want to see that they have taken the feedback given for their previous "performance" and employ it in their preparation and delivery of the second oral presentation.

The third, and highest stakes, speech adds an additional component to the previous ones. For this oral presentation, students work together with their classmates to create a lecture series for the community. They deliver their group presentations at a local church with a robust music and arts ministry whose mission supports the musical education of its participants. During some iterations of this project, the church was performing a musical, so the focus of the lectures was ready-made. In other years, I have worked with the members of the church's music community to choose an appropriate musical for the presentations either based on a show we can all attend in Denver and then discuss during the presentations, or simply a show they would like to study.[46] Although it has always been my goal to listen to the desires of our audience (the church members) to provide material of interest, some Broadway shows are easier to teach and research than others. Musical theatre scholarship is a relatively young academic field and because of this, there are some shows with much more scholarly consideration than others. In the years when we have studied a show with a dearth of secondary source materials available, the projects have not been as rich in content or have veered too far away from the musical theatre analysis I want from my students. I also think shows with interesting histories, like *Jesus Christ Superstar*, with its controversial content and unique path to the Broadway stage, tend to work better for pre- and post-show lectures. As I continue to modify the class, it is my intention to offer a list of specific show choices for the first-year students with an eye toward quality scholarship availability and material that will be of interest to an open-minded Christian community, instead of leaving the choice completely open.

Because the students have built trust within their learning community during their performance class sessions, the cooperation and respect needed to create a lecture series grow throughout the semester. Before students begin the now-familiar research and writing phase of the project, we study the benefits of community engagement in the arts along with social capital.[47] According to music educator, Dr. Donna Emmanuel, "engagement activities contain elements of shared benefit and reciprocity, in which all parties learn from one another over time."[48] Our first step toward creating a shared relationship occurs when the head of the Music and Arts Ministry, Judith Mitchell, visits our class, in order to introduce the educational mission of Trinity United Methodist Church's Music and Arts Ministries. This visit enables students to better understand the audience with which they will engage. Students then brainstorm possible topics appropriate for the series, taking into consideration the interests of the church community. They also arrange themselves into groups, research, write, and rehearse their presentations. Because this assignment is their final "performance," each group delivers their presentation in a dress rehearsal during class time before they present at the church. As is our practice, the presenting groups deliver their project as a performance class, are given comments both orally and in writing, and have a few days to adjust their content and/or delivery before the official, public lecture at the church. This ensures that each student group goes into the public feeling as confident as possible.

Although the most important part of their visit to the church is the oral presentation itself, the students also prepare for a few more elements of community engagement. Within each group presentation, the students develop an activity in which the audience can participate. This usually comes in the form of a discussion question, which initiates audience interaction with each other and with the students. Although discussion (both small and large group) is the most common mode of audience engagement, students have also created interactive quizzes and questionnaires to prime the audience for verbal participation. Sometimes these quizzes are as simple as a show of hands, while other groups have created pre- and post-presentation quizzes on paper to help demonstrate the audience's growth in understanding of the topic being presented. The discussions and quizzes tend to inspire questions from audience members, which in turn, create the environment of "shared benefit and reciprocity" for which we are striving.

In some cases, I can imagine taking students to a new or different venue may cause audiences to be reticent to participate in student-led activities. I have found, however, that bringing students to a community in which I already have an established relationship and one that Regis students have been visiting for over five years provides an audience that is prepared for dialogue. This expectation for interaction occurs for at least two reasons. First, when I introduce students to the audience before their presentations, it is helpful to include a description of their assignment. Because the audience is aware of the engagement piece of presentation, they become willing participants in order to help the students achieve success. Second, the practice of returning year after year to the same venue creates the desired reciprocity in community engagement work. Yes, audiences are learning about musical theatre from my students, but the students are experiencing what it is like to be part of a community because of the generous participation of Trinity members.

It is always exciting for me to return to the classroom and hear from the students that they expected to be teaching the audience about musical theatre, but instead, learned just as much from those in attendance. An example of this came in 2016 when one of my student groups was presenting on the AIDS crisis of the 1990s in conjunction with *RENT*. One of the audience members recounted a heart-wrenching story of caring for her partner with HIV/AIDS during that time and how difficult it was to find good medical care for him because of the misconceptions surrounding the disease. It was in that moment that everyone in the room truly realized the importance of *RENT*'s message to those who were and are affected by this cruel disease.

Although this course is currently being taught to mostly non-majors, I have plans to create another version of it for music majors. This more advanced iteration would ask students not only to research and present on various musicals but also to perform musical numbers from the shows from which they are studying in order to gain a deeper understanding of the material. For this class, I would also seek to partner with additional arts organizations (these might include a musical theatre troupe we have on campus and The Arvada Center, a performing arts facility located only ten minutes away) in order for music students to have more opportunities to share their knowledge and skills with the public. I can envision the format of this course working for any instructor interested in teaching the art of public speaking and coordinating opportunities for students to communicate with community organizations.

The communication-intensive Freshman Experience course is one of my favorites to teach because it brings together my scholarly focus of musical theatre studies and, with the performance class format, my former life as a classically trained singer. In that spirit of collaboration, I believe it stretches my students to engage with the intellect needed for academic inquiry and persuasive writing, as well as developing the practical skills of giving feedback to peers and practicing and delivering an excellent oral performance to multiple audiences. I have heard from my students that this is, indeed, the case. When asked on their Spring 2016 Student Evaluation of Faculty, "What aspects of this course contributed most to your learning?" 8 of the 17 students gave an answer about the public speaking projects. A few responses include phrases like, "The research I had to do for my speeches," "the feedback we received from peers about our presentations," "probably all of the speeches. It kind of forces you to know/learn the material," and "I think our speeches helped my writing and speaking skills, while boosting my confidence." Although not always mentioned in their course evaluations, each semester I offer this course, I see a marked improvement in both the writing and oral delivery skills of my students. I know that the lessons of preparation, performance, and community building that live at the heart of their learning, will not only help them through their remaining years of college, but also serve them as they grow into citizens of the greater world.

Notes

1. Compact.org.
2. Nerche.org.
3. Amy Driscoll, "Analysis of the Carnegie Classification of Community Engagement: Patterns and Impact on Institutions."
4. Ernest L. Boyer, *Scholarship Reconsidered: Priorities of the professoriate*.
5. Scott Jaschik, "Scholarship Reconsidered as Tenure Policy."
6. Driscoll, "Analysis of the Carnegie Classification of Community Engagement," 11.
7. Lee Nickoson and Kristine L Blair, "Intervening: The Value of Campus-Community Partnerships," 54–55.
8. Daniel Banks, "The Question of Cultural Diplomacy: Acting Ethically," 110.
9. Randy Stoecker, Elizabeth A. Tryon, and Amy Hilgendorf, eds., *The Unheard Voices: Community Organizations and Service-Learning*.
10. See thecpcp.org for more information about the Center for Performance and Civic Performance and examples of their powerful work engaging the arts in civic practice.
11. Michael Rohd and Shannon Scrofano, "Leadership, Change and Engagement: Theatre on Campus and in Community."

12. Rohd and Scrofano, "Leadership, Change and Engagement."
13. Banks, "The Question of Cultural Diplomacy," 116.
14. Graeme Evans and Jo Foord, "Cultural Mapping and Sustainable Communities: Planning for the Arts Revisited."
15. John Fenn and Douglas Blandy, T. J. Arnold, Johanna Lorbach, Stephanie Moore, Jay Shepherd, and Lauren Silberman, "Training Community-Engaged Culture Workers at a Public University," p. 358.
16. Fenn and Blandy, "Training Community-Engaged Culture Workers," 364.
17. Banks, "The Question of Cultural Diplomacy," 119.
18. SNAAP survey data.
19. For a justification for creating civically engaged theatre curricula, see Anne Berkeley, "Theatre in the 'Engaged University': A Context for Habermas's Communicative Action."
20. See Sharon L. Green, "Teaching Theatre in Precarious Times: Strategies for Survival in the Liberal Arts Curriculum," for an example of successful partnership with community members to offer symposia related to a performance season.
21. Marianne Bojer, Heiko Roehl, Mariane Knuth-Hollesen, and Colleen Magner, *Mapping Dialogue: Essentials Tools for Social Change*.
22. Victor Turner, *The Ritual Process: Structure and Anti-Structure*.
23. Dwight Conquergood, "Performing as a Moral Act: Ethical Dimensions of the Ethnography of Performance."
24. Nicolas Bourriaud, *Relational Aesthetics*, 1–13.
25. Iris Young, "Communication and the Other: Beyond Deliberative Democracy."
26. D. Soyini Madison, *Critical Ethnography: Method, Ethics, and Performance*, 191.
27. Madison, *Critical Ethnography*, 193.
28. Nopassport.org.
29. FGCU's staged reading of Caridad Svich's Spark was directed by student Armando Rivera and the student actors were Rachel Bennett (Evelyn), Jackie DeGraaff (Lexie), Hanny Zuniga (Ali), Adrian Serrano (Hector), Jake Scott-Hodes (Vaughn), and Clare Edlund (reader).
30. Bourriaud, *Relational Aesthetics*, 102.
31. Bourriaud, *Relational Aesthetics*, 109.
32. Young, "Communication and the Other: Beyond Deliberative Democracy," 53.
33. Akwugo Emejulu, "Re-theorizing Feminist Community Development: Towards a Radical Democratic Citizenship," 385.
34. Emejulu, "Re-theorizing Feminist Community Development," 380.
35. Augusto Boal, *Legislative Theatre*, 19.

36. Boal, *Legislative Theatre*, 19.
37. Susan Sci, "Communication-Intensive Core Course Introduction," 53.
38. Sci, "Communication-Intensive Core Course Introduction."
39. In any given semester I may teach a future music major or minor, but this course was designed to be taught to non-music majors. Along with my course counting toward their Freshman Experience credits, it also counts toward their Fine Arts undergraduate core requirement.
40. For more information on Trinity United Methodist Church's School for the Arts, see http://www.trinityumc.org/music-arts/school-for-the-arts accessed January 12, 2017.
41. George D. Kuh and Carol Geary Schneider, *High-Impact Educational Practices: What They Are, Who Has Access to Them, and Why They Matter*, 4.
42. Integration is when the elements of a musical—dialogue, song, and dance—all help to move the plot line forward. There are many musicals that have no integration at all, like many musical revues, and others, which strive for complete integration.
43. Since, in recent years, it has become popular to release movie-musicals during the holiday season, my classes have investigated *Les Miserables* (2012 film), *Into the Woods* (2014 film), *Sounds of Music Live!* (2013 television broadcast), *Peter Pan Live!* (2014 television broadcast), and *The Wiz Live!* (2015 television broadcast).
44. Our public speaking lesson is based on Jess K. Alberts, Thomas K. Nakayama and Judith N. Martin, "Speaking in Public."
45. These guidelines were created with the help of Dr. Susan Sci, Assistant Professor of Communications at Regis University and Dr. Ronald DiSanto, Professor of Philosophy at Regis University.
46. This community-based project began in 2013. The church's drama ministry was performing *Jesus Christ Superstar*. In 2014–2016 we focused on musicals suggested by participants in Trinity's music and arts ministry, *Carousel* (2014), *Sound of Music* (2015), and *Rent* (2016). In the current iteration of the class, we will return to *Jesus Christ Superstar* because it is being performed at a Denver-metro area theatre during the Lenten season. Both the participants in the music and arts ministry and the students in American Musical Theatre will attend productions.
47. We read Donna Emmanuel, "Community Engagement and Community Outreach: Aren't They the Same?", 4–7. A version of this reading is available on the College Music Society website http://www.music.org/index.php?option=com_content&view=article&id=1157&Itemid=1805 accessed January 20, 2017, and from the National

Endowment for the Arts, "The Arts and Civic Engagement: Involved in Arts, Involved in Life." We also study the principles of social capital in Robert Putnam, *Bowling Alone: The Collapse and Revival of American Community*, 15–28.
48. Emmanuel, "Community Engagement and Community Outreach," 2.

BIBLIOGRAPHY

Alberts, Jess K., Thomas K. Nakayama, and Judith N. Martin. 2010. Speaking in Public. In *Human Communication in Society*, 2nd ed., 385–413. Boston: Pearson Education Inc.

Banks, Daniel. 2011. The Question of Cultural Diplomacy: Acting Ethically. *Theatre Topics* 21 (2): 109–123.

Berkeley, Anne. 2007. Theatre in the 'Engaged University': A Context for Habermas's Communicative Action. *Journal of Dramatic Theory and Criticism* 22 (1): 9–28.

Boal, Augusto. 1998. *Legislative Theatre*. London: Routledge Books.

Bojer, Marianne, Heiko Roehl, Mariane Knuth-Hollesen, and Colleen Magner. 2008. *Mapping Dialogue: Essentials Tools for Social Change. Chagrin Falls*. Cleveland: Taos Institute Publications.

Bourriaud, Nicolas. 2007. *Relational Aesthetics*. Dijon: Les Presses du Reel. The Community Performance Reader, Kuppers & Robertson (eds.), New York: Taylor & Francis.

Boyer, Ernest L. 1990. *Scholarship Reconsidered: Priorities of the Professoriate*. Lawrenceville, NJ: Princeton University Press.

Campus Compact. Compact.org. https://compact.org/who-we-are/history/. Accessed 24 July 2017.

Center for Civic Practice. Thecpcp.org. http://www.thecpcp.org/about/. Accessed 21 Aug 2017.

Conquergood, Dwight. 1985. Performing as a Moral Act: Ethical Dimensions of the Ethnography of Performance. *Text and Performance Quarterly* 5: 1–13.

Driscoll, Amy. 2014. Analysis of the Carnegie Classification of Community Engagement: Patterns and Impact on Institutions. *New Directions for Institutional Research*(162): 3–15.

Emejulu, Akwugo. 2011. Re-theorizing Feminist Community Development: Towards a Radical Democratic Citizenship. *Community Development Journal*. 3 (46): 378–390.

Emmanuel, Donna. 2008. Community Engagement and Community Outreach: Aren't They the Same? In *College Music Society Newsletter*, 4–7. Missoula, MO: College Music Society.

Evans, Graeme, and Jo Foord. 2008. Cultural Mapping and Sustainable Communities: Planning for the Arts Revisited. *Cultural Trends* 17 (2): 65–96.

Fenn, John, Douglas Blandy, T.J. Arnold, Johanna Lorbach, Stephanie Moore, Jay Shepherd, and Lauren Silberman. 2015. Training Community-Engaged Culture Workers at a Public University. *Journal of American Folklore* 128 (509): 351–368.

Green, Sharon L. 2015. Teaching Theatre in Precarious Times: Strategies for Survival in the Liberal Arts Curriculum. *Theatre Topics* 25 (1): 37–49.

Jaschik, Scott. Scholarship Reconsidered as Tenure Policy. *Inside Higher Ed.* https://www.insidehighered.com/news/2007/10/02/wcu. Accessed 24 July 2017.

Kuh, George D., and Carol Geary Schneider. 2008. *High-Impact Educational Practices: What They Are, Who Has Access to Them, and Why They Matter.* Washington, DC: Association of American Colleges and Universities.

Madison, Soyini D. 2012. *Critical Ethnography: Method, Ethics and Performance.* 2nd ed. Los Angeles: Sage Publications.

National Endowment for the Arts. 2005. *The Arts and Civic Engagement: Involved in Arts, Involved in Life.* New York: National Endowment for the Arts.

New England Resource Center for Higher Education. Nerche.org. http://nerche.org/images/stories/projects/Carnegie/2015/2010_and_2015_CE_Classified_Institutions_revised_8_10_16.pdf. Accessed 24 July 2017.

Nickoson, Lee, and Kristine L. Blair. 2014. Intervening: The Value of Campus-Community Partnerships. *Feminist Teacher* 24 (1): 49–56.

Putnam, Robert. 2001. *Bowling Alone: The Collapse and Revival of American Community.* New York: Touchstone Books of Simon and Schuster.

Rohd, Michael, and Shannon Scrofano. 2017. Leadership, Change and Engagement: Theatre on Campus and in Community. Workshop presentation for Association for Theatre in Higher Education Leadership Institute, Las Vegas, NV, August 2.

Schaller, Kristi. 2002. *Principles of Effective Public Speaking Workbook.* Boston: McGraw Hill.

Sci, Susan. 2013. Communication-Intensive Core Course Introduction. In *Communication: First-Year Experience, Regis University*, 53–55. Boston: Pearson Learning Solutions.

Stoecker, Randy, Elizabeth A. Tryon, and Amy Hilgendorf, eds. 2009. *The Unheard Voices: Community Organizations and Service Learning.* Philadelphia, PA: Temple University Press.

Strategic National Arts Alumni Project. Snaap.indiana.edu. http://snaap.indiana.edu/pdf/2016/SNAAP15_16_Recent_Grads_Aggregate_Report.pdf. Accessed 24 July 2017.

Svich, Caridad. 2012. *Spark*. NoPassport Press. Print. Spark blog posts at http://www.nopassport.org/spark. Accessed 22 Aug 2017.
Turner, Victor. 1969. *The Ritual Process: Structure and Anti-structure*. Chicago: Aldine Pub. Co.
Young, Iris Marion. 1996. Communication and the Other: Beyond Deliberative Democracy. In *Democracy and Difference: Contesting the Boundaries of the Political*, ed. Seyla Behhabib, 120–136. Princeton: Princeton University Press.
Young, I.M. 2000. *Inclusion and Democracy*. Oxford: Oxford University Press.

CHAPTER 10

Internships

Internships, along with capstone experiences, are the high-impact practice (HIP) most often constructed within the major with little administrative oversight from outside the department. They are also the two HIPs generally not encountered until close to the end of a student's college career, and both challenge students to use all of the skills and knowledge gained through their curriculum and experience in other HIPs. Because they are generally located solidly within the major department, their structure, oversight, and assessment can vary widely even among departments in the same institution. Within the performing arts, both internships and capstones may be seen as redundant, since experiential learning is so much a part of the pedagogical process throughout the major. But as the Council for Advancement of Standards in Higher Education (CAS) asserts, "What distinguishes internships from other forms of active learning is that there is a degree of supervision and self-study that allows students to 'learn by doing' and to reflect upon that learning in a way that achieves certain learning goals and objectives."[1] Like faculty across the university, performing arts faculty may be reluctant to give up instructional oversight in internships, fearing that students might learn poor habits or techniques before their college training is complete. As Nancy O'Neill puts it, "[t]he idea that addressing career development in the context of the major would 'water down' the curriculum is a powerful one, with deep roots. ... What suffers,

© The Author(s) 2018
M. Hayford, S. Kattwinkel (eds.), *Performing Arts as High-Impact Practice*, The Arts in Higher Education, https://doi.org/10.1007/978-3-319-72944-2_10

as a result, are things like hands-on learning, developing marketable skills, or 'learning by doing'—exactly what internships can provide."[2] Nevertheless, the evidence of the importance of internships for student success after college continues to mount. According to a 2014 Association of American Colleges and Universities (AAC&U) survey of employers at private sector and nonprofit institutions, "[n]early all employers say they would be more likely to consider hiring a recent college graduate who had completed an internship or apprenticeship, including three in five (60%) who say their company would be much more likely to consider that candidate."[3]

Fortunately, the bias against "vocational" learning is perhaps more easily shaken in the performing arts, and internships in particular are a crucial experience for performing arts students to pursue while they are still students. The tendency of performing arts departments to be supportive, nurturing communities encourages risk-taking and confidence-building in students, but may not adequately prepare them for the often stressful, fast-paced atmosphere of the arts in the professional world. While we can argue that much of a performing arts major's undergraduate curriculum comes in the form of experiential learning, internships (and even brief externships) require students to test their practices in organizations with different structures than their academic department, and with the responsibilities of real-world employment. Internships provide students with an opportunity to transfer the experiential learning of their college work to the professional world, while still enjoying the support and guidance of their home department. Internships also provide opportunities for networking, community-building, and the cultivation of mentors—practices that are necessary in all fields but most especially in the arts. College students in the arts participate in internships at about the same rate as the general student body. The 2016 National Survey of Student Engagement (NSSE) found that exactly 50% of college seniors reported participating in an "internship or field experience," and in the 2015–2016 Strategic National Arts Alumni Project (SNAAP) survey of recent graduates (those who had graduated since 2006), 52% said they had participated in an internship while in college.[4] However, when students in arts majors outside the areas of performing arts practice (e.g., architecture, arts administration, arts education, visual arts, and digital media) are filtered out, the percentage of internships drops significantly. Only 18.7% of Dance, Music, and Theatre alumni reported having completed an internship in college.[5] The difference in these statistics should be disturbing to faculty and administrators.

Too many performing arts majors are graduating without an intentional internship experience. It's likely that many of the alumni who responded in the negative to this question did in fact have summer work or even work during the school year with performing arts organizations of the type that could be structured as an internship. But without a tie to their academic work and without faculty oversight, students may fail to see such work as experiential learning, and without intentionality and reflection, such work will likely not be high-impact. Performing arts departments clearly need to be more proactive about how they oversee internships and discuss them with their students. It is not sufficient to encourage students to apply for summer festival positions; those experiences should be incorporated into the curriculum, preferably as credit-bearing courses, with reflective assignments and coordination between faculty and organization supervisors.

Performing arts students applying for internships face the same roadblocks as students in other disciplines, but the season-bound existence of most arts organizations may present additional problems as well. The variation in internship types is as wide in the arts as in other disciplines in terms of duration, time of year, type of host organization, and compensation, but many arts internships are with summer arts festivals, making course connection and faculty oversight difficult. Professional theatre seasons do not generally match up with the academic schedule, so internship-offering companies must have a full understanding of the educational restrictions on interns who are still students. And while internships may be considered a HIP for the value they add to a student's educational experience, there are many ongoing debates about their value as career preparation. Studies suggest that unpaid internships are detrimental to students' quality of life and their career prospects, and that internships in general disproportionately favor students from wealthier backgrounds.[6] In light of these issues, it is crucial that performing arts departments closely guide their students through the internship process. Especially in the performing arts, where the exploitation of artists is a persistent and ongoing problem, it is vital that internship programs follow best practices so that they provide a true integrative learning experience and not just a line on a student's resume.

Research on internships and explorations of best practices has a history going back to John Dewey's calls for experiential learning in the mid-twentieth century, and departments seeking to construct efficacious ones should consult standards provided by groups such as the CAS and the National Society for Experiential Education (NSEE). Both groups provide research and best practices on or from their websites.[7] Best practices listed by those groups expand upon the characteristics of HIPs outlined by Kuh. In order for internships to truly integrate curricular learning and real-world practice and to be real learning experiences, they must involve high expectations, frequent feedback, substantive interactions with supervisors and faculty, and a clear structure that demands attention and reflection on the part of the student. Achieving these characteristics means intense participation by faculty. They must intentionally structure internship experiences so that they are connected to the student's education as a whole and not be presented as an "add-on" or a hoop through which students must jump in order to check all the boxes in their curriculum. Internships should be vetted by faculty, monitored for their continuing instructional and experiential value, and accompanied by regular faculty oversight and reflective work by students.

The internships described in the following case studies exhibit the best practices of effective internships and field experiences. The off-campus experiences described by Marissa Nesbit and Michele Volansky are well integrated into the major curriculum, anticipated with preparatory work earlier in the students' academic careers, accompanied by close faculty oversight, and both incorporate reflective writing to help students process and assess their experiences. Marissa Nesbit's case study examines an internship in dance education for dance majors that uses a scaffolded structure to help students build skills and confidence over the period of the internship. Frequent reflective assignments, both online and in person, help students to monitor their own progress. This particular experience also has the benefit of being structured as a course, so students have a community of support during the internship before they pursue greater responsibility in individual assignments in their senior year. Similarly, the internship in Michele Volansky's department is part of a culture of experiential learning that extends throughout the students' college careers. Intentionality is built into all aspects of the program, with students required to produce a clear plan and justification for their internship as well as a concluding reflective essay focused on how they will apply what they have learned from the experience. Both of these case studies are excellent models not only for the structure of the internships themselves but also for their incorporation into the program as a whole, and because they demonstrate the intentionality necessary to make internships truly high-impact.[8]

Call to action:

- Institutions of higher education should have standard requirements for internships that are to receive academic credit, and should encourage collaboration between offices of career services and academic departments. Internships in the performing arts do not always look like those in more traditional academic departments, and offices where students go to research internship opportunities often don't collect information on internships at arts organizations.
- Conversely, performing arts departments need to do a better job working with offices of career services to both collect and distribute appropriate internship information. All too often faculty take a one-on-one approach with students, and don't maintain collections of information about internships that have been vetted. Institutional staff who are well versed in the processes of internship acquisition and assessment can be invaluable resources for performing arts departments.
- Tying internships to academic learning outcomes is still an area where academic departments need to do better. Certainly, many students, especially those in theatre, get internships during the summers between their college years, but all too often those experiences are not arranged through or monitored by their home academic departments. The result is that those opportunities are not integrated into the students' curricular work, so valuable synthesis may be missed.

Experiential Learning in Dance Education: Collaborative Teaching to Develop Professional Practice

Marissa Beth Nesbit
East Carolina University
Greenville, NC, USA

Introduction

Gigi, short for "grocery-getter"—a clunky, worn minivan bearing the logo for East Carolina University's (ECU) Center for Leadership and Civic Engagement—pulls up outside the Messick Theatre Arts Center.

Tired from the morning's ballet class, dancers load in backpacks and water bottles, posters, and hand drums. After confirming that everyone's dancer attire has been suitably replaced with more modest clothing, someone gives the sliding door a shove, and Gigi departs from campus, her occupants mostly silent as they begin the weekly shift from student to teacher.

About two hours later, Gigi returns, this time ferrying a more exuberant bunch. In between bites of granola bars, they congratulate a classmate on a successful lesson, share funny anecdotes from work with the children, and brainstorm ideas for the next lesson. By the time we turn into the parking lot, someone checks her phone and announces an updated rehearsal schedule or the latest cast list and with that, identities shift back. Crawling out of the backseat, the teachers become students once again, headed toward the familiarity of the studio.

As students in a Bachelor of Fine Arts program, dance education candidates are expected to develop a high level of technical skill and artistry in theatrical dance forms while they simultaneously build the skills and dispositions that mark effective K12 educators. The weekly trips in Gigi traveling to partner schools represent a critical turning point where students work in a collaborative and supportive project to plan, deliver, and assess dance education in a real-world setting. The structure of a university course and the safety of camaraderie in a like-minded peer group (something many arts education students find scarce in foundations of education courses) create a scaffold for working within the unfamiliar terrain of K12 schooling.

Like many teacher education programs, the dance education curriculum requires a student teaching placement in the senior year where students work full time as an intern under the guidance of an experienced educator. However, students must begin to develop the professional identity of a dance educator far earlier as they learn to integrate theory and practice in meaningful ways. The *Dance in the Elementary School* and *Dance in the Secondary School* courses were developed to address the need for supported, hands-on field experiences prior to the student teaching year so that students begin to integrate content knowledge and general pedagogical knowledge within the specific context of dance education.

Course Descriptions

Both *Dance in the Elementary School* and *Dance in the Secondary School* are offered as 3-credit courses in the junior year. The courses are scheduled in two, two-hour blocks each week, meeting on campus one day per week and traveling to a school partner on the other day. The schedule is altered as needed to accommodate planning meetings and special activities with the school partners.

Students in these classes have completed one introductory dance education course that included observations in a school dance program along with lower-level courses in the Dance Bachelor of Fine Arts (BFA) program; many take introductory education courses concurrently. Enrollment in the dance education methods courses is quite small, averaging four students per course, which allows for significant feedback and collaboration.

Students are expected to develop skills in planning, delivering, and assessing dance instruction for elementary and secondary students following the NC Essential Standards for Dance[9] and the National Core Arts Standards.[10] The most significant activity in these courses is collaboratively teaching the weekly lesson at the partner schools. Other assignments include readings and associated discussion posts, written reflections on the lessons, written lesson plans and assessments of student work, and a final poster presentation where an aspect of the teaching project is shared.

School Partners

Building and maintaining mutually beneficial partnerships with local schools is essential for the success of these courses. Finding an appropriate setting for *Dance in the Elementary School* was an initial challenge because our county, while having several strong arts education programs, does not have any dance programs at the elementary level. By partnering with ECU's Center for Leadership and Civic Engagement, we located a school that had requested university involvement and accessed campus resources to assist with the project; teachers at the school worked with us to locate space and adjust schedules to facilitate a small dance program where there previously had been none.

Finding a school partner for *Dance in the Secondary School* was much easier, because most high schools and several middle schools in our county have dance programs led by licensed, full-time dance educators, many of whom are alumni of our program and maintain strong connections to the university. One dance educator at a rural, under-resourced school expressed interest in partnering with the university to provide additional opportunities for her students; additionally, her implementation of culturally responsive pedagogy within the dance curriculum provided a valuable setting for the university students to work within. Planning well in advance with our respective administrators, we could align the meeting times of our courses to facilitate this partnership.

Collaborative Teaching and Learning

Collaboration is a hallmark of the experiential learning in each of these courses, and it takes place across multiple dimensions: between professor and host teachers, between university students and professor, among university students, and between university students and K12 students. Initially, the collaboration between the university professor and the host teachers was critical to addressing both the logistical concerns that would make the work possible and pedagogical and curricular questions. This paved the way for the other collaborative relationships to develop and flourish.

Collaboration between professors and students is a common occurrence in the School of Theatre and Dance, where much of the faculty research and creative activity involves students as performers, production staff, and artistic collaborators. Students become accustomed to working closely with their professors and taking on significant responsibility for the success of large projects, and our work in these courses was similarly situated. Once the parameters of the teaching projects were established with the school partners, the university students made significant contributions to the ideas that shaped the direction of the teaching projects. Furthermore, the actual lessons presented in each course were taught through a highly collaborative co-teaching model where increasing responsibility was gradually transferred to the university students.

In *Dance in the Elementary School*, we taught second grade students lessons that integrated dance with language arts. In our most recent semester, the focus of the lessons was on the central concept of description, which is embedded in both content areas. Dancers and choreographers rely on clear descriptions to communicate their ideas in rehearsal and reflect on what they have created. In language arts, effective writers master the use of nouns, verbs, and adverbs to convey accurate descriptions of people and events. The university students worked together to plan lessons that paired specific topics in language arts with corresponding dance elements: nouns and body parts, verbs and actions, and adverbs and movement qualities. The lessons culminated with children creating short original dances accompanied by written accounts of their work.

The structure throughout the semester emphasized collaboration, modeling, and scaffolded practice. At the beginning of the course, many students had limited prior experience working with elementary age children; while most began dancing in childhood, their own experiences were in private dance schools. The K12 arts education environment was unfamiliar, and many students had concerns about their ability to connect with non-arts content, manage a classroom, and engage with young children. Therefore, the first lesson was taught primarily by the professor, with university students assigned specific tasks to assist, demonstrate, or work with small groups. Once the environment became familiar, university students selected activities to lead and worked together to transition from one teacher to the next. Additional duties included providing musical accompaniment, photo and video documentation, and movement demonstration. The professor remained ready to step in and assist, offering suggestions and reminders to enable the university students to feel confident and experience success in working with children. After the conclusion of the five-week unit, we began again with a new group of students. This time, the university students took on a more prominent teaching role from the beginning with each person assigned as the lead teacher for one full lesson.

In *Dance in the Secondary School*, we taught one weekly dance lesson to a class of high school students, primarily 9th and 10th graders who had little to no prior formal dance experience. While those students received a comprehensive curriculum through daily lessons with their regular dance educator, our project was specifically focused on providing additional experiences in dance composition. Our lessons addressed strategies for creating choreography connected to personal meanings and expression and were presented within a multicultural social justice framework emphasizing individual voice and ownership. One semester, following a university student's suggestion, we used the structure of "I am … /I am not" to generate gestural material based on ways students viewed themselves in contrast to the way they felt others perceived them. We then used a variety of choreographic strategies to elaborate the movement and shape it into group choreography. Another semester, we used the Language of Dance movement alphabet and motif symbols to introduce a variety of movement options and provide students with an initial vocabulary for describing dances they saw the university students perform. We worked with the theme of "Empowerment" to manipulate the basic movements to convey the students' ideas about power, community, and individual voice. In each semester, the university students worked with the high school dancers to shape their compositions into a finished, collaborative performance piece that was presented at both schools. High school students visited the university dance program at the end of the semester to share their dances and learn about the college environment, and university students assisted the high school teacher with a concert where they were also collaborative performers.

The structure of this course also emphasized collaboration and opportunities for the university students to take on increasing responsibility for instruction over the course of the semester. While many students felt comfortable with teenagers and had experience teaching this age group in dance studios and summer camp programs, only about half of the students themselves had experienced dance within a high school setting. The school we partnered with is in a low-income rural community and serves primarily African-American and Hispanic students; this cultural context is different from what many of our university dance students were familiar with, and some expressed concern about being able to connect meaningfully with the high school dancers. Consequently, the course emphasized many readings and discussions about the social and cultural dimensions of education. Our class structure often called for the university students to work closely with small groups of students as they developed, discussed, and refined their choreography in situations that allowed for the development of personal connections and mentoring relationships. The university students generally felt ready to take on leadership of the whole class activities, and their close work with groups of students provided important insights that they used for planning subsequent lessons. With an up-close view of students' reactions, they could tell when the high schoolers were bored and ready to move on or when they needed more time to work on a section of choreography.

In both courses, the element of reflection was a key component. After each lesson, students were expected to complete an online discussion board post responding to prompts about what happened and what they learned, which then became the starting point for discussion in class. Similarly, when students had reading assignments, we discussed how the text connected with our teaching. At midterm and final, students completed more formal Learning Statements where they reflected on important incidents that shaped their learning.

Preparation for Student Teaching Internship

The courses described here are typically taken in the junior year, and they serve as important preparation for the year-long student teaching internship that students complete as seniors. Candidates work in a school dance program with an assigned clinical teacher one day per week in the fall semester and full time in the spring semester. The intern-clinical teacher relationship is an important one, and to be successful, students should be prepared to understand the dynamics of a school environment, work collaboratively in the teaching context, reflect on their teaching practice, and voice their concerns and ideas respectfully. By embedding these skills into the junior year courses, we can more effectively transition students into their off-campus placements as they have already begun to shift from a student to a teacher identity.

One of the challenges we have encountered in the internship process is that, while the clinical teachers are all experts in the dance education field able to provide critical mentorship in teaching practice, they are not always aware of the requirements expected of our university students and may not consistently model the teaching strategies that candidates are expected to master. Our students are also required to complete the edTPA, an in-depth and challenging portfolio assessment that requires candidates to plan, deliver, and assess a unit of study and present substantial written and video evidence of their work.[11] Because many clinical teachers themselves did not have this requirement, they are not necessarily fully equipped to mentor interns through that process. While previous versions of the dance methods courses asked students to complete written lesson plan documents, students rarely had the opportunity to put these into action and practice refining and reflecting on them prior to the student teaching year. Embedding substantial and personally meaningful experiential learning activities into earlier coursework and providing structured opportunities for students to practice the planning, writing, and reflection skills that will be expected of them as interns create a useful framework within which faculty can guide and monitor their progress.

Assessment and Refinement

While the structure of these courses is established and experiential learning activities in the form of long-term teaching projects with partner schools will always be an integral part, the courses continue to be refined to be responsive to the needs of students, school partners, and program and curricular requirements.

In working with school partners, discussions have revealed the need to carefully consider the groups of children we involve to provide a quality arts education experience for the children and an easily manageable teaching situation that would enable the university students to feel successful as teachers. For instance, we have found it valuable to work with smaller groups of children and create focused, replicable lessons at the elementary level to give the university students more practice teaching in a calm and predictable context where they can readily see the impact of small changes in presenting material.

Discussions with school partners have also impacted the topics used for lessons. In the elementary course, our first semester of teaching included lessons based on science and literature topics; later, when the description lesson was proposed, the teachers found it especially useful to their work in the classroom and requested that we continue to work with that material. In the secondary course, regular feedback from the school partner has been used to refine the teaching strategies as well as the resulting choreography through more deliberate connections with the school's existing dance curriculum.

We have also found it to be helpful to involve the university students more directly in the planning for each project to help them become familiar with the school communities, gather important information that will shape the direction of the projects, and gain professional experience of collaborating with colleagues. At the beginning of each semester, we have added an orientation session where the university students meet with the school partners without the children present. Prior to that meeting, the university students discuss what they might need to know to be successful at each school and generate a list of questions. The meetings provide important opportunities to tour the schools, meet administrators, and gain insights. The university students develop professional relationships with the teachers; some have chosen to follow up independently by interviewing them for class projects or volunteering for additional activities.

Finally, an ongoing challenge we face is that our work in dance education—one of the smallest concentrations in the School of Theatre and Dance—is often invisible within our building. Owing to their performance backgrounds, many students thrive on the attention generated by the frequent productions happening on campus, but they do not receive any similar peer acknowledgment for the demanding and impactful work done in their teaching off campus. To address this, we have begun incorporating final projects that take the form of poster presentations delivered in the Studio Theatre just prior to one of the final choreography showings of the semester. Each dance education student chooses a research focus that relates to the teaching project; past topics have included arts integration, countering stereotypes, developing student leadership, and classroom management. Students develop a research poster following the guidelines of the National Dance Education Organization[12] and prepare short talks about their work to be shared with audience members. Through this activity, dance education as a profession becomes more visible within our campus community and the role of undergraduate research within our program is strengthened. Furthermore, students are encouraged to submit their posters for inclusion in state and national conferences, which further expands their understandings of the multitude of formats through which dance can be investigated and presented.

Conclusion

Purposefully embedding experiential learning within a collaborative course context has been a powerful pedagogical strategy to support student learning in dance education. Although dance education students will all complete a year-long internship, offering earlier, guided opportunities for experiential learning through school-based teaching projects has become an important component of our undergraduate curriculum. Such courses have the potential to deepen learning, provide scaffolding for the development of arts pedagogy, and facilitate the transition from student to teacher as dance education candidates make important steps toward their professional futures.

BEYOND THE PROSCENIUM: INTERNSHIPS
AT WASHINGTON COLLEGE

Michele Volansky
Washington College
Chestertown, MD, USA

Washington College (WC), a private, liberal-arts college in Chestertown, Maryland, has a culture of real-world preparedness that begins in a student's first year. Students are required to start thinking very early on about their career goals, what skills will be needed, and how to connect their career goals to their courses and to the opportunities available to them through WC. Such programming includes:

- First Year Career Awareness Program, which aims to prepare incoming freshmen from the summer before they enroll at WC through their freshmen year, to help them better understand their skills and interests and work toward a career involving these.
- In partnership with the Sophomore class officers, the Center for Career Development hosts a celebration of Sophomores (SOar), which includes an academic and activity resource fair, a series of interactive sessions to orient students to professional behaviors, and demonstrate personal and professional social interaction.

By the time students begin their junior year, they have had some experience and guidance in their pursuit of off-campus experiences. The College facilitates this through numerous signature programs, which offer internship opportunities and related funding open to WC students/alumni; in these cases, the host organizations give preference to our students, provided they meet the qualifications for the position. Such programs include "WC to Wall Street" (where students are mentored by alumni and friends of the College working in financial services), partnerships with institutions such as the National Archives, the Library of Congress and the National Park Service, and a robust alumni job shadowing program. The ultimate goal is to ensure that an internship is secured by a student's junior and senior year.

Academic departments across campus place a high value on experiential learning, with internships, study abroad semesters, and other off-campus activities built into major requirements. For example, students who major in either International Studies or Business Management are required to either study abroad or complete some other kind of hands-on learning activity, while students in science and mathematics conduct research with faculty members during the summer through the John S. Toll Fellows program. This kind of systematic approach to internships has been enormously successful; during the 2016–2017 academic year alone, over 200 WC students (or about 15% of the student body) had their internships supported through funding in excess of $240,000.

The Washington College Department of Theatre and Dance utilizes student experiential learning as a key component of our curriculum. Our program affords students the opportunity to explore breadth and depth of theatre studies through the following required core courses:

- Introduction to Acting
- Directing I

- Introduction to Design
- Technical Theatre
- Drama, Stage and Society I & II

From there, students are also required to take a Junior Seminar (which prepares them for their Senior Capstone project), one additional course in the theory/literature/history sequence and two electives.

The Department of Theatre and Dance has the following student learning outcomes:

1. Fluency in the vocabulary of the various disciplines (including acting, directing, design, playwriting, dramaturgy) within the field of theatre
2. Knowledge of the major trends, works, and individuals in the history of the theatre
3. Ability to contextualize theatre trends, works, and individuals in historic, geographic, artistic, political, and social terms
4. Ability to critique and analyze their work and the work of others in a productive and supportive way
5. Clear and persuasive communication skills: oral, written, and visual
6. Critical thinking through synthesis of textual and performance analysis and research
7. Skills in leadership, management, and collaboration
8. The importance of creativity in all aspects of their lives
9. A greater understanding and expansion of their own imaginative tools and resources

It is our belief that we are able to accomplish *all* of these outcomes through the *doing* of theatre and the majority of our classes, including the theory and literature courses, have this as a component. One of the strengths of our department, in our view, is the value we place on working collaboratively; decisions are made through rigorous discussion and evaluation that include faculty, students, and staff. Our efforts here reinforce the notion put forward by George Kuh that "working with a faculty member on research shows students firsthand how experts deal with the messy, unscripted problems that come up when experiments do not turn out as expected."[13] In our departmental productions—whether they are faculty or student directed—our students experience as close to a "real-world" production experience as possible. They routinely grapple with learning from mistakes, working with their peers, and ways of giving and receiving feedback. They articulate in post-mortem meetings the high value they place on accepting responsibility for choices that did and did not work, and are able to synthesize, in both written and oral form, what these choices were. We have discovered that on-campus production work prepares them for external internships in a thoughtful and deliberate manner.

Kuh's observation that internships "provide students with direct experience in a work setting—usually related to their career interests—and to give them the benefit of supervision and coaching from professionals in the field" is at the center of the Department's internship program, The Mary Martin Program in the Performing Arts. The internship arm of the program provides students a maximum of $1500 each to support an internship or experience away from campus. Students may apply for funding based on the following criteria:

1. To be eligible, students must have a minimum 3.0 GPA in either overall or within the major, and be in good academic standing.
2. Students may receive funding no more than twice over the course of their academic career, including for the summer after graduation.
3. Proposals are evaluated by the Theatre Department faculty and are subject to the availability of funds over the entire academic year. Preference may be given to first-time applicants.
4. Funds may not cover tuition for credit-bearing coursework.
5. The maximum amount awarded is $1500.
6. Recipients must write both a Final Report (minimum 750 words, summarizing their experience) and Thank You note(s) to the funder(s).

Students do not necessarily have to be upperclassmen to receive the funding, but we have discovered that securing an internship as a first year or sophomore is challenging because priority (in the case of the employers) is usually given to juniors or seniors.

Students who are interested in an internship work with faculty and their colleagues, alumni, and the Center for Career Development to identify theatres and programs to which they might apply. Since 2012, roughly half of the internships our students have conducted were as a direct result of a faculty member having a contact at the theatre or program. That being said, the students use the resources of the Center (such as internships.com and a discipline-specific curated list compiled by the staff that is updated annually) to find opportunities about which the faculty may not be aware.

The timeline for these activities usually coincides with advising sessions in the fall about spring courses (usually in early November); as students are thinking about their classes, they are also encouraged to explore plans for the winter and summer breaks. Though the Department Chair advises all Theatre majors, all members of the Theatre faculty play a role in working with students in their pursuit of internships, with students gravitating to the faculty member who shares their interests and connections. Some of the questions we ask in this discovery process include:

- Are you interested in digging deeper into a theatre practice with which you are very familiar or are you wanting to try something that is relatively new to you?
- Are you interested in exploring a particular city/region for life after graduation?
- Are you looking for a program that will help support your prospective Senior Capstone Experience (SCE)?
- Does the program provide the opportunity to learn skills that we do not offer here on campus?
- Does the program continue an already-started project?
- Are you interested in attending a conference or festival?

Students then apply for the funding—concurrent with their application to the internship/program—by completing an application that asks them to describe the internship, their personal and professional goals and a budget. The Center also asks the students to complete a series of questionnaires before, during, and after the internship, which include a "Learning Objective Worksheet" (before), a weekly journal and record of assignments/tasks (during), and a "Student Site Evaluation" (after).

Since the program was launched in 2015, we have funded 21 projects ranging from a student directing a play at their hometown community theatre to the support of internships and intensives at the Manhattan Theatre Club, the Bearded Ladies, Weston Playhouse, the Neighborhood Playhouse, the Shakespeare Academy, and the American Theatre Wing's Springboard program. Students have also, through the fund, attended the United States Institute for Theatre Technology and the National Dance Society annual conferences, done research in Italy on commedia dell'arte and in various archives about productions of *The Glass Menagerie* (both in support of SCE work), and worked with casting directors in New York to get a sense of how the professional casting process works.

Students who have been the recipients of these funds report that being asked to be "deliberate" in their personal and professional goals in the application process for the project sets them up for success. When asked "What was the impact of the internship/experience on what you learned in the classroom?" students responded as follows:

- "Training at The Neighborhood Playhouse helped take my acting, voice, and movement work to a level that I could not get at WAC. … My skill set has been enhanced, my work ethic and process have been informed and elevated by a range of teachers, exercises, and experiences (in and out of the classroom)."
- "Auditioning in New York with the Mary Martin funds changed the way I thought about theatre. In classes I was able to connect with scripts and recognize the artistic value of every aspect of a performance. The auditions stripped all of that away and made everything feel harsh and competitive in a way I was not expecting."
- "I learned how to approach plays and their production from different views and vantage points; how to take my critical thinking and allow it to be creative critical thinking, especially in regards to my academic design work. For me, practicality turned into possibility in the classroom, thanks to my experiences courtesy of the Mary Martin Grant."
- "The USITT trip pushed me to dive further into the technical side of theatre, making me more involved in the Theatre department's work calls and design ventures. Without the USITT, I doubt I would've seriously considered any theatre career as seriously as I do now. My hopes to work in lighting after graduation partially stem from that trip."
- "My internship showed me a great deal about collaboration and diplomacy while also giving a greater push for independence and a lack of a safety net."
- "I was able to see where I could most effectively put my own skill set to work."

Nancy O'Neill, at the Association of Colleges and Universities, quotes Kuh's assertions on particularly effective learning opportunities: "High-impact practices 'provide opportunities for students to see how what they are learning works in different settings, on and off campus. These opportunities to integrate, synthesize, and apply knowledge are essential to deep, meaningful learning experiences.'"[14] Based on our analysis, WC students are taking advantage of their internships to integrate and synthesize what they have learned in the classroom and apply it to their new workplaces and colleagues.

The mission of WC, which the current chair of the Department of Theatre and Dance helped to craft, is to "challenge and inspire emerging citizen leaders to discover lives of purpose and passion." Our departmental ethos is "yes/and," which is the first rule of improvisation. We embrace failure as a necessary part of the work that we do and encourage our students to take colossal risks to try things for which they do not always know the outcome. Though it does not come naturally to many students, we have discovered that our constant assessment, both in and out of the classroom, has proven valuable as they move from the confines of the campus to the various places of employ they experience upon graduation. Kuh states that the kinds of high-impact educational practices that are central to our curriculum provide students the unique opportunity to place themselves in the shoes of others, and that "they acquire the intellectual tools and ethical grounding to act with confidence for the betterment of the human condition."[15]

As noted above, part of the program asks students, upon completion of their internship, to submit a 750-word reflection on how the internship did or did not provide tools for networking and future work habits. Our students are thoughtful about their outcomes, echoing Kuh's emphasis on personal growth:

- "The summer program allowed me to connect with twenty other actors/creative people in the U.S. and abroad."
- "Perhaps, in the future, I'll be sure that I am better prepared for an audition. The preparation I did before each audition was definitely lacking."
- "Beyond production skills, I gained revolutionary tools for creating theatrical change and impact that I keep with me always as I approach theatre not only as an idea but a vehicle for expression, outreach, and improvement through storytelling."
- "Provided me with a network of contacts which would have provided me with plenty of job potentials, should I still be pursuing this

field. Also, nobody gives a damn if you're writing once you leave. Nobody is going to check in about your trip's itinerary, nobody is going to remind you to get a draft out or to work on edits. It has shown me how valuable and rare it is to have readers that are both reliable as well as helpful. And that some projects take time to understand themselves and to reach an audience."

- "USITT certainly taught me a lot about how to effectively network, collaborate with one's peers, and navigate an uncertain professional landscape. I learned that one must be proactive in order to be successful, and no other lesson has been made more apparent to me."
- "I would not have been able to hone in on my career goals without the internship experience, particularly because it forces young professionals to prioritize and discover what it is that makes them want to get up and go to work."

Recent graduates from our program have gone to medical and veterinary school, undertaken graduate study in sociology, political science, biology, and chemistry, worked for political campaigns (across all kinds of political spectrums), run non-profits and independent retailers, worked as teachers and in business, served in the military, and yes, even wound up as theatre-makers themselves.

Notes

1. Quoted in Nancy O'Neill, "Internships as a High-Impact Practice: Some Reflections on Quality," n.p.
2. O'Neill, "Internships as High-Impact Practice: Some Reflections on Quality," n.p.
3. Hart Research Associates, "Falling Short? College Learning and Career Success."
4. "NSSE 2016 High-Impact Practices"; "SNAAP 2015 & 2016 Recent Graduates Aggregate Frequency Report," 21.
5. From the SNAAP 2015 & 2016 Recent Graduates Aggregate Frequency Report. Data on performing arts majors extracted by SNAAP on request, provided July 2017.
6. See Greg Redlawsk, "Unpaid Internships, or Getting Your Foot in the Door of the American Theatre"; Rachel Burger, "Why Your Unpaid Internship Makes You Less Employable"; Alexander Frenette, "The Internship Divide: The Promise and Challenges of Internships in the Arts"; Phil Gardner, *The Debate over Unpaid College Internships*.

7. "Internship Programs Standards," Council for the Advancement of Standards in Higher Education, www.cas.edu; National Society for Experiential Education, www.nsee.org.
8. Readers might also want to consult Doug Risner, "Research, Design, and Implementation of an Internship Course in Dance: Turning Student Knowledge into Professional Know-How." This article offers reflections on the challenges and benefits of constructing a dance internship at a "large, urban, research-intensive university" (70) and provides a table of contents for a prototype internship manual.
9. North Carolina State Board of Education, Department of Public Instruction, *Arts Education Standard Course of Study*.
10. National Coalition for Core Arts Standards, *National Core Arts Standards*.
11. American Association for Colleges of Teacher Education, *About edTPA*.
12. National Dance Education Organization, *Conference Poster Presentations*.
13. George D. Kuh and Carol Geary Schneider, *High-Impact Educational Practices: What They Are, Who Has Access to Them, and Why They Matter*, 17.
14. Quoted in O'Neill, "Internships as a High-Impact Practice: Some Reflections on Quality," n.p.
15. Kuh and Schneider, *High-Impact Educational Practices*, 17.

BIBLIOGRAPHY

About edTPA. edTPA. American Association for Colleges of Teacher Education. http://edtpa.aacte.org/about-edtpa. Accessed 1 Aug 2017.

Arts Education Standard Course of Study. North Carolina State Board of Education, Department of Public Instruction. http://www.ncpublicschools.org/curriculum/artsed/scos/support-tools/. Accessed 1 Aug 2017.

Burger, Rachel. 2014. Why Your Unpaid Internship Makes You Less Employable. *Forbes*. January 16. https://www.forbes.com/sites/realspin/2014/01/16/why-your-unpaid-internship-makes-you-less-employable/#f97f46d75017. Accessed 6 July 2017.

Conference Poster Presentations. National Dance Education Organization. http://www.ndeo.org/content.aspx?page_id=22&club_id=893257&module_id=196192#PosterResources. Accessed 1 Aug 2017.

Frenette, Alexander. The Internship Divide: The Promise and Challenges of Internships in the Arts. *Strategic National Arts Alumni Project*. http://snaap.indiana.edu/pdf/SNAAP15/SNAAP_Special_Report_2015.pdf. Accessed July 2017.

Gardner, Phil. 2011. *The Debate over Unpaid College Internships*. Intern Bridge. http://www.ceri.msu.edu/wp-content/uploads/2010/01/Intern-Bridge-Unpaid-College-Internship-Report-FINAL.pdf. Accessed 6 July 2017.

Hart Research Associates. Falling Short? College Learning and Career Success. *Association of American Colleges and Universities.* https://www.aacu.org/leap/public-opinion-research/2015-survey-results. Accessed 11 Aug 2017.

Internship Programs Standards. Council for the Advancement of Standards in Higher Education. www.cas.edu.

Kuh, George D., and Carol Geary Schneider. 2008. *High-Impact Educational Practices: What They Are, Who Has Access to Them, and Why They Matter.* Washington, DC: Association of American Colleges and Universities.

National Core Arts Standards. National Coalition for Core Arts Standards. State Education Agency Directors of Arts Education. www.nationalartsstandards.org. Last Modified 2014.

National Society for Experiential Education. www.nsee.org.

NSSE 2016 High-Impact Practices. http://nsse.indiana.edu/20"16_institutional_report/pdf/HIPTables/HIP.pdf. Accessed 6 July 2017.

O'Neill, Nancy. 2010. Internships as a High-Impact Practice: Some Reflections on Quality. *Peer Review* 12 (4): 4–8. http://aacu.org.895elmp01.blackmesh.com/publications-research/periodicals/internships-high-impact-practice-some-reflections-quality. Accessed 1 July 2017.

Redlawsk, Greg. Unpaid Internships, or Getting Your Foot in the Door of the American Theatre. *HowlRound.* http://howlround.com/unpaid-internships-or-getting-your-foot-in-the-door-of-the-american-theatre. Accessed 6 July 2017.

Risner, Doug. 2015. Research, Design, and Implementation of an Internship Course in Dance: Turning Student Knowledge into Professional Know-How. *Journal of Dance Education* 15 (2): 60–71.

SNAAP 2015 & 2016 Recent Graduates Aggregate Frequency Report. http://snaap.indiana.edu/pdf/2016/SNAAP15_16_Recent_Grads_Aggregate_Report.pdf, 21. Accessed 6 July 2017.

CHAPTER 11

Capstone Courses and Projects

Capstone courses and projects are the only high-impact practice expressly intended for the final year of a student's undergraduate degree program, and performing arts departments have embraced them for the benefits they provide students in terms of skills synthesis and intense time on task. Performing arts students have always tended to have their most intensive performative experience, with all the attending responsibility, collaborative work, and deep research, toward the end of their college careers, but in recent years departments have worked to make these experiences intentional and reflective. A review of the literature confirms that we have high expectations of what the capstone is supposed to achieve, regardless of discipline. A capstone should be collaborative and team-based, faculty mentored, serve as a transition to graduate school or the professions, utilize all skills learned in the major, self-reflective about past experiences and future goals, include presentation, and problem solve community issues.[1]

With such demands on one course or project, there are bound to be ways the capstone experience comes up short, even as students can reflect on the overall value of the experience. The truth is that most individual faculty do not have the expertise or the capacity to meet all of the above elements, which is why capstone courses or projects are often mentored by more than one faculty member. Because there is often a sharing of faculty mentorship and an expectation of student self-sufficiency, capstone projects

© The Author(s) 2018
M. Hayford, S. Kattwinkel (eds.), *Performing Arts as High-Impact Practice*, The Arts in Higher Education,
https://doi.org/10.1007/978-3-319-72944-2_11

and courses have a tendency to become inconsistent or unruly in their delivery, resulting in students feeling overwhelmed and under supported in their efforts. "Understanding the Capstone Experience Through the Voices of Students" is an illuminating study by Patsy Tinsley McGill that captured student feedback about their capstone experience in numerous disciplines at California State University Monterey Bay. The results are not surprising to anyone who has faculty mentored a capstone course or project. Tinsley McGill confirmed what many of us already know about the typical capstone experience. A summary of her findings includes the following:

- Students need to be better prepared for the capstone, with expected content scaffolded throughout the curriculum, so that the work of the capstone is not surprisingly rigorous by comparison, or assuming knowledge that seniors had not previously studied.
- Students want faculty support from multiple faculty members in pursuing their capstone projects, regardless of who the designated mentor/advisor/teacher may be. Students need to have various kinds of faculty mentorship and want support for capstone experiences from diverse faculty members.[2]
- When the capstone is faculty mentored by more than one faculty member, students need consistency in grading and standards applied, as well as shared understanding of capstone goals.
- Students want regular class meetings, even though many capstone experiences are treated like independent studies and do not meet on a regular class schedule.
- Students want to follow a syllabus, even though the course may be designed to be student co-created, or expect the students to take initiative.
- Students prefer smaller teams (five or fewer) to larger teams.
- Students prefer capstones that are longer than one semester, as the work expected is more demanding and they want more time to complete it.
- Students need sufficient time with faculty mentors. Many students feel that faculty are too overburdened with other responsibilities and do not have the time to meet that they would prefer. They would like faculty to have an agreed-upon understanding of the time commitment required to mentor capstone projects.

Resource implications of meeting the students' reasonable requests above are enormous. A common issue at many campuses is that capstones, especially when mentored by multiple faculty, are often not considered part of a faculty member's teaching load. Not surprisingly then, faculty are not as available as they would like to be to mentor capstone projects when this is the case. The idea that the overall curriculum should support and prepare students for the capstone has implications on academic freedom for any one faculty member to consider how their course offerings are aligned with the curriculum as a whole, and may require faculty to have difficult conversations in thinking about integrating common learning objectives across the curriculum. The feedback tells us that students still crave the structure and syllabus of a regular course (or two courses over the entire senior year), even though the capstone is often designed to require more self-direction. Encouraging our students to be more self-sufficient while also being available for consistent mentorship is a delicate balance.

The demands on performing arts faculty to appropriately resource the capstone experience for students are significant. Many faculty make personal sacrifices and unpaid efforts to support graduating seniors because we know how beneficial the capstone experience can be for our students. Preparing our students for careers outside of performance, providing skills in arts administration and entrepreneurship, and considering how the capstone can also be a site for critical ethical reflection are a few additional capstone goals acknowledged in the arts.

In "Developing Realistic Notions of Career in the Performing Arts," Dawn Bennett describes the career path that many performing arts majors pursue post-graduation as "protean":

> Protean careers are at the extreme end of portfolio careers and are named after the mythological Greek sea god Proteus who was able to change form at will in order to avoid danger: something that increasing numbers of people need to do in order to remain employable. The creative industries workforce has long engaged in protean careers, which necessitate the continual development of new opportunities and the attainment of the corresponding skills required to meet each new challenge.[3]

Bennett acknowledges that many performance-based curriculums are assumed to have more prestige than curriculums that incorporate broader and practical coursework, and therefore devalue the development of non-performance skills. It is a disservice to our students to not prepare them in the broadest way possible for common career paths they may take upon graduation. These career paths often require skills in self-promotion and marketing, teaching, running a small business, and negotiation. Students often come into higher education already perceiving performance as the pinnacle of their career aspirations (especially when they have successfully auditioned to gain admittance). They do not need their faculty to further reify professional performance as the only way to measure success, but rather need exposure to other likely and realistic career paths they will be prepared for upon graduation. There is no need to fear that students will no longer appreciate "art for art's sake," or devalue performance, when galvanized with other skill sets during their college careers. Instead, they will be better prepared to succeed, and more likely to find performance opportunities if that is their ambition, when they have the tools they need to broaden their career portfolio.

Arts management or arts administration has long been a known quantity in the performing arts and one can find various degree programs that include arts management content; however, entrepreneurship is a more recently embraced approach in the performing arts higher education landscape. Entrepreneurship differs from arts management in meaningful ways, as detailed by Linda Essig in "Suffusing Entrepreneurship Education throughout the Theatre Curriculum." Essig notes that arts management or arts administration programs "focus on how to run an arts organization, not on how to manage the innovation, ambiguity, and change required to *launch* an arts-based venture or support creativity in the performing arts."[4] Entrepreneurship training in the arts requires curriculum that enables students to become content creators and position themselves as artists with skin in the game, taking risks in a safe environment where failure won't mean destitution. Essig gives an example of a course at Arizona State University wherein the students comprise a theatre board, and treat a black box theatre as their own venue in which they produce and market a season of plays, keeping the ticket proceeds for their own company. Giving students this kind of agency to practice entrepreneurship skills is a high value for capstone experiences. Students invested in their own success through entrepreneurial ventures get the hands-on experiential practice of transferrable skills to various career paths upon graduation.

"Transferrable skills" is not a bad word. In fact, having students learn how their skills gained in performance majors relate to additional careers outside or related to the arts will only enhance their prospects upon graduation. Additionally, understanding how their talents can be harnessed in the service of others as they are considering career opportunities is a necessary component of transformative learning in a capstone experience. Incorporating deep critical thinking about life purpose and ethical artistic practice are meaningful additions to any capstone.

Encouraging students to articulate an artist identity that includes ethical reflection and more pervasive understandings of what practicing their art may include will serve their future goals. How the performing arts may serve local communities, in partnership with local social service agencies, health, museum and tourism industries, are all creative career paths that have currency now and will continue to grow as the applied performing arts movement becomes more entrenched and understood as an effective method of building capacity and creating change in communities. Applied performing arts curriculum can include coursework in applied theatre and dance, teaching in the arts (outside of education majors and catered to the independent contracting of teaching that artists often pursue), and music therapy programs.

Within the capstone experience, providing graduating seniors the opportunity for self-reflection is paramount. Assignments or projects that require a student to look back on what they have learned and project forward to consider future goals is commonplace in a capstone. In addition, the capstone can serve as a site for transformational learning, in which students are able to reframe past experience in light of reflection on ethics and newly acquired knowledge. Transformational learning in the capstone sets the stage for the ability to recognize that one is a lifelong learner, and that personal growth continues past graduation. While it may seem that graduating students would welcome the opportunity to pause and reflect on their education, ethics, and future goals, Jason Martin and Michael G. Strawser remind us in "Transforming the Capstone: Transformative Learning as a Pedagogical Framework and Vehicle for Ethical Reflection in the Capstone Course" that these students are also in a hurry:

> True internal reflection and transformative musing do not occur naturally. In fact, as students progress in their college education they may be less inclined to pause and think about their college experience and more devoted to finishing the degree as quickly as possible.[5]

It is up to performing arts faculty to build reflection into capstone course assignments, projects, and class dialogue so that we ensure time for the valuable practice of self-reflexivity. Reflection needs to become a habit for our students, who as artists will often take great risks. With attention to the value of the capstone, hopefully we prepare our student artists to take those risks with increased capacity for self-knowing and resilience.

The following case studies demonstrate effective capstone coursework and projects that include opportunities for students' self-exploration and collaborative work. Gretchen McLaine utilizes individual capstone projects in dance that demonstrate longitudinal progress toward student learning outcomes (SLOs). Marc Ernesti focuses on the often neglected support of early career transition for music graduates, with professional development opportunities that are relevant to the current music industries.

Call to action:

- Performing arts faculty need to build reflection on the students' entire academic career and future goals into the capstone.
- Performing arts faculty should consider the capstone as a site for transformational learning, where students can reflect on their ethics and have opportunities for reframing and applying their ethics accordingly.
- Performing arts faculty need to maintain their professional networks and professional development as artists, so that productive student experiences through internships and partnerships with those contacts can be fostered. The opportunities opened up by faculty who are practicing artists for experiential learning and mentoring cannot be overstated.
- Performing arts faculty must review and revise curriculum to ensure proper scaffolding of skills expected in the capstone experience.
- Performing arts faculty must seek faculty development training opportunities on the capstone experience. Preparing to meet the numerous demands of a capstone course is imperative and administrators should acknowledge the cost benefit of investing in such professional development of faculty.
- Performing arts units must have an intentional approach to the capstone among all faculty (not just those assigned as capstone instructors or mentors), so that students' needs are met and common capstone pitfalls are avoided.
- Performing arts faculty should consider implementing e-portfolios into the capstone experience, as an online presence is essential to

artistic success. E-portfolios have been called the "eleventh high impact practice."[6]
- Performing arts faculty need to include entrepreneurial training as part of the capstone experience. Allowing students to take risks, succeed, and potentially fail in a secure and safe environment of the academy is critical to their future artistic ventures. Making grant monies available, providing resources such as venues/set materials/costumes, or providing a workshop with a Certified Public Accountant, are a few ways that faculty can support entrepreneurial training.
- Performing arts departments should work to incorporate and formalize senior-year experiences that students are self-selecting and creating on their own (directing, choreographing, conducting, organizing student arts organizations) into the curriculum to make those experiences intentional and reflective.

Cultivating a Successful Dance Capstone Course

Gretchen S. McLaine
College of Charleston
Charleston, SC, USA

The intelligent intersection where theory and experience meet is known as praxis.[7] Capstones are traditionally used in postsecondary education as a means to integrate students' educational experiences and foster the transition to the professional world which they will experience after graduation.[8] It is in this praxis where capstone courses have their greatest value. While approximately 85% of capstone courses are discipline specific, they are similarly designed to include a variety of educational praxes that positively affect application, synthesis, and reflection of students' knowledge base. If designed purposefully, capstone courses allow students to engage in several academically beneficial practices and understand real-world applicability.[9] This chapter will provide a brief overview of capstone practices used in the College of Charleston's (C of C) DANC 441: Dance Capstone course, and will then focus on two major assignments in this course: the capstone project and the e-portfolio.

The dance capstone course offered at C of C is taken during the final fall semester of a student's matriculation, and is carefully integrated into the curriculum.[10] C of C is a liberal arts institution offering a Bachelor of Arts degree, and the number of credit hours designated for major-specific courses is limited. Therefore, as the curriculum was developed, deliberate attention was given to integrating key concepts and multiple high-impact practices throughout several majors-level courses; for example, the development and maintenance of an online portfolio to document longitudinal growth of the student. The capstone class consists of traditional class meetings and individual consultations. The major capstone project emanates from a pedagogical rationale and recognition of the importance in having students connect their dance scholarship with other fields of study.

Educational theorists such as Kuh[11] consider capstone courses as high-impact practices because these experiences foster students' abilities to integrate research and apply the knowledge learned to real-world situations. Capstones also tie into Bloom's taxonomy and the use of higher-order thinking skills—create, evaluate, analyze—which are reinforced and demonstrated in multiple ways throughout the capstone course. Through data analysis, including data from the National Survey of Student Engagement (NSSE), Kinzie found that students who completed a capstone course experienced more growth in reflective and integrative learning than those who did not, and concluded that capstones allow for student engagement in purposeful, educational practice.[12] Kolb's theory of experiential learning, which is based on the work of foundational education theorists Dewey, Piaget, and Freire, explains how cognitive processes are engaged during active learning experiences: "Learning is the process whereby knowledge is created through the transformation of experience."[13]

In higher education, capstone courses often develop through faculty evaluation of student learning and program assessment. Noting deficiencies within an undergraduate education that is often fragmented in content delivery and fails to prepare students for the world's complexities, college campuses are now investing in integrative learning so that students may embrace a more holistic view of their education.[14] The capstone course required for all dance majors at C of C serves as a bridge between students' past and/or present educational experiences and career opportunities. Goals of this praxis-based course are fourfold: develop critical thinking and problem-solving skills, synthesize discipline-specific knowledge into a significant culminating project, connect curriculum to career transition and preparedness, and engage in academic research.

Critical thinking and problem-solving skills are integrated into the dance major curriculum so that students have multiple opportunities to experience the upper levels of Bloom's taxonomy. The conception, development, and implementation of a major capstone project require students to reflect upon their own strengths, weaknesses, and goals, and to foresee potential issues which may arise during the execution of their project. When problems inevitably arise, students must find and use creative solutions in order to satisfactorily complete their projects. Students are also required to merge their major fields of study or design a project that is otherwise directly related to their major and career prospects. This requires them to tap into previous knowledge gained throughout their academic career, which may be both co-curricular and cross-curricular as appropriate.

Engagement in academic research is another skill required in multiple dance majors' courses and reinforced in the capstone. All students are expected to engage in academic research, whether traditional, participatory-action research (PAR), public scholarship, or creative scholarly work. For students who engage in PAR, the capstone experience may be the first time their academic work has moved beyond the classroom walls, and marks their introduction into public scholarship. Broadening the oftentimes narrow definition that is ascribed to research is of particular importance to the discipline, where there are many forms of creative scholarly work that are largely undervalued in traditional academic circles. Prominent dance scholars Fraleigh and Hanstein define research as a process that is inherently creative; as a process, it means to search and re-search.[15] By informing and inspiring students to engage in this type of research, we serve our field by creating advocates for non-traditional modes of scholarship. We must create a culture of value for creative scholarship, encouraging and mentoring students to establish and pursue their own research profile. Through exhaustive examination and reflection, research helps us build a critical analysis of a problem or issue. In dance, we also use Boyer's expanded definition of research that reaches across the four domains: teaching, discovery, integration, and application.[16]

The purpose of the dance capstone course at C of C is to prepare students to succeed in life after graduation, whether they pursue graduate studies, enter the world of the professional dancer, or work as freelance artists. One of the most significant assignments which address professional competencies and preparation is the e-portfolio. These not only serve as a visual reminder of a student's growth but also facilitate integrative learning.[17] We encourage, but do not yet require, that students use this e-portfolio for documenting growth in dance technique classes, writing and critical reflection, and maintaining an updated resume. The establishment and maintenance of an e-portfolio is also one method of addressing SLOs and assessing student growth and achievement.

Longitudinal SLOs are addressed within various classes throughout the entire dance curriculum; students are also afforded various opportunities within the program to tailor their educational experiences for career preparation in other majors or fields of study. The SLOs for the dance capstone course at C of C are:

- students research and define various content areas of dance while coordinating and integrating these within an individually designed dance project;
- students research, create/design, and present a dance capstone project suitable to their career goals in the field of dance, and to defend the project in oral, creative, and written formats;
- students articulate substantial knowledge of historical perspectives and current issues/trends in the dance field;
- students model professional values and behaviors of the field (deadline adherence, effective communication, creative problem solving, collaboration, etc.);
- students articulate the importance and responsibility taken upon oneself with desired career path;
- students write and speak thoughtfully about dance, dancers, and dancing; and
- students create a website/e-portfolio based on professional career goals.

Students' cumulative experiences throughout the dance curriculum are carefully scaffolded to create multiple high-impact praxis and reflective self-assessment opportunities. Dancers enter into the capstone course with an ongoing, substantive evaluation and documentation of their undergraduate work in dance. They can clearly articulate career goals, and more specifically, possess a greater understanding of how their two majors may intersect with each other. As freshmen, all C of C students are required to enroll in either a first-year seminar or learning community, both of which are established high-impact practices. Dance majors approach the capstone class with a working knowledge of anatomy, history, composition/choreography, experiences in performance and production, basic research practices, and technical proficiency in dance. Additionally, they have taken elective classes such as Career Seminar and Dance Pedagogy and Practice. The projects in these and other courses deepen their knowledge of and experience in working with others, creative problem solving, conflict resolution, and research. Therefore, these prior experiences establish a baseline of scholarship and high-impact praxis, which allows for a greater amount of time for reflective self-assessment practices in the capstone course.

The Capstone Project

Studies have shown that faculty engagement with students is an important factor in student satisfaction and perceived growth with capstones[18]; therefore, consultation with and final approval from a faculty member is required for their projects. While there is an understanding that the student and professor consistently interact throughout the semester, each student is responsible for designing, researching, analyzing, and presenting his/her individual capstone project.

One example of an effective capstone project experience merged a student's two majors: dance and computer science. Rebecca[19] entered the capstone class with research experience in both content areas, but was unsure of how to combine the two into a useful capstone project. After consulting with the faculty member, she decided to attempt the use of motion capture software to record dance movements into a language known as Labanotation.[20] Rebecca completed a literature review to analyze current advancements in using motion capture technology to notate movement. After further discussion with her professor, she revised her original project to make it more feasible.[21] Rebecca developed the computer coding that would make this project possible, and after working with the motion capture equipment, she was able to analyze the program's difficulties in recognizing certain movement patterns. The professor attended recording sessions in the motion capture lab to evaluate Rebecca's work and assess her work. At the conclusion of the project, the professor and student agreed to continue working on this, with the eventual goal of creating a computer program that can translate motion into Labanotation. The opportunity to combine the fields of computer science and dance was meaningful for Rebecca, who found herself with an established research agenda as she entered a PhD program in computer science.

Another capstone project involved Susan's combination of her majors in dance and arts management. With an interest in dance education and community engagement, Susan developed a capstone project in which she created a comprehensive public relations guide for establishing a summer arts-integration program for the community. This guide included information on how to understand your audience, effectively market and price your program, promote its benefits to the community and individuals, and so on. The guide was adapted by the dance program and used to plan a summer community outreach program. Susan is currently working in an arts management position at a major international dance festival, and credits getting the job directly to the work she did in the capstone course.

Michael was a dance major who did not begin serious dance training until his sophomore year in college. As a student in the Dance Pedagogy and Practice course, he displayed a natural affinity for teaching and developing creative lesson plans. He also developed a passion to teach dance to children. After much discussion and self-reflection, Michael concluded that he should pursue something related to teaching children. Michael utilized the knowledge from the Pedagogy class, the teaching experiences he had in Classical Ballet Technique,[22] and his training in choreography and kinesiology to develop his curriculum. In order to further validate his work to public school administrators, he used the opportunity to infuse concepts in math, science, and literature which were requisite knowledge for eighth-grade students. His capstone project culminated in the creation of a dance curriculum for eighth-grade boys. Michael used the lesson plans he created during the course, along with his e-portfolio, when he interviewed for and secured the dance teacher position at a local arts magnet school.

After this course was offered for many years, several modifications were made to its content and delivery. First was the need to allow for greater flexibility in project design. Approximately 85% of dance majors at C of C are also pursuing a second major or dual degree, making their interests and career goals quite varied. Because of this, we allow each individual student to explore what interests him/her and what he/she wants from the class. Therefore, a flexible approach to capstone project content and methodology is necessary. Flexibility in how the capstone project is conceived and implemented necessitated a refinement of project assessment rubrics, and the ability, to a certain extent, of each student to tweak the rubric which more accurately reflects his/her SLOs. An example of a project rubric is seen in Table 11.1.

The second change dealt with the project proposal. Faculty should help students find the cross and co-curricular connections, without allowing the capstone proposal to be too vague or have too few parameters. The proposal should include a general statement of approach, method, working thesis, timeline, procedures, assumptions, definitions, and limitations/delimitations. However, the proposal is a living, breathing document that inherently requires flexibility. The element of a formal presentation of this

Table 11.1 DANC 441 Capstone Project Rubric (sample) for *Motion Capture for Labanotation*

Measure	Excellent (10–9.0)	Very good (8.9–8.0)	Average (7.9–7.0)	Deficient (6.9–6.0)	Failing (<6.0)
Professionalism and presentation (mid-term) (10%)	Student conducted him/herself in a professional, eloquent, and engaging manner; confident delivery of presentation, with ability to remain on topic	Student conducted him/herself in a fairly professional manner; may have shown eloquence, confidence, relevance, or engagement, but was not consistent	Student conducted him/herself in a generally acceptable manner, but showed deficiencies in confidence, eloquence, relevance, engagement, and/or professionalism	Student did not conduct him/herself in a generally acceptable manner, as demonstrated through a clear lack of confidence, eloquence, relevance, engagement, and/or professionalism	Student did not conduct him/herself in an acceptable manner; demonstrated blatant disregard for significance of the assignment and its function in the course

Measure	Excellent (20–18)	Very good (17–16)	Average (15–14)	Deficient (13–12)	Failing (<11)
Research proposal (20%)	Research of topic was thorough and evident; student was clear on thesis or purpose of project; proposal contained required information and was formatted to specifications	Research of topic was thorough and/or evident; student may not have been clearly articulated thesis or purpose of project; proposal contained required information, but there may have been errors in organization, format, or grammar	Proposal was completed, but may be missing key information; there may also be a lack of understanding the significance of this project; thesis was not articulated clearly	Proposal was submitted late or was missing many key components; thesis or purpose of project was not clear; several errors in proposal structure, grammar, spelling; minimal effort was placed into this proposal	Proposal was very late or not submitted; no understanding of the assignment and apparent lack of interest on behalf of the student

(*continued*)

Table 11.1 (continued)

Measure	Excellent (50–45)	Very good (44–40)	Average (39–35)	Deficient (34–30)	Failing (<30)
Research and Preparedness (includes literature review) (50%)	Preparation was extensive and evident; organization of content and thesis were well-developed	Preparation was evident; thesis was clear, and content was largely organized, but may have shown weakness in lack of depth	Demonstrated an acceptable level of preparation, but had problems with depth of content and/or its organization	Preparation was significantly lacking; information presented was not relevant and/or thorough, with unclear thesis	Very little to no prior preparation was apparent; content was unorganized, inaccurate, and/or grossly lacking in scholarship

Measure	Excellent (10–9.0)	Very good (8.9–8.0)	Average (7.9–7.0)	Deficient (6.9–6.0)	Failing (<6.0)
Professionalism and presentation (final) (10%)	Student conducted him/herself in a professional, eloquent, and engaging manner; confident delivery of presentation, with ability to remain on topic	Student conducted him/herself in a fairly professional manner; may have shown eloquence, confidence, relevance, or engagement, but was not consistent	Student conducted him/herself in a generally acceptable manner, but showed deficiencies in confidence, eloquence, relevance, engagement, and/or professionalism	Student did not conduct him/herself in a generally acceptable manner, as demonstrated through a clear lack of confidence, eloquence, relevance, engagement, and/or professionalism	Student did not conduct him/herself in an acceptable manner; demonstrated blatant disregard for significance of the assignment and its function in the course

Comments:

proposal was added to the course requirements. Forcing students to articulate and defend their ideas to their peers earlier in the process made them think more critically about those ideas, and eventually develop stronger proposals. Finally, students were required to conduct a literature review of their topic within the first three weeks of class, and fold this into both their peer proposal and the final project presentation. These changes allowed for greater clarity both from the students in articulating their work and in the grading/assessment of these projects.

The E-Portfolio

The other major component of the DANC 441 capstone course is the establishment and upkeep of an e-portfolio. E-portfolios showcase curricular and professional experiences, while providing multiple opportunities for frequent dialog between teacher and student. They not only allow for frequent feedback but also allow students to see how their own understanding and developmental gains increase over time.[23] While the dance program does not require students to maintain an e-portfolio throughout their entire academic career, they are highly encouraged to do so, and e-portfolios are being utilized in a greater number of dance major courses at C of C. The e-portfolios serve as an archive of student artifacts: videos, writing samples, resumes, and photos. The early establishment of an e-portfolio underscores its integrative nature of curricular content and reinforcing praxis value. It should be a space for thoughtful reflection on behalf of the student about their own educational experiences, skills, and growth. The e-portfolio also provides students with a completed site to use in job preparation, self-promotion, and professional interviews. The students are required to make their portfolios public, which not only serves to educate them about the permanence of data in the digital world, it is also a great motivator to take the related assignments seriously. Students are encouraged to use a platform that offers free storage space and with which they are comfortable. Most students choose to maintain a wiki, or use either Weebly or Wix webpage editors to create and maintain their portfolio.

E-portfolios are most effective when strongly aligned with course and department learning outcomes. Prompts provided to the students must allow for the significant practice of higher-order thinking skills. Assignments must intentionally engage students in reflection in order to reap the greatest benefits.[24] Assessments must also be clear and thorough, demonstrating that evidence of student learning and growth has occurred. The self-reflection prompt for the e-portfolio is completed at the end of the semester, and includes the following questions: How has your capstone class affected or changed you or your beliefs? What did you learn about yourself by composing this portfolio? What personal weaknesses or challenges did you discover through this assignment? What lessons from this experience are you going to carry forward? If given the opportunity, what would you do differently? Table 11.2 shows the required elements of the e-portfolio in the dance capstone course.

Structured in a purposeful way, capstone courses provide educators with a rich environment in which to stimulate and hone students' higher-order thinking skills. If students enter the classroom with an understanding of the capstone's purpose and perhaps having previous high-impact experiences, then the integrative learning they embark upon allows students to meaningfully reflect on their past and present work. The sophisticated cognitive development that occurs in such high-impact practices aligns with workforce

Table 11.2 Required elements of e-portfolio for DANC 441

Required elements of e-portfolio	Include in performance/dance resume?	Include in teaching application?	Include in graduate school application?
Cover page/introduction	Yes	Yes	Yes
Resume (includes contact information)	Performance resume (include height and weight)	CV or resume	CV or resume
Two professional photos	Yes	No	Only if directed
Five minute professional video/promo reel	Yes	Only if directed	Only if directed
Two examples of scholarly research and writing	No	Yes	Yes
Final self-reflection (write as a personal philosophy)	No	Yes, but frame as teaching philosophy	Yes
Subfolder containing all class assignments: literature review, reflection papers, reading responses, and so on	No	No	Include one or two only if requested
Sample of professional work	Only if requested	Yes	Yes

demands for employees who are creative problem-solvers and holistic thinkers. However, in order to reap maximum benefits, the deliberate curricular development and pedagogical methods of the faculty must be met by the intentional effort of students.[25] If these challenges can be met, a capstone course or experience is a proven way to increase integrative learning, metacognition, and career preparedness.

(NEVER) MIND THE GAP: PREPARING PROFESSIONAL MUSICIANS AT THE ROYAL ACADEMY OF MUSIC, LONDON

Marc Ernesti
The State University of New York at Potsdam
Potsdam, NY, USA

Despite their high profile, record companies are remarkably small and only recruit people with very specific skills. Producers and others in the Artists and Repertoire Department usually have a degree in music; PR and sales and marketing personnel might have an arts degree and a diploma or in-service training in marketing; a legal training is necessary for contracts and royalties; while for recording engineers there are courses such as the Tonmeister course at Surrey University. Competition is tough. You must get to know the record industry and gain experience in any related field, such as a recording studio or publishing. It is sometimes possible to get work experience through a placement with a record company. Even once you are working for a record company, success in a particular area does not guarantee promotion.[26]

Establishing the Field

Only a few would doubt that, even over the past 20 years, the music sector as a whole and the recording industry in particular have changed dramatically and, acknowledging this fundamental truth, that somehow it would need to reflect from the way we think about, and indeed teach skills needed for the music profession in capstone courses and projects.

In reality, however, industry bodies and institutions alike so far proved unable to respond to the challenges other than stating a "crisis" and, more often than not, holding on to mechanisms and business models increasingly under threat. The debacle of a Recording Industry failing, among other issues, to swiftly respond to the digital market is also a failure to understand structural mechanisms of the music business, and anticipate strategic consequences—in other words, respond with critical understanding and resourcefulness that should be hallmarks of an education in arts and humanities.

There is some irony in the fact that Music Business—not least due to the decidedly critical reading of the culture industry as bourgeois capitalism, by Adorno—has long struggled, and in fact still is struggling to find its place in the academy.[27] At least in mainland Europe, conventionally its agenda is absorbed by the Sociology of Music.[28] Going by key texts in musicology or standard reference tools such as *New Grove*, a classical music industry appears not even to be in existence.

Whether knowingly or not, this perception has been kept alive in the classical music sector, from curricula to the media, as an antagonism between the "pure music" (i.e., what you study or perform) and the "dirty market" (which potentially compromises and abuses it).[29]

Unsurprisingly, the few existing dedicated studies have not found their way into mainstream accounts of Western music history nor in the teaching of the business of music. The latter, in fact, is mostly surrendered to "hands-on" accounts penned by practitioners in popular and recorded music, with modest academic ambition and, hence, limited analytical powers to actually penetrate any mechanisms of the music market beyond typically un-reflected "how-to" advice.

With a little-defined identity as a subject, then, both the label for and the content delivered under what essentially is, in one form or another, music business varies considerably in the United Kingdom, and beyond. Equally, associated knowledge and skills would come under banners as diverse as music business, music industry studies, career advancement, vocational training, arts and event management, professional development, and the like.

Soundings and Echoes

The sector is indeed undergoing change—in fact, it is moving far too quickly to catch and condense every (short-lived) industry trend into formal academic teaching. What results, is a marked correspondence between trial-and-error mentalities in the music business, and the lack of coherent research and theory underpinning the teaching of music business and related professional skills.

Two major trends appear to be dominating the music industry across North America and Europe. First, there is the sharp decline of traditional, often public-funded institutions, such as orchestras, music schools, and universities, with freelance and self-employed musicians—who typically juggle simultaneous careers in both music and related industries—becoming the norm.[30] Second, there is the crisis of the recording industry, only in part compensated by the digital distribution, and, at the same time, a dynamic renaissance of the concert and live industry.[31]

Both trends have been registered within academia; and institutions are beginning to consider how to integrate industry symptoms into music teaching and curricula but, by and large, do not answer the implicit call for careful investigation of the bigger picture, and leadership—in other words, they follow the course of a ship that is rudderless itself. As a result, academic institutions on both sides of the Atlantic run music industry and professional development programs without being able to know, with certainty, whether program objectives and course content correspond at all.[32]

When drafting an approach to the professional development of young musicians in mostly classical and jazz, for the Royal Academy of Music London, therefore, two major risks associated with the current approach to professional education were identified. The first is caused by the lack of basic research, and can be felt in what Mike Jones has described as "instruction is preceding understanding": young professionals may end up disempowered because they have been instructed in a narrow *know how* rather than *know why*.[33]

The second risk, hindering the professionalization of conservatoire-based education in particular, stems from an anachronistic focus on masterclass-style training for solo or orchestral careers where preparation for realistic jobs of less prestige, in the changing environment that is the self-employed portfolio musician of today, more often than not is neglected.[34]

The young professionals themselves, so early in their careers, are naturally not fully aware of these complexities and, in their majority, baffled that the music business, to an extent, operates like other creative industries. The further they advance in their studies; however, they come to realize that only "a small percentage of graduates will fall into jobs/steady income, but a majority will struggle to make ends meet"[35] as a top-achieving graduate student and recipient of major awards noted.

This is echoed by some current debate about conservatoire training and, specifically, its relevance to and teaching of professionalism, across Europe.[36] The focus here has been on internationalization; student-driven initiatives, under the sometimes vaguely applied concept of "entrepreneurship"[37]; and the effort to add new content within traditional degree courses, often on a project basis, and "vocational-ize" minor subjects such as aural training, and make them immediately relevant to the realities of the profession.[38] Complex as the status quo might have seemed, the point of departure was remarkably easy to identify.

Listening to the Students' Needs

As the doctoral research by Magdalena Bork and a recent report by the Musicians Benevolent Fund document,[39] young music graduates are very much aware of specific areas that would help them compete more successfully in the professional world.

Identified areas that, by and large, were not part of the graduates' curricula include[40]:

- How to cope with stress, whether performance-related anxieties or motivated by failed attempts at securing bookings;
- Efficient study and practice techniques fit for the pressurized diary of a professional musician;
- How to pitch for and secure a gig, and mount a concert;
- The practicalities of self-employment and associated skills needed to operate, for example, tax, accounting, and negotiating contracts;
- Managing a career, including self-promotion (CV-writing, portfolio-making, demo tracks, publicity), building a profile and creating employment opportunities, working with agents, and networking skills and opportunities;
- Working abroad; and
- A broad understanding for the need to diversify, and be versatile and dynamic.[41]

As Bork's research suggests, the disparity between conservatoire and professional world is felt most acutely if, during the studies including their academic grades, a strong sense of expectation is created. The expectation might be, for example, to secure an orchestra job and then "be told" how to play while, in reality, the young professionals are faced with the need to be independent, conceptualize ideas into fund-able projects, and organize themselves.[42] "Getting ahead," as clarinetist Stuart Eminson discovered soon, "is about good social skills and business skills as well as being a good player."[43]

The most critical moment in the process, and the period needing careful preparation, then, is the transition from (graduate) studies to professional life, and the first few years in the business.[44]

Further research and pilot events I carried out at the Royal Academy of Music in 2012, confirmed that, while most departments had robust principal study-specific activities in place, the biggest gap at the institutional level was indeed perceived in supporting early career transition, and transferable skills.

Professional Development Portfolio and Logbook as Real-World Capstones

It seemed obvious, therefore, to combine training skills and employability needs, and focus them in one product that would be tangible, and meaningful to the students' professional life.

Introduced in 2013–2014, the professional development portfolio is a vessel to hold the items required in order to engage successfully with the musical business: a CV for either teaching, performance, or music administration; a short biography; a program brochure for a real-life public event; and a proposal ready to go to a promoter; plus one of four choice items, a funding application, a website, a live recording, or an entrepreneurial project (typically, a self-organized event).

In addition, students reflect on their achievements and further career steps, in a Logbook that would also document which modules—from a menu of various sessions per topic—they have chosen to study, with options including mental skills for performers, outreach sessions, basic finance, digital marketing, or an internship that could be with either an ensemble, within teaching, or in the arts industry, and any topic in between and beyond.

In the accompanying advisory sessions with artist faculty and with the careers and professional development service, students are encouraged to explore new learning experiences, and challenge themselves to go out of their comfort zone: the Logbook, therefore, also serves to track student progression, and ensure marking is respectful of individual starting points.

The ranking of intended learning outcomes for either—with the Logbook typically fore-grounded in years 1 and 2, the portfolio the prime focus for years 3 and 4—does vary in practice, and depends on how much individual students embrace the concept of "counter-cyclical" experiences. That said, they have been designed to enable students to project their distinctive musical personality; engage in productive critical self-evaluation and self-assessment; communicate with confidence and insight; manage time and prioritize tasks by working to strict deadlines; use appropriate technology creatively and effectively; and, in particular, work autonomously and take responsibility for their own personal/professional development and self-promotion.

The vision is to help all students develop their existing and discover new talents, and to equip them as musical leaders according to their aptitude, which may go well beyond their immediate principal study, and beyond immediate degree course requirements. In daily life at the academy, this buffet offering—time-tabled during reading/projects week, and during two dedicated professional development weeks, respectively—aims to provide a truly balanced musical education that responds to, and advances professional expectations, through three tiers:

- Inspire students to realize the full range of their talents, analyze individual potential, and advise students accordingly on career development;
- Create a positive environment that supports their professional development in all areas principal study-specific (e.g., playing with click tracks); related skills that extend those (e.g., setting scores with notation software for a violist arranging parts for her string quartet); and supporting industry-relevant and transferable skills (e.g., project management);
- Offer an in-depth, critical awareness and understanding of the music business and, through mostly practice-led research, ensure there is interaction with state-of-the-art industry practice, and academy teaching and advising in this area is relevant.

As described above, a student's journey will be very much a process of clarifying, identifying, and developing individual talents, which is a process that may be shorter in some and take longer in other cases but typically consists of the following stages:

- B1 and B2—create awareness and analyze potential and needs, and acquire basic professional protocols, documented in the Logbook;

- B3 and B4—develop relevant supporting skills from a choice selection of offerings, through the portfolio work, and academic electives in music business, and music and arts management.

This is further developed at graduate level, where first- and second-year masters students explore professional avenues in an even more self-directed environment; but, in practice, there is a good cross-over between year cohorts, which leads to the added benefits of collaborative learning and projects in mixed-age, cross-faculty student groups that are composed only after individual study choices. Essentially, students manage their own progress and level of engagement: their studies are defined by the outcomes described above, but students themselves are in control. Although there are virtually no compulsory sessions, nonetheless attendance is excellent and, importantly, driven by the students' own individual career needs.

How Do We Know?

Like all UK higher education institutions, the Royal Academy of Music is expected to keep track of graduate employability; and it has been able to secure an enviable position, with 100% either in employment or further studies.

Internal responses, collected in the annual BM Program Feedback, underline these findings: in the feedback for 2015–2016, 77.78% of students considered that the five portfolio items would indeed test the right skills.

Beyond quantitative evidence, however, the voluntary student feedback suggests that the culminating experience, professional development portfolio, and associated support sessions also hold the potential to catalyze students' own career planning:

- "A brief email to thank you for the great "Fundraising Clinic" session today—it was most inspiring! I am wondering if it might be possible to make an appointment to see you in the near future—I would be grateful for your advice on the starting points of forming a charity?" (PhD1 student, 2016–2017)
- "It has been a very interested [*recte*: interesting] Professional Development week and very beneficial to me. Today I've spoken

with … about copyrights. I was wondering if I could book a slot to talk about my songwriting project." (B4 student, 2015–2016)
- "I have already got a note from (…) that contains when started … where I teach …, so I will attach it with my portfolio." (B3 student, 2015–2016)
- "I hope the Professional Development [Days] are going well, I have had really positive feedback from Students commenting on how interesting and useful the sessions are!" (Student Union President, 2015–2016)
- "Please can I extend a personal thanks to you for this week. It's be[en] completely enlightening, and has really changed my outlook on how I run my business." (M2 student, 2014–2015)
- "Just a quick note to say thanks to … for the Website design study date. I found it very helpful. I need to look at my content more, I think." (B3 student, 2013–2014)

Catherine Moore has once likened career and professional development to a river that has to be crossed, on graduation—narrow or wide, depending on how successful the student has, and has been, prepared. Every student in London, in fact, every visitor is well familiar with this concept: "Mind the Gap!," warn the loudspeakers in the underground, to watch out for the sometimes frighteningly large void between the cars and the platform.

Watching our young musicians succeed, we like to think that they do indeed manage forward and upward progression.

Notes

1. See Ernest L. Boyer, *Reinventing Undergraduate Education*; Randy Brooks, Jodi Benton-Kupper, and Deborah Slayton, "Curricular Aims: Assessment of a University Capstone Course"; Richard Olsen, David Weber, and Frank Trimble, "Cornerstones and Capstones: A Case Study on the Value of a Holistic Core in the Discipline of Communication Studies"; Connie J. Rowles, Daphene Cyr Koch, Stephen P. Hundley, and Sharon J. Hamilton, "Toward a Model for Capstone Experiences: Mountaintops, Magnets, and Mandates"; Bryce F. Sullivan and Susan L. Thomas, "Documenting Student Learning Outcomes through a Research-Intensive Senior Capstone Experience: Bringing the Data Together to Demonstrate Progress"; Peter J. Collier, "The Effects of Completing a Capstone Course on Student Identity. Sociology of Education."
2. Patsy Tinsley McGill, "Understanding the Capstone Experience Through the Voices of Students."

3. Dawn Bennett, "Developing Realistic Notions of Career in the Performing Arts," 311.
4. Linda Essig, "Suffusing Entrepreneurship Education throughout the Theatre Curriculum," 118–119.
5. Jason M. Martin and Michael G. Strawser, "Transforming the Capstone: Transformative Learning as a Pedagogical Framework and Vehicle for Ethical Reflection in the Capstone Course," 17.
6. Edward C. Watson, George D. Kuh, Terrel Rhodes, Tracy Penny Light, and Helen L. Chen, "ePortfolios—The Eleventh High Impact Practice."
7. Robin Nelson. *Practice as Research in the Arts: Principles, Protocols, Pedagogies, Resistances.*
8. Jillian Kinzie, "Taking Stock of Capstones and Integrative Learning."
9. Kinzie, "Taking Stock of Capstones and Integrative Learning," 28.
10. The course was originally taught in the spring (final) semester, but faculty felt that students were too overwhelmed with post-graduation employment and plans. Changing the course offering to the fall allows students more time to reflect on their capstone experiences and better understand how to translate these experiences into action.
11. George D. Kuh and Carol Geary Schneider, *High-Impact Educational Practices: What They Are, Who Has Access to Them, and Why They Matter.*
12. Kinzie, "Taking Stock of Capstones and Integrative Learning."
13. David Kolb, *Experiential Learning: Experiences as the Source of Learning and Development*, 38.
14. Kinzie, "Taking Stock of Capstones and Integrative Learning," 29.
15. Sondra Fraleigh and Penelope Hanstein. *Researching Dance: Evolving Modes of Inquiry*, 25.
16. Lynnette Overby, *Public Scholarship in Dance*, 4.
17. Kathleen Harring and Tian Luo, "Eportfolios: Supporting Reflection and Deep Learning in High-Impact Practices."
18. Kinzie, "Taking Stock of Capstones and Integrative Learning," 28.
19. Pseudonyms are provided for all student names.
20. Labanotation is a symbol based system of writing and analyzing movement, and parallels music notation. While the student was not proficient in Labanotation, the professor is an experienced Labanotation re-stager. In this situation, the student was the computer science expert and the professor functioned as the Laban expert.
21. Rebecca's original plan was to focus on the limbs and torso in space; the spatial aspect of the proposal was dropped because of a lack of necessary equipment.
22. Students who are accepted into the Performance and Choreography concentration in the program are expected to develop one lesson plan per each advanced level course in which they are enrolled, and teach that

lesson plan to their peers. The pedagogical justification is that teaching movement and developing a critical eye is a skill necessary for all performers and choreographers, as most of them also end up teaching dance to supplement their income.

23. Harring and Luo, "Eportfolios: Supporting Reflection and Deep Learning in High-Impact Practices," 9.
24. Harring and Luo, "Eportfolios: Supporting Reflection and Deep Learning in High-Impact Practices," 9.
25. Kinzie, "Taking Stock of Capstones and Integrative Learning," 29–30.
26. Incorporated Society of Musicians, "Record Companies," in *Careers With Music*, edited by the Incorporated Society of Musicians (London: ISM, 1991), 11.
27. For a critique of modern musicologists' failure to concern themselves with professional musicians and the music business, see David Baskerville, *Music Business Handbook and Career Guide*.
28. In addition, the economics of music are confused with, or explored almost exclusively in the context of the Recording Industry, and Popular Music. For an example, see Marius Carboni, *The Classical Music Business*.
29. The study of only Popular Music through creative and economic aspects is also articulated by the Standing Committee of Principals of German university schools of music (*Musikhochschulen*); see Martin Pfeffer, *Ausbildung für Musikberufe*, 2. For a historical survey of the perceived tensions between idealistic and economic values in music, see Christian Kaden, "Professionalismus in der Musik."
30. Pfeffer, *Ausbildung für Musikberufe*, 9; Magdalena Bork, "Von der Berufung zum Beruf: Musikerausbildung in Österreich auf dem Prüfstein," 33; Musicians Benevolent Fund, *Supporting Emerging Professional Musicians*, 5.
31. For a snapshot of the industry, see Phillip Sommerich, "In the Doldrums: Worst Year for Classical Record Sales," 6; Richard Fawkes, "Proms Ticket Website Helps Record-Breaking Sales Classical Music," 7; Phillip Sommerich, "Live Music Offsetting CD Decline," 9.
32. Mike Jones identifies "tensions" around course content and, occasionally, rather opportunistic motivation for creating the degrees in the first place; Mike Jones, "Learning to Crawl: The Rapid Rise of Music Industry Education." This is echoed by David Baskerville's dictum: "This field of education is relatively new, and faculty continue to search for the 'ideal' curriculum"; David Baskerville, "Music Business Studies in Higher Education," 18.
33. Mike Jones, "Learning to Crawl."
34. Raoul Mörchen, *Kernthesen der Diskussionsreihe "Musik und Beruf" des LandesMusikRates*. It may be safe to say that arts and humanities are still slow to analyze the impact of over-saturated job markets on individual students' careers and accept the new role, of helping make student success—in the emerging markets—possible.

35. Musicians Benevolent Fund, *Supporting Emerging Professional Musicians*, 13.
36. See Pfeffer, *Ausbildung für Musikberufe*; Bork, "Von der Berufung zum Beruf."
37. For a mature approach to this topic, see the New England Conservatory's approach, formalized as Entrepreneurial Musicianship.
38. Sandra Sinsch, "Erfolgreich?: Musikerausbildung in Deutschland."
39. Bork, *Von der Berufung zum Beruf.*
40. Both studies operate on a small number of samples and, consequently, represent tendencies not generalizations; Bork, "Von der Berufung zum Beruf"; Musicians Benevolent Fund, *Supporting Emerging Professional Musicians*. It also should be noted that the latter report contains some disparities, for example, the graduates' perceived need for professional skills that however do not reflect from their answers to current training needs, which pass uncommented; Musicians Benevolent Fund, *Supporting Emerging Professional Musicians*, 11. For a detailed analysis of one musician's first years in the profession, see Tom Walker, "Getting Started."
41. Versatility as a key attribute also for young leaders in the music business is singled out by David Baskerville; see David Baskerville, "Music Business Studies in Higher Education," 19. These findings are confirmed for young professionals in the creative industries in a wider context, by Jo Wilkinson who emphasizes the importance of networking especially in the music sector; Jo Wilkinson, "First Steps."
42. Student responses to the Musicians Benevolent Fund survey confirm this finding, suggesting the conservatoires did not give them a realistic picture of the music business or would even create "false expectations about the ease of getting work"; Musicians Benevolent Fund, *Supporting Emerging Professional Musicians*, 9.
43. Walker, "Getting Started."
44. Musicians Benevolent Fund, *Supporting Emerging Professional Musicians*, 14.

Bibliography

Baskerville, David. 1995. Music Business Studies in Higher Education. In *Music Business Handbook and Career Guide*, ed. David Baskerville, 6th ed., 17–19. Thousand Oaks, CA: Sage.

———. 2001. *Music Business Handbook and Career Guide*. 7th ed. Thousand Oaks, CA: Sage.

Bennett, Dawn. 2009. Academy and the Real World: Developing Realistic Notions of Career in the Performing Arts. *Arts and Humanities in Higher Education* 8 (3): 309–327.

Bork, Magdalena. 2009. Von der Berufung zum Beruf: Musikerausbildung in Österreich auf dem Prüfstein. *Das Orchester*, April.

Boyer, Ernest L. 1998. *The Boyer Commission on Educating Undergraduates in the Research University, Reinventing Undergraduate Education: A Blueprint for America's Research Universities*. Stony Brook, NY 46.

Brooks, Randy, Jodi Benton-Kupper, and Deborah Slayton. 2004. Curricular Aims: Assessment of a University Capstone Course. *The Journal of General Education* 53 (3): 275–287.

Brown, John, Allan Collins, and Paul Duguid. 1989. Situated Cognition and the Culture of Learning. *Educational Researcher* 18 (1): 32–42.

Carboni, Marius. 2011. The Classical Music Business. In *The Music Industry Handbook*, ed. Paul Rutter, 195–223. Abingdon and New York: Routledge.

Collier, Peter J. 2000. The Effects of Completing a Capstone Course on Student Identity. *Sociology of Education* 73: 285–299.

Essig, Linda. 2009. Suffusing Entrepreneurship Education Throughout the Theatre Curriculum. *Theatre Topics* 19 (2): 117–124.

Fawkes, Richard. 2010. Proms Ticket Website Helps Record-Breaking Sales. *Classical Music*. May 22, p. 7.

Fraleigh, Sondra, and Penelope Hanstein, eds. 1999. *Researching Dance: Evolving Modes of Inquiry*. Pittsburgh: University of Pittsburgh Press.

Harring, Kathleen, and Tian Luo. 2016. Eportfolios: Supporting Reflection and Deep Learning in High-Impact Practices. *Peer Review* 18 (3): 9–12.

Incorporated Society of Musicians. 1991. Record Companies. In *Careers with Music*, ed. The Incorporated Society of Musicians, 11. London: ISM.

Jones, Mike. 2002. Learning to Crawl: The Rapid Rise of Music Industry Education. In *The Business of Music*, ed. Michael Talbot, 292–310. Liverpool: Liverpool University Press.

Kaden, Christian. 1999. Professionalismus in der Musik. In *Professionalismus in der Musik*, ed. Christian Kaden and Volker Kalisch. Essen: Blaue Eule.

Kassing, Gayle. 2010. New Challenges in 21st Century Dance Education. *Journal of Physical Education, Recreation, and Dance* 81 (6): 21–27.

Kinzie, Jillian. 2013. Taking Stock of Capstones and Integrative Learning. *Peer Review* 15 (4): 27–30.

Kolb, David. 1984. *Experiential Learning: Experiences as the Source of Learning and Development*. Englewood Cliffs, NJ: Prentice Hall.

Kuh, George D., and Carol Geary Schneider. 2009. *High-Impact Educational Practices: What They Are, Who Has Access to Them, and Why They Matter*. Washington, DC: Association of American Colleges and Universities.

Martin, Jason M., and Michael G. Strawser. 2017. Transforming the Capstone: Transformative Learning as a Pedagogical Framework and Vehicle for Ethical Reflection in the Capstone Course. *The Journal of Faculty Development* 31 (1): 25–34.

Marzano, Robert, Debra Pickering, and Jane Pollock. 2001. *Classroom Instruction That Works: Research-Based Strategies for Increasing Student Achievement*. Alexandria, VA: Association for Supervision and Curriculum Development.

May, Shaun. 2015. *Rethinking Practice as Research and the Cognitive Turn*. New York: Palgrave Macmillan.
McGill, Patsy Tinsley. 2012. Understanding the Capstone Experience Through the Voices of Students. *The Journal of General Education* 61 (4): 488–504.
Mörchen, Raoul. 2005. *Kernthesen der Diskussionsreihe 'Musik und Beruf' des LandesMusikRates NRW e.V.* Düsseldorf: Landesmusikrat NRW.
Musicians Benevolent Fund. 2012. *Supporting Emerging Professional Musicians: Survey Report*. London: Musicians Benevolent Fund.
Nelson, Robin. 2013. *Practice as Research in the Arts: Principles, Protocols, Pedagogies, Resistances*. New York: Palgrave Macmillan.
Olsen, Richard, David Weber, and Frank Trimble. 2002. Cornerstones and Capstones: A Case Study on the Value of a Holistic Core in the Discipline of Communication Studies. *Communication Education* 51 (1): 65–80.
Overby, Lynnette. 2016. *Public Scholarship in Dance*. Champaign, IL: Human Kinetics.
Pfeffer, Martin. 2006. *Ausbildung für Musikberufe*. Bonn: Deutscher Musikrat.
Rowles, Connie J., Daphene Cyr Koch, Stephen P. Hundley, and Sharon J. Hamilton. 2004. Toward a Model for Capstone Experiences: Mountaintops, Magnets, and Mandates. *Assessment Update* 16 (1): 1–2.
Rutter, Paul. 2011. Into the Future. In *The Music Industry Handbook*, ed. Paul Rutter, 264–274. Abingdon and New York: Routledge.
Scott, Derek B., ed. 2000. *Music, Culture, and Society: A Reader*. New York: Oxford University Press.
Sinsch, Sandra. 2009. Erfolgreich?: Musikerausbildung in Deutschland. *Das Orchester*. April, pp. 10–12.
Sommerich, Phillip. 2010. In the Doldrums: Worst Year for Classical Record Sales. *Classical Music*. May 22, p. 6.
———. 2012. Live Music Offsetting CD Decline. *Classical Music*. June 30, p. 9.
Stewart, Andrew. 2008. Musical Life: Get the Facts. *Classical Music*. November 22, pp. 36–37.
Sullivan, Bryce F., and Susan L. Thomas. 2007. Documenting Student Learning Outcomes Through a Research-Intensive Senior Capstone Experience: Bringing the Data Together to Demonstrate Progress. *North American Journal of Psychology* 9 (2): 321–329.
Walker, Tom. 2006. Getting Started. *Classical Music*. October 14, p. 27.
Watson, C. Edward, George D. Kuh, Terrel Rhodes, Tracy Penny Light, and Helen L. Chen. 2016. ePortfolios–The Eleventh High Impact Practice. *International Journal* 6 (2): 65–69.
Wilkinson, Jo. 2006. First Steps. *Arts Professional*. July 17, p. 5.
von Zahn, Robert. 2005. *Selbständige Berufsmusiker zwischen Innovation und Überleben*. Düsseldorf: Landesmusikrat NRW.

Index[1]

A
Acting, 39, 66, 117, 134, 166, 203, 204, 208, 241, 264, 265, 268
Action research, 165–167, 173
Adaptation, 69, 71, 73, 110–111, 155
Administrators, 2, 3, 9, 12–14, 22, 24, 45, 49, 53, 57, 60n9, 65, 66, 118, 124, 147, 154, 189, 212n40, 218, 223, 224, 231, 252, 258, 262, 278, 284
Advocacy, 2, 51, 52, 55, 221
Advocate, 7, 13, 15, 103, 148, 153, 154, 189, 209, 219, 223, 281
Aesthetic, 8, 11, 34, 68, 69, 76, 77, 126, 141, 142, 164, 172, 173
Aha, 84, 85, 92
Alignment, 14
Alternate writing assignments, 105
Alternative ways of knowing, 3
Applied dance, 124, 188, 222, 277
Applied music, 188, 222
Applied theatre, 188, 199, 222, 225–230, 233, 277
Artistic literacy, 125, 126, 158, 159
Arts
 administration, 252, 275, 276
 education, 2–4, 8, 9, 13, 35, 36, 47, 123, 153, 252, 256, 257, 262
 educators, 14, 121
 integration, 3, 263, 283
 as public practice, 11
 therapies, 11
Assessment, 2, 4, 14, 32, 46, 65–67, 93, 109–110, 133, 135, 137, 157, 168–171, 200, 201, 209, 218–220, 240, 251, 255, 257, 261–263, 269, 280, 284, 287, 288
Association for Theatre in Higher Education (ATHE), 17n32, 220
Association of American Colleges and Universities (AAC&U), 1–4, 6, 9, 10, 12–14, 16n12, 45, 46, 60n9, 70, 200, 252

[1] Note: Page numbers followed by 'n' refer to notes.

Audience, 11, 25, 29, 32, 40, 41, 51, 57, 58, 84, 101–105, 107, 111, 112, 118, 123, 130–134, 139, 155, 173, 182, 183, 188, 189, 195, 197, 203, 221, 228, 229, 231, 235, 238, 241–244, 263, 270, 283
Auditions, 129, 130, 133, 183, 186, 190, 268, 269, 276
Autism Spectrum Disorder (ASD), 189, 198–208

B
Bachelor of Arts (BA), 155, 187, 279
Bachelor of Fine Arts (BFA), 155, 187, 256, 257
Beginning College Survey of Student Engagement (BCSSE), 41n6
Best practices, 1–4, 13, 122, 137, 220, 253, 254
Better practice, 220
Bias, 12, 127, 183, 189, 190, 210n6, 211n27, 252
Bigger Than Me, 7
Boal, Augusto, 11, 27, 233, 245n35, 246n36
Boyer, Ernest, 218, 244n4, 281, 296n1
Business, 6, 10, 12, 14, 33, 65, 264, 270, 276, 289, 293, 296
Business leaders, 6, 9
Business School, 130, 270

C
Call to action, 13–16, 24, 49, 66, 104–105, 124, 154, 189–190, 223–224, 255, 278–279
Campus Compact, 217, 219
Campus–community partnership, 225, 226
Capacity building, 221

Capstone courses and projects, 16, 273–296
Capstone experience, 49, 134, 251, 273–279, 281, 297n10
Career
  development, 251, 294
  paths, 3, 16, 101, 121, 275–277, 282
Carnegie Community Engagement Classification, 218, 219
Casting, 15, 128, 130, 131, 133, 134, 183, 188, 268
Center for Performance and Civic Practice, The (CPCP), 11, 220, 221
Characteristic of high-impact practice, 5, 70, 254
Chief Academic Officers (CAOs), 6, 10, 45
Chronicle of Higher Education, 7
Civic
  application, 221
  dialogue, 225, 227, 228
  engagement, 11, 188, 226, 235
  leadership, 223, 225–227
  practice, 11, 14, 221, 244n10
Collaboration, 6, 12, 23, 27, 32, 65, 70, 73, 74, 81, 86, 116, 118, 121, 123, 124, 131, 133, 140, 145n8, 173, 199, 200, 204, 221, 227, 243, 255, 257, 258, 260, 265, 268, 282
Collaborative assignments, 15, 87, 121, 125
Collaborative learning, 1, 21, 65–67, 93, 121–125, 258–260, 295
Collaborative projects, 70
Collaborative teaching, 87, 121, 258–260
Collage, 72, 157–159, 175n19
Collective, 7, 59, 65, 86, 122, 123, 188, 202, 204, 208, 209, 227, 229, 233, 240

College, 2, 6, 7, 9, 13–15, 21–25, 29, 33, 34, 36–38, 40, 47, 48, 50, 53, 58, 64, 65, 67, 80, 86, 94n4, 126, 128, 134, 141, 148, 152, 153, 156, 167, 181, 182, 184, 185, 187, 189, 191, 200, 205, 211n22, 217–219, 222, 224, 230, 231, 234, 235, 244, 251, 252, 254, 255, 260, 263, 264, 273, 276, 277, 280, 284
College Music Society, 152
Common intellectual experiences, 15, 45–49, 87, 155, 191
Common read, 36, 48, 49
Communication, 46, 53–54, 57–59, 70, 86, 106, 132, 133, 136, 137, 155, 157–161, 198, 199, 202, 203, 206–208, 220, 222, 230, 232–235, 265, 282
Community
 engagement, 27, 217–219, 222, 223, 225, 226, 229, 230, 233–235, 242, 243, 283
 partners, 67, 124, 130, 134, 188, 199, 219–222, 224
Community-based learning, 15, 17n32, 27, 217–244
Compromise, 23, 38, 128, 133, 204, 208, 227, 290
Computer coding, 66, 283
Computer music, 70
Computer programming, 68, 69, 77–80
Computing in the arts, 81
Conquergood, Dwight, 164, 177n39, 245n23
Council for Advancement of Standards in Higher Education (CAS), 200, 251, 253
Council of Public Liberal Arts Colleges (COPLAC), 47

Council on Undergraduate Research (CUR), 148, 155
Course goals, 23
Creative
 activity, 147–156, 175n9, 258
 capacity, 13, 174
 economy, 12
 process, 3, 47, 50, 121, 123, 124, 126, 138, 141, 161, 165, 202, 205
 scholarship, 15, 124, 151, 154, 182, 281
Creativity, 2, 6–7, 10, 15, 28, 32, 51, 52, 59, 65–67, 86, 93, 105, 149, 164, 166, 170, 171, 173, 265, 276
Crisis, 8, 83, 137, 152, 243, 289, 291
Critical thinking, 16n5, 21, 22, 34, 46, 48, 86, 87, 106, 149, 150, 158, 164, 181, 234, 265, 268, 277, 280
Critique sessions, 133
Cross-sector innovation, 221
Cultural competence, 15, 189, 224
Cultural diplomacy, 222, 223
Cultural diversity, 48, 210n15
Cultural history, 158
Cultural immersion, 186, 210n15
Cultural literacy, 13, 105, 154
Culturally relevant pedagogy, 257
Cultural mapping, 222
Curricula/Curriculum, 2, 3, 6–9, 14, 15, 21, 22, 24, 27, 33, 35, 45, 46, 48, 49, 51, 70, 80–82, 93, 101, 106, 111, 121, 123, 125, 141, 145n8, 150, 151, 153, 155, 176n37, 183–187, 189, 190, 211n22, 218, 221, 223, 224, 251–254, 256, 257, 259, 262–264, 269, 274–280, 282, 284, 290–292

D

Dance, 4, 8, 32, 34, 50, 52, 102, 103, 124, 148, 153, 154, 163–166, 168, 170–174, 176–177n37, 177n51, 183, 184, 186–189, 199, 212n40, 222, 235, 246n42, 252, 254, 256–263, 277–284, 287, 288
   education, 173, 174, 176n37, 186, 187, 256, 257, 261–263, 277, 283
   studies, 164, 166, 176n37, 186–187
Democracy, 225, 227, 230
Democratic practice, 188, 233
Devised theatre, 24
Devising, 25–32, 117, 153–155, 170
Dialogical performance, 226
Dialogue, 37, 39, 117, 151, 164, 183, 188, 189, 206, 221–233, 243, 246n42, 277
Digital music, 75
Disabilities, 170, 186, 187, 200, 209
Discovery, 104, 112, 114, 117, 147, 164, 166, 168, 209, 267, 281
Disruption, 84, 90, 193
Dissemination, 4, 123, 147, 149, 150, 155
Diversity, 5, 15, 39, 51, 59, 125, 126, 181–209, 222
Dramaturgy, 154, 156–163, 175n19, 176n30, 265
Dress rehearsal, 142, 242

E

Early career transition, 278, 293
Elbow, Peter, 112, 113, 119n10
Embodied learning, 35, 65–67
Embodied pedagogy, 11, 24, 41
Empathy, 7, 32, 40, 66, 84, 90, 188, 199, 202, 208, 209, 223, 225–227, 229–233

Engagement, 3, 4, 11, 14, 27, 35, 46, 51, 65, 67, 69, 74, 94n5, 95n19, 95n26, 102, 112, 137, 141, 142, 181, 188, 189, 191, 194, 201, 217–220, 222, 223, 225, 226, 229–235, 242, 243, 280, 281, 283, 295
Entrepreneurship, 275, 276, 292
e-portfolios, 48, 287
Ethical practice, 218, 223
Ethical Reflection, 275, 277
Ethics, 22, 36–38, 48, 165, 166, 229, 277, 278
Ethnomusicology, 184, 185
Every Student Succeeds Act, 35
Experiential learning, 16, 51, 54, 83, 153, 181, 189, 251–254, 264, 278, 280
Expression, 7, 10, 47, 52, 66, 69, 81, 104, 105, 172, 231, 232, 237, 259, 269

F

Faculty, 4, 6, 9, 12–15, 21–26, 33–35, 40, 48, 49, 51–59, 63–65, 67, 73, 74, 101, 104, 105, 121, 123–125, 127, 129, 130, 133, 134, 136–138, 143, 144, 145n7, 147, 149–152, 154, 155, 157, 160, 182, 185, 189, 190, 199, 200, 209, 217–220, 223, 224, 231, 234, 251–255, 258, 261, 265–267, 273–280, 283, 284, 289, 293, 298n32
   mentorship, 273–275
Failure, 85, 87, 90, 115, 203, 204, 269, 276, 290, 298n27
Feedback, 5, 108–110, 132, 133, 139–143, 152, 157, 159, 160, 219, 220, 224, 240, 241, 244, 254, 257, 262, 266, 274, 275, 287, 295, 296

Feminist, 219, 225, 226, 229, 230, 232, 233
Field experience, 48, 252, 254, 256
Final performance, 36, 201, 205
First-year experience (FYE), 21–25, 33–41, 45, 64, 66
First-year seminar, 15, 21–41, 234, 282
First-year students, 22–27, 29–32, 40, 48, 49, 64
Freshman Experience, 243, 246n39

G

Gaston, Paul, 17n34, 46, 60n7
Gender, 85, 188, 190
General education, 1, 2, 4, 7, 10, 12–15, 25, 45–49, 64, 67, 104, 185
General Education Maps and Markers (GEMs), 46
Given circumstances, 156, 157, 162
Global learning, 15, 26, 125, 181–209
Global reach, 127
Goals, 2, 12, 13, 21–23, 27, 33, 34, 36, 37, 48, 54, 65, 67, 90, 126, 139, 157, 181, 182, 188, 189, 200, 202, 207, 209, 221, 234, 251, 263, 267, 268, 270, 273–275, 277, 278, 280–282, 284
Good practices, 4
Grade Point Average (GPA), 26, 266
Graduates, 2, 3, 6, 9, 10, 13, 86, 176n36, 182, 183, 224, 252, 278, 291, 292, 299n40
Great Books, 8
Group presentations, 241

H

Harvard Taskforce on the Arts, 7
Higher education, 1–4, 7–13, 15, 21, 46, 48, 51, 70, 74, 85, 86, 95n19, 95n26, 106, 151, 164, 165, 173, 176n37, 182, 184, 186, 209n2, 217, 219, 255, 276, 280, 295

High-impact practices, 1–16, 22, 46, 64, 65, 93, 135, 157, 158, 190, 200, 201, 224, 251, 268, 273, 280, 282, 288
High-Impact Practices for Administrators Tool, 14
Hip hop pedagogy, 190
Historical context, 15, 50, 52, 158, 188
Humanities, 3, 9–12, 14, 15, 33, 47, 50–53, 55, 56, 58, 65, 87, 105, 106, 132, 150, 193, 223, 290, 298n34

I

Ideation, 84, 90, 91
Identity, 39, 85, 102, 153, 176n37, 182, 189–198, 218, 232, 256, 261, 277, 290
Imagination, 3, 7, 93, 203, 204
Inclusive arts, 207
Inclusive political communication, 226
Individual expression, 7
Individual research, 154, 158, 160–163
Information literacy, 21, 33, 34, 36
Innovation, 2, 10, 16, 21, 50, 58, 65, 67, 82–93, 136, 276
Innovative, 6, 10, 59, 83–85, 124, 189, 199, 220
Integrating research, 159, 160
Integrative learning, 33, 34, 36, 253, 280, 281, 288, 289
Intentional, 13, 14, 18n38, 46, 63, 67, 121, 124, 154, 227, 253, 273, 278, 279, 289
Intercultural competence, 190
Interdependence, 123
Interdisciplinary, 10, 23, 24, 49, 64, 66, 67, 123, 124, 126, 151, 154, 155, 176n37, 188
Interdisciplinary learning community, 68–81

Internationalization, 291
Internships, 15, 22, 251–270, 278, 293
Interracial interaction, 181

K
Kindelan, Nancy, 125, 145n10, 158, 159, 175n24, 176n29
K12 education, 23, 256, 258, 259
Kuh, George, D., 5, 16n7, 16n8, 16n10, 21, 41n2, 45, 59n2, 94n6, 94n13, 101, 119n1, 133, 145n9, 145n12, 145n13, 145n14, 145n18, 157, 158, 175n17, 175n20, 175n21, 176n26, 176n32, 181, 209n1, 246n41, 254, 265, 266, 268, 269, 271n13, 271n15, 280, 297n6, 297n11

L
Labor, 124, 136–144, 164, 192
Laptop orchestra, 73–75
Leadership, 22, 23, 125, 131, 181, 220, 223, 225–234, 255, 257, 260, 263, 265, 291
Leadership Institute, 220
Learning community, 15, 26, 27, 29, 33, 34, 45, 63–67, 125, 134, 189, 241, 282
Learning outcomes, 6, 9, 10, 12–15, 21–23, 26, 27, 32, 34, 36, 46, 54, 65, 70, 80, 81, 133, 137, 140, 156, 158, 235, 255, 265, 278, 287, 293
Lerman, Liz, 7, 11
Liberal arts, 2–4, 8, 9, 12–14, 47, 126, 128, 134, 135, 148, 153, 154, 156, 191, 234, 263, 279
Liberal Education and America's Promise (LEAP), 8–13

Liminal space, 225, 228
Literature, 10, 11, 13, 14, 34, 47, 52, 103, 111, 122, 156, 165, 262, 265, 273, 283, 284, 287

M
Major, 2, 4, 8, 13, 15, 21, 24–26, 29–31, 33, 34, 38, 45, 46, 53, 55, 56, 64, 67, 79, 104, 108, 129, 136–138, 150, 155, 156, 159, 182, 186, 217, 228, 234, 243, 251, 252, 254, 264–266, 276, 277, 279–284, 287, 291
Media, 7, 75, 79, 81, 124, 125, 149, 151, 153, 155, 188, 194, 197, 198
Mentoring, 149, 219, 260, 261, 278, 281
Metacognition, 289
Mission, 2, 14, 26, 27, 48, 51, 54, 58, 87, 134, 155–157, 182, 184, 190, 218, 221, 226, 241, 242, 269
Mistakes, 35, 115, 116, 204, 205, 240, 266
Motivation, 3, 74
Multicultural, 124, 125, 134, 135, 186, 259
Music, 4, 9, 11, 27, 50–52, 54, 55, 58, 66, 68–77, 79–81, 103–108, 110–111, 124, 141, 148–150, 152, 153, 155, 182–189, 222, 228, 235, 238, 241–243, 252, 277, 278, 289–293, 295
  business, 290, 291, 294, 295
  composition, 66, 76, 80, 105, 110, 148
  education, 69, 74, 106, 184, 185, 241
  theory, 69, 81
  therapy, 185, 277
Musical theatre studies, 243

Musicology, 73, 234, 290
Mutual reciprocity, 219
Mutual understanding, 225

N
National Conference of Undergraduate Research (NCUR), 148–150, 152, 154
National Dance Education Organization (NDEO), 263
National Dance Society (NDS), 267
National Resource Center for Learning Communities, 63, 64
National Society for Experiential Education, 253
National Survey of Student Engagement (NSSE), 4, 252, 280
Neurodiversity, 199
Neurotypical, 202
No Child Left Behind, 23
Non-majors, 2, 25, 65, 104, 105, 154, 243
Non-profit, 15, 148, 226, 270

O
O'Neill, Nancy, 251, 268, 270n1, 270n2, 271n14
Oral communications, 157, 158, 234, 235
Oral presentation, 151, 158, 223, 234–238, 240–242

P
Partnership, 63, 67, 219–221, 225, 226, 257, 258, 264, 277, 278
Payscale, 6, 86
Pedagogy, 2, 4, 6, 9, 11–13, 15, 22–26, 33–35, 41, 47, 48, 63–67, 74, 83, 84, 93, 112, 113, 116, 121, 123–126, 139, 155, 156, 158, 173, 187, 189, 190, 218, 223, 224, 257, 263, 282, 284
Peer evaluation, 240–244
Peer model, 202, 208
Performance class, 23, 240–243
Performance expectations, 5
Performance of possibilities, 226, 227
Performing arts
 departments, 11, 13, 14, 24, 25, 49, 67, 123, 187, 189, 252, 253, 255, 273, 279
 faculty, 13, 14, 24, 49, 65, 67, 104, 121, 123–125, 150–152, 154, 155, 188–190, 224, 251, 275, 277–279
 majors, 16, 154, 155, 182, 224, 252, 253, 275
 programs, 1, 2, 15, 24, 47, 49, 152, 183, 220
Perspective, 7, 49, 51–55, 57, 58, 63, 69, 79, 83, 84, 86, 87, 93, 106, 111–113, 134, 141, 148, 153, 157, 171, 183, 191, 194, 196–198, 208, 227, 230, 232, 282
Plays, 9, 25, 27, 30, 36–40, 49, 55, 75, 82–85, 117, 124–129, 131, 133–135, 143, 144, 148, 153, 155–164, 170, 197, 202, 203, 208, 225, 227, 232–234, 267, 276, 292
Poetry writing, 116
Portfolio, 261, 275, 280, 287, 288, 291–295
 See also e-portfolios
Post-colonial identity, 191, 192, 194–197
Poster presentation, 151, 257, 262
Postmodern, 8, 102, 198
Post-performance panel, 229, 230, 233
Post-traumatic stress (PTS), 225, 231
Potency, 123
Practical, 1, 16, 21–23, 104, 117, 121, 122, 124, 131, 137, 140, 153, 168, 170, 173, 187, 222, 232, 235, 244, 275

Practice, as research, 164, 165, 174
Praxis, 34, 164, 173, 219, 279, 280, 282, 283, 287
Preparation, 38, 75, 149, 236, 240, 241, 244, 253, 260–261, 281, 282, 287, 291, 293
Problem solve/problem-solving, 34, 64–66, 85, 159, 168, 198, 273, 280, 289
Process, 3, 4, 10, 23, 27, 28, 30, 31, 33, 34, 37, 39, 46, 47, 50, 51, 56, 57, 65, 68, 75, 76, 79, 82–85, 91, 102–104, 106, 108, 112–114, 117, 118, 122–124, 126, 128–130, 132, 134, 138, 139, 141, 143, 144, 151, 160, 161, 165, 166, 168, 170–173, 183, 191, 193, 202, 203, 205, 207, 221, 223, 226–230, 234, 237, 251, 253–255, 261, 267, 268, 280, 281, 287, 293, 294
Professional development, 12, 124, 161, 189, 224, 278, 290, 291, 293–296
Professional identity, 256
Professional practice, 14
Program notes, 50, 103–111, 135
Project-based learning, 124
Promotion, 58, 154, 190, 218, 223, 229, 289
Psychological safety, 123
Public dissemination, 4, 103, 123
Public narrative, 223, 225–227, 230
Public performance, 6, 11, 127
Public practice, 10, 11
Public speaking, 10, 234, 240, 243, 244
Purpose, 7, 11, 22, 47, 48, 83, 87, 107, 111, 121, 201, 223, 232, 269, 277, 281, 288

Q
Queer theory, 188

R
Race, 30, 39, 181, 188–190, 192, 194
Ranking card, 132
Reach, 127
Real-world application, 5, 12
Reciprocity, 83, 220, 229, 233, 242, 243
Recording industry, 289, 291
Recordings, 71, 72, 75, 115, 116, 118, 138, 283, 289, 293
Reflection, 41, 54, 59, 87, 125, 171, 173, 174, 190, 194, 223, 230, 253, 254, 260, 261, 269, 275, 277–279, 281, 287
Refugee, 188, 189
Rehearsal process, 131, 134
Reimer, Bennett, 9, 17n24, 184, 185, 210n12, 210n13
Representation, 71, 75, 102, 153, 154, 158, 182, 188, 194, 228
Research, 1, 21, 48, 103, 139, 218, 253, 273
Research profile, 15, 148, 152, 154, 281
Research with faculty, 4, 200, 264
Resilience, 208, 209, 278
Resulting, 262
Retention, 4, 21, 24, 64, 149, 181, 190
Rohd, Michael, 220, 221, 244n11, 245n12
Role-play, 201, 202, 208
Rubric, 9, 104, 109, 116, 157, 161, 237, 240, 284

S
Sawyer, R. Keith, 17n27
Scaffolded curriculum, 274
Scholarship, 2, 10, 12, 15, 49, 102, 124, 148, 150–154, 182, 218, 219, 225, 226, 241, 280, 281, 283
Scholartist, 152, 153

Script analysis, 158
Self-awareness, 164
Self-employment, 292
Self-evaluation, 112
Self-reflection, 22, 23, 36, 126, 160, 189, 223, 224, 233, 277, 284, 288
Self-reflexivity, 15, 224
Sensory, 207
Service learning, 190, 217–244
Shared benefit, 242
Shared reciprocity, 242
Skills, 3, 6, 9–15, 21–23, 25–27, 32–36, 39, 45, 46, 64, 66, 67, 69–71, 74, 83, 86, 103–107, 109–111, 116, 121, 124–126, 135, 137–141, 143, 154, 158, 160–164, 166, 172–173, 181, 198–202, 204, 208, 209, 221, 223, 235, 238, 241, 243, 244, 251, 252, 254, 256, 257, 261, 263–265, 267, 273, 275, 276, 278, 280, 281, 287–290, 292–295
Slam poetry, 115
Social competence, 208
Social dynamics, 123
Social interaction, 74, 122, 144n2, 203, 208, 264
Social justice, 184, 186, 188, 219, 220, 232, 259
Social practice, 221
Social service, 15, 277
Socioeconomic, 186, 187
Sonification, 75–79, 81
Spoken word, 32, 114, 115
Stafford, William, 113, 116, 119n11, 119n12
Staged reading, 225, 227–229
Statistics, 130, 252
STEAM (Science, technology, engineering, ARTS, mathematics), 2, 147, 175n4
STEM (Science, technology, engineering, mathematics), 2, 3, 10, 23, 150, 175n4

Stige, Brynjulf, 11, 17n31
Story-sharing, 221
Storytelling, 85, 204, 233, 269
Strategic National Arts Alumni Project (SNAAP), 16n4, 17n35, 182, 210n8, 224, 245n18, 252
Student engagement, 4, 65, 67, 74, 137, 141, 181, 280
Student–faculty interaction, 4, 65
Student learning outcomes (SLOs), 6, 14, 46, 101, 137, 265, 278, 281, 282, 284
Student teaching, 256, 260–261
Studio habits, 3
Studio practice, 221
Study abroad, 4, 181, 264
Subjectivity, 22, 35, 39, 191, 196, 197, 226, 227, 229
Survey, 6, 7, 10, 12, 24, 28, 29, 32, 45, 46, 79, 80, 105, 107, 110, 209, 224, 252
Sustained contact between faculty and students, 6
Synthesis, 34, 36, 40, 71, 74, 77, 79, 109, 160, 162, 255, 265, 273, 279

T
Task cohesion, 123
Teacher education, 188, 256
Team, 6, 53, 57, 63, 87, 121–125, 131, 136, 140–142, 148, 149, 204, 205, 274
Team-based capstone courses and projects, 273
Teamwork, 6, 9, 86, 121, 124, 125, 235
Technology, 45, 70, 79, 124, 155, 204, 283, 294
Tenure, 151, 152, 218
and promotion, 154, 190, 218, 223
Tepper, Steven J., 7, 17n16
Theatre, 4, 24, 51, 66, 103, 121, 148, 183, 220, 252, 276
Theatre for social change, 227

Theatre games, 30, 205, 206
Theatre majors, 137, 159, 228, 267
Theatre Practicum, 137
Theatre semiotics, 206
Timely feedback, 5
Transdisciplinary, 15, 82, 83, 86, 87, 90
Transferable skills, 74, 293, 294
Transformative learning, 189, 277
Trial and error, 148, 205, 208, 290

U
Undergraduate research, 1, 15, 22, 147–174, 263
United States Institute for Theatre Technology (USITT), 267, 268, 270
University, 1, 24, 47, 63, 124, 147, 184, 217, 251, 276

V
VALUE rubric, 9
Veterans, 223, 225–229, 231–233
Vetting process, 128, 129, 134
Vocational learning, 252
Vocational training, 14, 153, 290
Voice, 7, 40, 71, 93, 103, 104, 108, 112–119, 135, 193, 204, 206, 208, 226, 227, 234, 237, 259, 261, 268

W
Western music, 184, 185, 290
Workshop, 55, 70, 112, 114, 124, 140, 164, 166, 170–172, 202, 220, 240
World dance, 284
World music, 111, 183, 184
World theatre, 183, 188
Writing genres, 105
Writing-intensive courses, 15, 101